Patent Case Management Judicial Guide

Third Edition

2016

Volume III

Patent Case Management Judicial Guide

Third Edition

Peter S. Menell
Koret Professor of Law
Berkeley Center for Law & Technology
University of California, Berkeley School of Law

Lynn H. Pasahow
Fenwick & West LLP

James Pooley
Orrick, Herrington & Sutcliffe LLP

Matthew D. Powers
Tensegrity Law Group LLP

Steven C. Carlson
Kasowitz, Benson, Torres & Friedman LLP

Jeffrey G. Homrig
Latham & Watkins LLP

George F. Pappas
Covington & Burling LLP

Carolyn Chang
Fenwick & West LLP

Colette Reiner Mayer
Morrison & Foerster LLP

Marc David Peters
Morrison & Foerster LLP

in collaboration with

Anita Choi
Morrison & Foerster LLP

John Fargo
U.S. Department of Justice

Michael Sawyer
Covington & Burling LLP

Allison A. Schmitt
University of California, Berkeley

Michael R. Ward
Morrison & Foerster LLP

Patricia Young
Latham & Watkins LLP

Federal Judicial Center 2016

email: pmenell@law.berkeley.edu

A print version of *Patent Case Management Judicial Guide* (3d ed. 2016), including all appendices, is available through Clause 8 Publishing (Clause8Publishing.com). The treatise is also available through the Lexis online database.

Summary Table of Contents

Table of Contents

Appendix A
Patent Glossary

Note: Many of these definitions are derived from the USPTO glossary, available at http://www.uspto.gov/main/glossary/index.html.

abandonment: A patent application becomes abandoned for failure to file a complete and proper reply within the time period provided under 37 C.F.R. § 1.134 and § 1.136 unless an office action indicates otherwise. Abandonment may be either of the invention or of an application. An abandoned application, in accordance with 37 C.F.R. §§ 1.135 and 1.138, is one which is removed from the Patent Office docket of pending applications. *See* § 14.3.4.1.6.

abstract of the disclosure: A concise statement of the technical disclosure, including that which is new in the art to which the invention pertains.

agent (practitioner, representative): One who is not an attorney but is authorized to act for or in place of the applicant(s) before the USPTO, that is, an individual who is registered to practice before the USPTO.

all-limitation rule (all-elements rule): A doctrine requiring that an allegedly infringing device contain every element of a claim to establish infringement, either literally or under the doctrine of equivalents. *See* § 14.4.1.4.2.1.1.

analogous art (pertinent art, relevant art): In a nonobviousness analysis, art that a person having ordinary skill in the art would have consulted in attempting to solve the problem addressed by the innovation. Analogous art must be either within the same field of endeavor as the invention, or from a different field but reasonably pertinent to the same problem. *See* § 14.3.5.3.2.

antedate (swearing behind a reference): A procedure whereby a patent applicant can establish an invention date earlier than the effective date of prior art that has been cited against his claims in a rejection for non-obviousness (§ 103) or lack of novelty (§§ 102(a) or (e)).

anticipation: A single prior art reference anticipates a claim when it contains all the elements of the claim. The claim is rejected for lack of novelty under § 102.

assignment: A transfer of ownership of a patent application or patent from one entity to another. Record all assignments with the USPTO Assignment Services Division to maintain clear title to pending patent applications and patents.

benefit claim: The claiming by an applicant in a nonprovisional application of a benefit of an invention disclosed in a prior-filed, co-pending (under examination at the same time), provisional, or nonprovisional application, or international application designating the United States for the purposes of securing an earlier effective filing date for the nonprovisional application.

best mode: The specification must set forth the best mode, or preferred embodiment, contemplated by the inventor at the time of filing, of making and using his or her invention (§ 112), or the patent may be declared invalid. *See* § 14.3.3.3. The AIA eliminated failure to set forth best mode as a basis for patent invalidity.

blocking patent: Two or more patented inventions block each other when one cannot be practiced without infringing the other, and vice versa. Blocking patents often arise when an improvement on an invention is patented: the improvement cannot be practiced without infringing the original patent, and the original inventor cannot practice the improvement without infringing the improvement patent. The parties commonly agree to a cross-license to resolve the issue.

central claiming: A claiming regime in which a claim recites the preferred embodiment of the invention but is deemed to cover a range of equivalents to that preferred embodiment.

Certificate of Correction: Minor errors in an issued patent can be corrected with a Certificate of Correction. *See* § 254 (correction of USPTO mistake); § 255 (correction of applicant mistake).

claim restriction: A discretely claimed component of a patent claim. *See also element.*

claim vitiation: An accused device cannot be infringing if it would effectively vitiate (or eliminate) any claim limitation. This doctrine is a corollary of the all-elements rule. *See* § 14.4.1.4.2.1.1.1.

claims: Claims delineate the patented invention. The patent specification must conclude with a claim or claims particularly pointing out and distinctly claiming the subject matter that the applicant regards as his or her invention or discovery.

classification: Patents are classified by a system using a three-digit class and a three-digit subclass to describe every similar grouping of patent art. Multiple classification codes may describe a single invention.

combination patent: A patent granted for an invention that unites existing components in a novel way.

composed of (used when defining the scope of a claim): A transitional phrase that is interpreted in the same manner as either *consisting of* or *consisting essentially of*, depending on the facts of the particular case.

comprising (used when defining the scope of a claim): A transitional phrase that is synonymous with *including*, *containing* or *characterized by*; is inclusive or open-ended and does not exclude additional, unrecited elements or method steps. *Comprising* is a term of art used in claim language that means that the named elements are essential in describing the invention.

conception: The formation in the mind of the inventor of the definite and permanent idea of the complete invention that is thereafter reduced to practice. *See* § 14.3.4.1.2.1.

consisting essentially of (used when defining the scope of a claim): A transitional phrase that limits the scope of a claim to the specified materials or steps and those that do not materially affect the basic and novel characteristics of the claimed invention. For the purposes of searching for and applying prior art under §§ 102 and 103, absent a clear indication in the specification or claims of what the basic and novel characteristics actually are, *consisting essentially of* will be construed as equivalent to *comprising*.

consisting of (used when defining the scope of a claim): A transitional phrase that is closed and excludes any element, step, or ingredient not specified in the claim.

continuation: A second application for the same invention claimed in a prior non-provisional application and filed before the first application becomes abandoned or patented.

continuation-in-part (CIP): An application filed during the lifetime of an earlier nonprovisional application that repeats some substantial portion or all of the earlier nonprovisional application and adds matter not disclosed in the earlier non-provisional application. *See* § 14.2.3.4.

contributory infringement: Section 271(c) imposes liability when a party "offers to sell or sell within the United States or imports into the United States a component of a patented machine, manufacture, combination or composition, or a material or apparatus for use in practicing a patented process, constituting a material part of the invention, knowing the same to be especially made or especially adapted for use in an infringement of such patent, and not a staple article or commodity of commerce suitable for substantial noninfringing use, shall be liable as a contributory infringer." *See* § 14.4.1.3.2.

counterpart: An application filed in a foreign patent office that is substantially similar to the patent application filed with the USPTO and is based on some or all of the same invention. The two applications would generally have the same applicant.

covered business method review (CBMR): The America Invents Act instituted a variant of the postgrant review process for business method patents of all filing dates. Patent validity can be challenged on any ground, and covered business method review is broader than inter partes review. *See* § 14.2.5.8.1.

critical date: The date one year prior to the date a patent application is filed. The patent will be invalid for lack of novelty if the invention was in public use in the United States, or patented or described anywhere in the world, prior to the critical date. *See* § 102(b); § 14.3.4.1.5.

declaration (of inventor): A document in which an applicant for patent declares that he or she (1) made or authorized the application, (2) believes that he or she is the original inventor or an original joint inventor of a claimed invention in the application; and (3) acknowledges that any willful false statement made in the declaration is punishable under 18 U.S.C. § 1001 by fine or imprisonment of not more than five (5) years, or both. These requirements apply to applications filed after September 15, 2012. *See* M.P.E.P § 602.01(a)–(b). For applications filed prior to that date, the declaration also required the inventor's country of citizenship. An oath or declaration must be filed in each nonprovisional patent application.

definiteness: Shorthand for the requirement, under § 112(b), that the claims particularly point out and distinctly claim the subject matter that the applicant regards as his or her invention. *See* § 14.3.3.4.

dependent claim: A claim that refers back to and further limits a preceding dependent or independent claim. A dependent claim includes by reference every limitation of the claim from which it depends.

derivation proceeding: The AIA established this new proceeding to allow an inventor to challenge an earlier-filed third-party application or patent claiming subject matter that was derived from the inventor's own work. This proceeding partially substitutes for interference proceedings. *See* § 14.3.4.2.5.

design patent: A patent for a new, original, and ornamental design for an article of manufacture.

designation: A selection made by the applicant, in the Request for an International Application filed under the Patent Cooperation Treaty (PCT), as to the countries in which protection for an invention is desired.

diligence: To establish a conception date as the date of invention, the inventor must have worked diligently following conception to reduce the invention to practice. In the course of an interference, a party can establish its conception date as the date of invention by showing reasonable diligence from before the other's conception until their own reduction to practice date. *See* § 102(g); § 14.3.4.1.2.3.

direct infringement: A person is liable for direct infringement if he or she "without authority makes, uses, offers to sell, or sells any patented invention, within the United States or imports into the United States any patented invention during the term of the patent therefore." § 271(a). An accused infringer's intent is immaterial, as patent infringement is a strict liability offense. *See* § 14.4.1.1.

disclaimer: There are two types of disclaimers under § 253: statutory disclaimers and terminal disclaimers. A patentee may make a statutory disclaimer of any complete claim, stating therein the extent of his or her interest in such patent. A patentee may make a terminal disclaimer to disclaim or dedicate to the public the remaining time of the term of the patent granted. A terminal disclaimer may be filed for the purpose of overcoming a judicially created double-patenting rejection. Disclaimers are required to be in writing and recorded in the USPTO, and are considered part of the original patent to the extent of the interest actually possessed by the disclaimant and by those claiming under him or her.

disclosure: In return for a patent, the inventor gives as consideration a complete disclosure of the invention for which protection is sought. *See* § 14.3.3.

divisional application: A later application for an independent or distinct invention disclosing and claiming only a portion of the subject matter disclosed in the earlier or parent application.

doctrine of equivalents: A judicially developed principle for finding patent infringement when the accused process or product falls outside the literal scope of the patent claims. The essential objective inquiry is: "Does the accused product or process contain elements equivalent to each claimed element of the patented invention?" *See* § 14.4.1.4.2.

double patenting: An inventor may not obtain claims in more than one patent directed either to the same invention or an obvious variation of the same invention. A rejection by the USPTO based on obviousness can be overcome by filing a terminal disclaimer stating that the additional patents will expire on the same date as the first patent. A terminal disclaimer, therefore, eliminates any improper extension of the initial patent term. *See* § 14.4.2.4.1.

effective filing date: The filing date of an earlier-filed application accorded under §§ 119/365(a)/365(b) (foreign filing or domestic provisional application), 120/365(c) (earlier U.S. filing date), or 121 (divisional applications), or if none of these sections is satisfied, the actual filing date of the patent.

electronic file wrapper: A system that provides a way to access electronic copies of the correspondence, documents, and other pertinent records used in considering a particular patent application.

element: A discretely claimed component of a patent claim. *See also claim restriction.*

embodiment: A manner in which an invention can be made, used, practiced, or expressed. *See best mode.*

enablement: The specification must describe in "full, clear, concise, and exact terms" how to make and use the invention such that any person skilled in the art can do so without undue experimentation. *See* § 14.3.3.2.

ex parte reexamination: A procedure whereby patentees and third parties can seek reexamination of issued patents. *See* § 14.2.5.5.2.

experimental use: Experimental use has two distinct meanings within patent law. First, experimental use is an exception to the public-use statutory bar under § 102(b). So long as the public use was to test or experiment with the invention, it is not counted in computing the one-year statutory bar. Second, experimental use is a defense to infringement and requires that the construction and use of the patented invention be for scientific purposes only. *See* § 14.3.4.1.5.1.

express abandonment: *See abandonment.*

file wrapper: The folder into which papers for a particular application are collected and maintained. It contains a complete record of proceedings in the USPTO from the filing of the initial patent application to the issued patent. The file wrapper of a patent application that is maintained by the USPTO is the official record.

file wrapper estoppel: *See prosecution history estoppel.*

filing date: The date of receipt in the USPTO of an application which includes (1) a specification containing a description and, if the application is a nonprovisional application, at least one claim, and (2) any required drawings.

final office action: A USPTO action on the second or any subsequent examination or consideration by an examiner that is intended to close the prosecution of a nonprovisional patent application.

First Sale Doctrine/Exhaustion Principle: The first unrestricted sale of a patented product exhausts the patentee's control over that product, and it can be resold and repaired without implicating the patent owner's rights. This is a form of implied license. *See* § 14.4.2.2.1.1.

grace period: The one-year period between the critical date and the filing date, during which the invention may be offered for sale or used publicly in the United States, or described in a printed publication or patented anywhere in the world without invalidating the patent under § 102(b).

***Handgards* claim**: An antitrust counterclaim to a patent infringement suit, alleging that the patentee either knew the patent was invalid or was not being infringed. *See Handgards, Inc. v. Ethicon, Inc.*, 601 F.2d 986 (9th Cir. 1979).

having (used when defining the scope of a claim): A transitional phrase that is synonymous with *including*, *containing*, or *characterized by*; is inclusive or open-ended and does not exclude additional, unrecited elements or method steps.

improvement patent: A patent based on an improvement to a preexisting invention.

indefiniteness: *See definiteness.*

independent claim: A claim that does not refer back to or depend on another claim.

indirect infringement: Indirect infringement covers conduct by a person who assists or supports another's direct infringement of a patented invention. Direct infringement must be established as a predicate for each act of indirect infringement. *See* § 14.4.1.3.

inducement: Section 271(b) provides that "[w]hoever actively induces infringement of a patent shall be liable as an infringer." A finding of inducement requires that a patent owner establish evidence of culpable conduct directed toward encouraging another's infringement. *See* § 14.4.1.3.1.

inequitable conduct: Where a patent applicant breaches the duty to prosecute a patent application in good faith and candor. *See* 37 C.F.R. § 1.56; *see also* § 14.4.2.3.1.

information disclosure statement (IDS): A list of patents, publications, U.S. applications, or other information submitted for consideration by the USPTO in a nonprovisional patent application filed under § 111(a) to comply with applicant's duty to submit information that is material to the patentability of the claimed invention. *See* § 14.2.2.1.

inter partes reexamination: A procedure allowing third parties to seek invalidation by the USPTO of patents granted on applications filed on or after November 29, 1999. It was phased out beginning on September 16, 2011, and replaced by the AIA's inter partes review procedure. *See* § 14.2.5.5.3.

inter partes review (IPR): A procedure established by the AIA for third parties to seek invalidation of patents. *See* § 14.2.5.6.

interference: A proceeding, typically conducted before the Board of Patent Appeals and Interferences or in certain circumstances before a district court, to determine priority of invention between a pending application and/or one or more unexpired patents.

intervening rights: Claims that were modified at reissue, for any reason, are subject to a reliance-type interest (intervening rights). Third parties may rely on the claims of an issued patent. *See* § 14.2.5.4.2.2.

invention: Any art or process, machine, manufacture, design, or composition of matter, or any new and useful improvement thereof, or any variety of plant, which is or may be patentable under the patent laws of the United States.

invention date: The date either on which an invention is reduced to practice or conceived, so long as the inventor can show reasonable diligence from conception until reduction to practice.

issue date: The date that a patent application becomes a U.S. patent. The issue date is the date that patent rights can be exercised.

***Jepson* claim format**: A claim containing a preamble explaining the current state of the art, followed by a description of the claimed patentable improvement.

joint infringement: Liability for joint infringement can be found only where one party controlled or directed each step in the process. *See* § 14.4.1.3.3.

joint inventor: An inventor who is named with at least one other inventor in a patent application, wherein each inventor contributes to the conception of the invention set forth in at least one claim in a patent application.

laches: An equitable defense that the plaintiff unreasonably delayed in asserting an infringement claim. If a patentee files suit more than six years after he or she became (or reasonably should have become) aware of the alleged infringement, a presumption of laches arises, and the patentee must establish legitimate reasons for the delay. This defense does not bar the plaintiff's action entirely, but prevents the recovery of any damages accrued prior to the filing of the action. *See* § 14.4.2.3.4.

license: An agreement between a patent owner and a licensee that the patent owner will not sue the licensee for acts that would otherwise constitute infringement.

limitation: A component of an invention described in a patent claim. *See element.*

literal infringement: Literal infringement requires an accused device to satisfy every element of the asserted patent claim precisely. *See* § 14.4.1.4.1.

***Markush* claim format**: A *Markush* claim claims a genus of inventions in a single claim where the family of inventions all share a common trait, for example, "a chemical compound of the formula COOH–CH2-R, where R is selected from the group consisting of ________." *Markush* claims normally do not occur outside of the field of chemistry.

means-plus-function claim format: A means-plus-function claim defines one or more elements of the claim as a "means for [performing a function]." This special type of limitation is interpreted to cover the structure(s) described in the specification for performing the claimed function as well as equivalents of that/those structure(s) as of the time of filing. *See* § 112(f); § 14.4.1.4.1.1.

method claim: A claim covering a way of doing something, typically conveyed as a series of steps.

multiple dependent claim: A dependent claim that further limits and refers back in the alternative to more than one preceding independent or dependent claim. Acceptable multiple dependent claims shall refer to preceding claims using the terms *or*, *any one of*, *one of*, *any of*, *either*. A multiple dependent claim may not depend on another multiple dependent claim, either directly or indirectly.

national stage application: An application that has entered the national phase of the Patent Cooperation Treaty by the fulfillment of certain requirements in a national patent office. Such an application is filed under § 371 in the United States and is referred to as a "371 application."

new matter: Information in an amendment to a pending patent that departs from the original disclosure. Under § 132, amendments cannot introduce new matter into the disclosure of the invention.

nonfinal office action: An office action made by the examiner where the applicant is entitled to reply and request reconsideration or further examination, with or without making an amendment.

nonobviousness: The requirement that to be patentable, an invention be sufficiently different from the prior art that, at the time it was made, it would not have been obvious to a person having ordinary skill in the art. *See* § 14.3.5.

nonpatent literature: Documents and publications that are not patents or published patent applications but are cited as references for being relevant in a patent prosecution. For example, a magazine article or doctoral thesis relevant to a claimed invention might be cited as nonpatent literature. Typically, references cited in an application are grouped into domestic patents and patent application publications, foreign patents, and nonpatent literature.

nonprovisional application: The "regular" type of patent applications, as distinct from provisional applications filed under § 111(b), often referred to simply as "applications." *See* § 14.2.2.2.1.

nonresponsive amendment: An amendment filed by the applicant that does not fully respond to the examiner's office action in accordance with 37 C.F.R. § 1.111.

normal publication: Regular 18-month publication or redacted publication of a nonprovisional application.

notice: The practice of marking a patented article with the word *patent* followed by the patent number. Without notice, the patentee may recover only for damages that occurred after the infringer received a charge of patent infringement.

notice of abandonment: A written notification from the USPTO that an application has been declared abandoned or, in other words, is no longer pending. If the application was abandoned unintentionally or due to USPTO error, the applicant has a deadline of two months from the issue date of the notice of abandonment to file either (1) a petition to revive the application or (2) a request to reinstate the application.

notice of allowance: A notification to the applicant that he or she is entitled to a patent under the law and requesting payment of a specified issue fee (and possibly a publication fee as well) within three months (non-extendable) from the mailing date of the notice of allowance.

notice of references cited (also known as a PTO-892 form): A list of relevant references cited by a patent examiner in an office action. The following are some examples of such references: domestic patents, domestic patent application publications, foreign patents or patent publications, publications, electronic documents, and affidavits.

novelty: The requirement under § 102 that an invention be sufficiently new relative to the prior art. *See* § 14.3.4.

oath: *See declaration (of inventor).*

obviousness: *See nonobviousness.*

office action: The patent examiner's responses to the patent application and subsequent amendments.

on-sale bar: Section 102(b) specifies an on-sale bar, such that if an invention has been on sale for over one year, it is no longer patentable. *See* § 14.3.4.1.5.2.

opposition: A procedure allowing a third party to request a patent application's refusal or an issued patent's annulment.

original application: *Original* is used in the patent statute and rules to refer to an application that is not a reissue application. An original application may be a first filing or a continuing application.

parent application: The term *parent* is applied to an earlier application of the inventor disclosing a given invention.

patent: A quasi-property right granted by the government of the United States to an inventor "to exclude others from making, using, offering for sale, or selling the invention throughout the United States or importing the invention into the United States" for a limited time in exchange for public disclosure of the invention.

Patent Cooperation Treaty (PCT): A mechanism by which an applicant can file a single application that, when certain requirements have been fulfilled, is equivalent to a regular national filing in each designated country. There are currently over 130 PCT contracting states.

patent pending: A phrase that often appears on manufactured items. It means that someone has applied for a patent on an invention that is contained in the manufactured item. It serves as a warning that a patent may issue that would cover the item and that copiers should be careful because they might infringe if the patent issues. Once the patent issues, the patent owner will stop using the phrase "patent pending" and start using a phrase such as "covered by U.S. Patent Number XXXXXXX."

patent term: The period of time during which a patent is enforceable. For patent applications filed after June 8, 1995, the expiration date is twenty years from the earliest effective filing date, subject to various extensions for delays occurring during prosecution and regulatory approval for drug-related patents. *See* § 14.2.4.

Patent Trial and Appeal Board (PTAB): The AIA created this administrative body to replace the Board of Patent Appeals and Interferences (BPAI). It hears appeals by a patent applicant from a USPTO patent examiner's final refusal to allow a patent application or adverse decision in an ex parte patent reexamination proceeding, inter partes and postgrant review proceedings filed by a party challenging the validity of an issued patent, derivation proceedings filed by a subsequent patent applicant claiming that an earlier patent applicant for the same invention derived the invention from the subsequent patent applicant, and interference proceedings to determine the first inventor of an invention commenced before September 16, 2012. PTAB decisions concerning inter partes and postgrant reviews and ex parte reexamination proceedings may be appealed only to the U.S. Court of Appeals for the Federal Circuit. In several circumstances, a civil action against the USPTO in the U.S. District Court for the Eastern District of Virginia may be instituted after a final

PTAB decision: (1) where a patent applicant is dissatisfied with a PTAB decision concerning the final rejection of the patent application unless the applicant has appealed to the Federal Circuit (*see* § 145); (2) in a derivation proceeding where the losing party initially filed a notice of appeal from the PTAB decision to the Federal Circuit, the adverse party may request that further proceedings instead be conducted in the Eastern District of Virginia (*see* AIA § 7); and (3) where a party is dissatisfied with the decision in an interference proceeding over which the PTAB has jurisdiction, unless that party has appealed to the Federal Circuit (*see* § 146).

peripheral claiming: A regime in which an applicant delineates the precise boundaries of the claimed area of exclusivity, in contrast to central claiming in which the applicant defines the claim directly.

person: For purposes of small entity determination, a person is defined as any inventor or other individual (e.g., an individual to whom an inventor has transferred some rights in the invention) who has not assigned, granted, conveyed, or licensed, and is under no obligation under contract or law to assign, grant, convey, or license any rights in the invention.

person having ordinary skill in the art (PHOSITA): A hypothetical person with knowledge of all analogous art from whose perspective nonobviousness, written description, and enablement are analyzed. *See* §§ 103, 112; *see also* §§ 14.3.3, 14.3.5.3.1.

petition to make special (PTMS): An applicant may petition the USPTO to examine his or her application ahead of other pending applications. A petition to make special may be granted on the basis of an inventor's age or poor health, that the patent will enable manufacture of the invention, is presently being infringed, relates to certain fields including superconductivity, HIV/AIDS, and counter-terrorism, or several other reasons.

post-grant review (PGR): Under this new procedure added by the AIA, third parties may file a petition seeking to cancel one or more patent claims within nine months of a patent's issue or reissue date. *See* § 14.2.5.8.

preferred embodiment: How the inventor sets forth the best mode for carrying out the claimed invention in the application.

printed publication: A reference that is sufficiently accessible to the public interested in the invention. *See* § 14.3.4.1.1.2.

prior art: The general category of technologies and events against which novelty and nonobviousness are evaluated. What qualifies as prior art is specified in §§ 102 and 103.

priority claim: Claims under §§ 119(a)–(e) and 120 for the benefit of the filing date of earlier filed applications.

priority date: The first filing of a patent application anywhere in the world describing an enabled invention usually establishes the priority date for that invention. *See* § 14.2.2.2.3.

pro se: Used to designate an independent inventor who has elected to file an application by himself or herself without the services of a licensed representative.

prosecution: The process for applying for and obtaining a patent from the USPTO.

prosecution history estoppel: A doctrine that prevents a patentee from obtaining coverage through the doctrine of equivalents over subject matter that was surrendered during prosecution. *See* § 14.4.1.4.2.1.2.

provisional application: A provisional application for patent is a U.S. national application for patent filed in the USPTO under § 111(b), which allows filing without a formal patent claim, oath or declaration, or any information disclosure (prior art) statement. A provisional application can establish an early effective filing date in a nonprovisional patent application filed under § 111(a) and automatically becomes abandoned after one year. It also allows the term *patent pending* to be applied. *See* § 14.2.2.2.4.

reads on: An accused device, manufacture, composition, or process "reads on" (and hence infringes) a patent claim if it embodies each of the claim limitations. Similarly, a patent claim "reads on" a prior art reference (and hence is invalid) if the prior art reference contains each of the claim limitations.

reasonable diligence: First-to-conceive inventor must have been reasonably diligent in working to reduce the invention to practice between the time "just prior" to the later inventor's date of conception until the first-to-conceive inventor's reduction to practice. Reasonable diligence is only at issue when the inventor was first to conceive but second to reduce to practice. *See* § 14.3.4.1.2.3.

recapture rule: Bars a patentee from seeking reissue claims that regain subject matter that was surrendered to obtain allowance during the original prosecution. *See* § 14.2.5.4.2.1. This rule is similar to prosecution history estoppel. *See* § 14.4.1.4.2.1.2.

record copy: Original copy of an international application filed under the Patent Cooperation Treaty maintained by the International Bureau of the World Intellectual Property Organization.

redacted publication: A patent application publication that omits material that was present in the specification or claims of the nonprovisional patent application filed in the USPTO. *See* 37 C.F.R. § 1.217 and MPEP § 1132.

reduction to practice: Following conception, reduction to practice is the final step in the inventive process. Reduction to practice can be actual (by constructing a physical embodiment of the invention) or constructive (by filing a patent application that satisfies the disclosure requirements of § 112). *See* § 14.3.4.1.2.2.

reexamination proceeding: At any time during the enforceability of a patent, any person may file a request for the USPTO to conduct a second examination of any claim of the patent on the basis of prior art patents or printed publications which that person states to be pertinent and applicable to the patent and believes to have a bearing on the patentability (*see* 37 C.F.R. § 1.501). For the request for reexamination to be granted, a substantial new question of patentability must be present with regard to at least one patent claim. The request must be in writing and must be accompanied by payment of a reexamination request filing fee as set forth in 37 C.F.R. § 1.20(c). *See* § 14.2.5.5.

reference: *See prior art.*

reissue application: An application for a patent to take the place of an unexpired patent that is defective in one or more particulars. Resissues may narrow or broaden the application. *See* § 14.2.5.4.

rejoinder: The returning to active consideration of claims previously withdrawn from consideration to due to a restriction requirement—i.e., a determination by the USPTO that an application contains more than one invention.

request for continued examination (RCE): A request filed in an application in which prosecution is closed (e.g., the application is under final rejection or a notice of allowance) that is filed to reopen prosecution and continue examination of the application.

restriction: If two or more independent and distinct inventions are claimed in a single application, the examiner may require the applicant to elect a single invention to which the claims will be restricted. This requirement is known as a requirement for restriction (also known as a requirement for division). Such requirement will normally be made before any action on the merits; however, it may be made at any time before final action (final rejection).

reverse doctrine of equivalents: A doctrine excusing infringement where an accused device literally infringes a patent, but should nonetheless be excused because it substantially differs in operative principle and results. Although it has not been applied in over a century to excuse infringement, it continues to be raised. *See* § 14.4.1.4.3.

specification: A written description of the invention and the manner and process of making and using the same.

statutory disclaimer: *See disclaimer.*

submarine patent: An informal term for a patent that is intentionally delayed in prosecution by the applicant to let an infringing user continue to develop its business, with the intention of claiming later-invented technology once the patent finally "surfaces" from the PTO. As of November 29, 2000, most patent applications must be published within eighteen months of filing, so submarine patents have become less common.

substitute patent application: An application that is, in essence, a duplicate of a prior application by the same applicant abandoned before the filing of the substitute application. A substitute application does not obtain the benefit of the filing date of the prior application.

supplemental Examination: A procedure added by the AIA authorizing a patentee to seek further consideration of additional information relevant to patentability. *See* § 14.2.5.3.

terminal disclaimer: *See disclaimer.*

utility: To be patentable, an invention must have specific, substantial, and credible utility. *See* § 14.3.2.

***Walker Process* claim**: An antitrust counterclaim to a patent infringement suit, alleging that the patent was fraudulently obtained so as to exert monopolistic power and is therefore invalid. *See Walker Process Equip., Inc. v. Food Mach. & Chem. Corp.*, 382 U.S. 172 (1965).

written description: The portion of a patent specification, as required by § 112(a), describing the background of the invention, a summary of the invention, and a detailed description of the invention. The patentee must convey with reasonable clarity to those skilled in the art that, as of the filing date sought, he or she was in possession of the invention, and the written description must enable a person having ordinary skill in the art to practice the invention without undue experimentation. *See* § 14.3.3.1.

Appendix B
Acronyms

AIA: America Invents Act
AIPA: American Inventors Protection Act of 1999
AIPLA: American Intellectual Property Law Association
ANDA: Abbreviated New Drug Application
AOUSC: Administrative Office of the United States Courts
AU: (Group) Art Unit
BLA: Biologic License Application
BPAI: Board of Patent Appeals and Interferences
BPCIA: Biologics Price Competition and Innovation Act
CAPC: civil action to obtain patent certainty
CBM: covered business method
CBMR: covered business method review
CC: claim construction
CCPA: United States Court of Customs and Patent Appeals
CIP: continuation-in-part
CMC: case-management conference
CPA: continued prosecution application
CRU: Central Reexamination Unit
DOE: Doctrine of Equivalents
EAST: examiner automated search tools
EFD: effective filing date
EFS: electronic filing system
ePAS: Electronic Patent Assignment System
EPO: European Patent Office
ESD: examination support document
ESI: electronically stored information
FAR: Federal Acquisitions Regulations
FCBA: Federal Circuit Bar Association
FDA: Food and Drug Administration
FDCA: Food, Drug, and Cosmetic Act
FRAND: fair, reasonable and non-discriminatory
FTC: Federal Trade Commission
FTF: first-to-file
FTI: first-to-invent
GAU: Group Art Unit
IDS: information disclosure statement
INID: Internationally agreed Numbers for the Identification of bibliographic Data
IPR: inter partes review
IT: information technology
ITC: International Trade Commission

JMDL: Judicial Panel on Multidistrict Litigation
JSPR: joint preliminary status report
MDL: multidistrict litigation
MPEP: Manual of Patent Examining Procedure
MSJ: motion for summary judgment
NCE: new chemical entity
NDA: new drug application
NOA: notice of allowance
NPE: nonpracticing entity
NPL: non-patent literature
OG: Official Gazette
OIPE: Office of Initial Patent Examination
PAIR: Patent Application Information Retrieval
PCT: Patent Cooperation Treaty
PGR: postgrant review
PHOSITA: person having ordinary skill in the art
PHSA: Public Health and Safety Act
PLR(s): patent local rule(s)
PPA: Plant Patent Act
PTA: patent term adjustment
PTAB: Patent Trial and Appeal Board
PTE: patent term extension
PTMS: petition to make special
PTO: Patent and Trademark Office
PVP: plant variety protection
PVPA: Plant Variety Protection Act
RAND: reasonable and nondiscriminatory
RCE: request for continued examination
RCFC: Rules of the United States Court of Federal Claims
RLD: Reference Listed Drug
SEP: standard-essential patents
SNQ: substantial new question of patentability
SSO: standard setting organization
TD: terminal disclaimer
TSM: teaching, suggestion, or motivation
UPOV: Convention of the International Union for the Protection of New Plant Varieties
USITC: United States International Trade Commission
USPTO: United States Patent and Trademark Office
WIPO: World Intellectual Property Organization
WTO: World Trade Organization

Appendix C
Patent Resources

Organizations

ABA Section of Intellectual Property Law
http://www.abanet.org/intelprop

American Intellectual Property Law Association
http://www.aipla.org/

Federal Circuit Bar Association
http://www.fedcirbar.org/olc/pub/LVFC/

Intellectual Property Owners Association
http://www.ipo.org

Online Resources

Federal Judicial Center (Patent Law Resources)
http://fjconline.fjc.dcn/node/253794

http://www.google.com/patents

Manual of Patent Examining Procedure (MPEP)
http://www.uspto.gov/web/offices/pac/mpep/mpep.htm

Orange Book Blog ("At the Intersection of Patent and FDA Law")
http://www.orangebookblog.typepad.com/

Patent Trade Office (Patent Full-Page Databases)
http://patft.uspto.gov/

PatentlyO ("The nation's leading patent law blog")
http://www.patentlyo.com/

Promote the Progress ("The patent education portal")
http://promotetheprogress.com/

Publications

Anatomy of a Patent Case (American College of Trial Lawyers, 2d ed. 2012) (copies available to the federal judiciary from the Federal Judicial Center)

Donald S. Chisum, Chisum on Patents: A Treatise on the Law of Patentability, Validity, and Infringement (New York : LEXIS Pub., 1978)

Civil Litigation Management Manual (Judicial Conference of the United States, 2d ed. 2010) (208 pages) (copies available to the federal judiciary from the Federal Judicial Center)
This manual provides trial judges with a guide to managing civil cases. It sets out a wide array of case-management techniques, beginning with case filing and conclud-

ing with steps for streamlining trials, and it discusses a number of special topics, including pro se and high-visibility cases, the role of staff, and automation that supports case management.

Effective Use of Courtroom Technology: A Judge's Guide to Pretrial and Trial (Federal Judicial Center 2001) (358 pages)
This publication, a joint project between the FJC and the National Institute for Trial Advocacy, describes the substantive and procedural considerations that may arise when lawyers bring electronic equipment to the courtroom or use court-provided equipment for displaying or playing evidentiary exhibits or illustrative aids during trial.

Federal Circuit Bar Journal (http://www.law.gmu.edu/fcbj/)

Robert J. Goldman, Schwartz's Patent Law and Practice (Bloomberg BNA 8th ed. 2015) (available online to the federal judiciary from the Federal Judicial Center at http://fjconline.fjc.dcn)

Manual for Complex Litigation, Fourth Edition (Federal Judicial Center 2004) (798 pages)
This manual describes approaches that trial judges have found useful in managing complex cases. This edition updates the treatment of electronic discovery and other aspects of pretrial management and describes major changes in the substantive and procedural law affecting case management in mass tort, class action, intellectual property, employment discrimination, and other types of litigation. A new chapter deals with managing scientific evidence.

Moy's Walker on Patents (4th ed., Thomson Reuters)

Barbara J. Rothstein, Ronald J. Hedges & Elizabeth C. Wiggins, Managing Discovery of Electronic Information: A Pocket Guide for Judges (Federal Judicial Center 2d ed. 2012) (40 pages)
This pocket guide covers issues unique to the discovery of electronically stored information (ESI), including its scope, the allocation of costs, the form of production, the waiver of privilege and work product protection, and the preservation of data and spoliation.

Video

The Patent Process: An Overview for Jurors (Federal Judicial Center 2013) (17 minutes) (sample patent) (https://www.youtube.com/watch?v=ax7QHQTbKQE)
This brief video provides jurors in a patent case an explanation of what a patent is and the process for obtaining it. It has been carefully crafted, in consultation with judges and members of the bar, to present a balanced view of the patent process, but individual judges will want to review it carefully and consult with counsel before deciding whether to use it in a particular case. A sample patent, developed to accompany the video, is available at http://www.fjc.gov/public/pdf.nsf/lookup/PatentSystemSample2.pdf/$file/PatentSystemSample2.pdf

Appendix D
Patent Local Rules

Patent Local Rules (PLRs) date back to December 1, 2000, when the Northern District of California promulgated the first set of rules governing the content and timing of disclosures in patent cases. These rules established a default regime for operationalizing the claim construction process that developed following the Supreme Court's decision in *Markman v. Westview Instruments*, 515 U.S. 1192 (1995). *See generally* James Ware & Brian Davy, *The History, Content, Application, and Influence of the Northern District of California's Patent Local Rules*, 25 Santa Clara Computer & High Tech. L.J. 965 (2009). The Northern District of California has since updated its PLRs. Thirty-one district courts now have some form of Patent Local Rules. Many follow the Northern District of California model. Some districts have augmented the model to address distinctive aspects of their docket. For example, the District of New Jersey, which is home to many pharmaceutical companies, developed rules specific to Hatch-Waxman ANDA cases. Other districts, such as the District of Massachusetts, implement somewhat different approaches. Some districts also include model scheduling orders and protective orders in their local rules. This appendix lists the PLRs that have been implemented as of March 11, 2015. The documents in bold are contained herein.

California

- **Northern District (last updated Nov. 1, 2014)**
- Southern District (last updated Feb. 2, 2015)

Colorado (adopted Aug. 1, 2014)

Delaware

- **Chief Judge Stark scheduling order (non-ANDA issued June 2014, ANDA issued July 1, 2014) — included in Chapter 7 (non-ANDA), Chapter 10 (ANDA)**
- Judge Robinson scheduling order (last updated Feb. 5, 2015)
- Judge Sleet scheduling order (patent) (last updated Feb. 25, 2014)
- Judge Andrews Rule 16 patent scheduling order (last updated April 2012)

Georgia

- Northern District (effective July 15, 2004)

Idaho (revised Jan. 2, 2015)

Illinois

- Northern District (last updated Apr. 28, 2015)

Indiana

- Northern District (last updated Aug. 15, 2014)
- Southern District Patent Case Management Plan (revised Nov. 3, 2014)

Maryland (revised July 1, 2014)

Massachusetts (updated through Jan. 6, 2015)

Minnesota: uses Form 4 for patent cases (special Rule 26(f) report) (last updated May 14, 2013)

Missouri

- Eastern District (effective Jan. 1, 2011)

Nevada (effective Aug. 1, 2011)

New Hampshire (last updated Dec. 1, 2013)

New Jersey (last updated Apr. 3, 2014)

New York

- Eastern District (effective Apr. 8, 2013)
- Northern District (effective Jan. 1, 2012)
- Southern District (updated Jan. 30, 2015)

North Carolina

- Eastern District (last updated Aug. 2013)
- Middle District (last updated Mar. 1, 2014)
- Western District (effective Mar. 31, 2011)

Ohio

- Northern District (effective Oct. 22, 2009)
- Southern District (effective June 1, 2010)

Pennsylvania

- Western District (effective Dec. 1, 2009)

Tennessee

- Western District (last updated Jan. 1, 2014)

Texas

- **Eastern District (last updated May 19, 2015)**
- Northern District (Dallas Div.) (last updated Dec. 1, 2009)
- Southern District (last updated Dec. 1, 2009)

Utah (effective Dec. 1, 2013)

Washington

- Eastern District (effective Nov. 10, 2010)
- Western District (effective Jan. 1, 2009)

The website localpatentrules.com provides many useful comparisons between the rules, as well as updated copies of the rules. Many of these districts additionally have blogs covering changes to their local rules, including patent local rules. The best source for checking for updates to patent local rules remains the official website of each district court of interest.

The Northern District of California and the District of New Jersey have similar rules in many areas. Both jurisdictions require infringement claim charts and enforce § 271 rules and § 101 defenses on invalidity contentions in the same way. The jurisdictions differ in the required timing for infringement and invalidity contentions, as well as rules for document disclosure and claim construction.

In addition, several federal districts are known as "rocket dockets"—districts in which cases are typically disposed of much faster than in other federal districts. Typically these districts have special rules for handling patent cases, go to trial within a year of filing the complaint, are willing to resolve cases on summary judgment motions, and tend to view discovery disputes harshly. The Eastern District of Texas, Eastern District of Virginia, and the Western District of Wisconsin are commonly viewed as rocket dockets (along with the International Trade Commission). Many of these districts have judges who establish standing orders to move cases forward in a rapid fashion, and the local rules in these jurisdictions (even if not specific to patents) tend to support efficient management of the docket.

However, each venue is unique. In the Eastern District of Texas, local counsel is generally needed, and the local patent rules must be observed. Notably, infringement contentions are due no later than ten days before the initial case-management conference. The Western District of Wisconsin does not have local patent rules, but judges do have specific procedures for patent cases—including mandating that infringement contentions be served within five weeks of the first scheduling conference. In the Eastern District of Virginia, all cases proceed quickly, and there are no specific rules for patent cases.

UNITED STATES DISTRICT COURT
Northern District of California

PATENT LOCAL RULES

TABLE OF CONTENTS

1. SCOPE OF RULES

1-1. Title

These are the Local Rules of Practice for Patent Cases before the United States District Court for the Northern District of California. They should be cited as "Patent L.R. __."

1-2. Scope and Construction

These rules apply to all civil actions filed in or transferred to this Court which allege infringement of a utility patent in a complaint, counterclaim, cross-claim or third party claim, or which seek a declaratory judgment that a utility patent is not infringed, is invalid or is unenforceable. The Civil Local Rules of this Court shall also apply to such actions, except to the extent that they are inconsistent with these Patent Local Rules. If the filings or actions in a case do not trigger the application of these Patent Local Rules under the terms set forth herein, the parties shall, as soon as such circumstances become known, meet and confer for the purpose of agreeing on the application of these Patent Local Rules to the case and promptly report the results of the meet and confer to the Court.

1-3. Modification of these Rules

The Court may modify the obligations or deadlines set forth in these Patent Local Rules based on the circumstances of any particular case, including, without limitation, the simplicity or complexity of the case as shown by the patents, claims, products, or parties involved. Such modifications shall, in most cases, be made at the initial case management conference, but may be made at other times upon a showing of good cause. In advance of submission of any request for a modification, the parties shall meet and confer for purposes of reaching an agreement, if possible, upon any modification.

1-4. Effective Date

These Patent Local Rules take effect on December 1, 2009. They govern patent cases filed on or after that date. For actions pending prior to December 1, 2009, the provisions of the Patent Local Rules that were in effect on November 30, 2009, shall apply, except that the time periods for actions pending before December 1, 2009 shall be those set forth in and computed as in the Federal Rules of Civil Procedure and the Patent Local Rules that took effect on December 1, 2009.

2. GENERAL PROVISIONS

2-1. Governing Procedure

(a) Notice of Pendency of Other Action Involving Same Patent.

(1) When actions concerning the same patent are filed within two years of each other by the same plaintiff, they will be deemed related.

(2) Whenever a party knows or learns that actions concerning the same patent have been filed within two years of each other by the same plaintiff, the party must promptly file in each such case A Notice of Pendency of Other Action Involving Same Patent.

(3) Pursuant to the Assignment Plan, the Clerk will reassign the related higher-numbered cases to the Judge assigned to the lowest-numbered case and will file the appropriate notification on the docket of each reassigned case.

(4) If the Judge determines that the reassignment is not in compliance with subsection (1), the Judge may refer the matter to the Executive Committee for resolution.

(5) Even if a case is not deemed related to a pending case pursuant to this rule, a party may still seek a related case determination pursuant to Civil L.R. 3-12.

(6) If the lowest-numbered case is assigned to a magistrate judge to whom the parties have consented to preside over the action, the magistrate judge will retain that case even if consent is not entered in higher-numbered cases deemed related pursuant to subsection (1).

(b) Initial Case Management Conference. When the parties confer pursuant to Fed. R. Civ. P. 26(f), in addition to the matters covered by Fed. R. Civ. P. 26, the parties shall discuss and address in the Case Management Statement filed pursuant to Fed. R. Civ. P. 26(f) and Civil L.R. 16-9, the following topics:

(1) Proposed modification of the obligations or deadlines set forth in these Patent Local Rules to ensure that they are suitable for the circumstances of the particular case (see Patent L.R. 1-3);

(2) The scope and timing of any claim construction discovery including disclosure of and discovery from any expert witness permitted by the court;

(3) The format of the Claim Construction Hearing, including whether the Court will hear live testimony, the order of presentation, and the estimated length of the hearing; and

(4) How the parties intend to educate the court on the technology at issue.

2-2. Confidentiality

Discovery cannot be withheld on the basis of confidentiality absent Court order. The Protective Order authorized by the Northern District of California shall govern discovery unless the Court enters a different protective order. The approved Protective Order can be found on the Court's website.

2-3. Certification of Disclosures

All statements, disclosures, or charts filed or served in accordance with these Patent Local Rules shall be dated and signed by counsel of record. Counsel's signature shall constitute a certification that to the best of his or her knowledge, information, and belief, formed after an inquiry that is reasonable under the circumstances, the information contained in the statement, disclosure, or chart is complete and correct at the time it is made.

2-4. Admissibility of Disclosures

Statements, disclosures, or charts governed by these Patent Local Rules are admissible to the extent permitted by the Federal Rules of Evidence or Procedure. However, the statements and disclosures provided for in Patent L.R. 4-1 and 4-2 are not admissible for any purpose other than in connection with motions seeking an extension or modification of the time periods within which actions contemplated by these Patent Local Rules shall be taken.

2-5. Relationship to Federal Rules of Civil Procedure

Except as provided in this paragraph or as otherwise ordered, it shall not be a ground for objecting to an opposing party's discovery request (e.g., interrogatory, document request, request for admission, deposition question) or declining to provide information otherwise required to be disclosed pursuant to Fed. R. Civ. P. 26(a)(1) that the discovery request or disclosure requirement is premature in light of, or otherwise conflicts with, these Patent Local Rules, absent other legitimate objection. A party may object, however, to responding to the following categories of discovery requests (or decline to provide information in its initial disclosures under Fed. R. Civ. P. 26(a)(1)) on the ground that they are premature in light of the timetable provided in the Patent Local Rules:

(a) Requests seeking to elicit a party's claim construction position;

(b) Requests seeking to elicit from the patent claimant a comparison of the asserted claims and the accused apparatus, product, device, process, method, act, or other instrumentality;

(c) Requests seeking to elicit from an accused infringer a comparison of the asserted claims and the prior art; and

(d) Requests seeking to elicit from an accused infringer the identification of any advice of counsel, and related documents.

Where a party properly objects to a discovery request (or declines to provide information in its initial disclosures under Fed. R. Civ. P. 26(a)(1)) as set forth above, that party shall provide the requested information on the date on which it is required to be provided to an opposing party under these Patent Local Rules or as set by the Court, unless there exists another legitimate ground for objection.

3. PATENT DISCLOSURES

3-1. Disclosure of Asserted Claims and Infringement Contentions

Not later than 14 days after the Initial Case Management Conference, a party claiming patent infringement shall serve on all parties a "Disclosure of Asserted Claims and Infringement Contentions." Separately for each opposing party, the "Disclosure of Asserted Claims and Infringement Contentions" shall contain the following information:

(a) Each claim of each patent in suit that is allegedly infringed by each opposing party, including for each claim the applicable statutory subsections of 35 U.S.C. § 271 asserted;

(b) Separately for each asserted claim, each accused apparatus, product, device, process, method, act, or other instrumentality ("Accused Instrumentality") of each opposing party of which the party is aware. This identification shall be as specific as possible. Each product, device, and apparatus shall be identified by name or model number, if known. Each method or process shall be identified by name, if known, or by any product, device, or apparatus which, when used, allegedly results in the practice of the claimed method or process;

(c) A chart identifying specifically where each limitation of each asserted claim is found within each Accused Instrumentality, including for each limitation that such party contends is governed by 35 U.S.C. § 112(6), the identity of the structure(s), act(s), or material(s) in the Accused Instrumentality that performs the claimed function.

(d) For each claim which is alleged to have been indirectly infringed, an identification of any direct infringement and a description of the acts of the alleged indirect infringer that contribute to or are inducing that direct infringement. Insofar as alleged direct infringement is based on joint acts of multiple parties, the role of each such party in the direct infringement must be described.

(e) Whether each limitation of each asserted claim is alleged to be literally present or present under the doctrine of equivalents in the Accused Instrumentality;

(f) For any patent that claims priority to an earlier application, the priority date to which each asserted claim allegedly is entitled; and

(g) If a party claiming patent infringement wishes to preserve the right to rely, for any purpose, on the assertion that its own apparatus, product, device, process, method, act, or other instrumentality practices the claimed invention, the party shall identify, separately for each asserted claim, each such apparatus, product, device, process, method, act, or other instrumentality that incorporates or reflects that particular claim.

(h) If a party claiming patent infringement alleges willful infringement, the basis for such allegation.

3-2. Document Production Accompanying Disclosure

With the "Disclosure of Asserted Claims and Infringement Contentions," the party claiming patent infringement shall produce to each opposing party or make available for inspection and copying:

(a) Documents (e.g., contracts, purchase orders, invoices, advertisements, marketing materials, offer letters, beta site testing agreements, and third party or joint development agreements) sufficient to evidence each discussion with, disclosure to, or other manner of providing to a third party, or sale of or offer to sell, or any public use of, the claimed invention prior to the date of application for the patent in suit. A party's production of a document as required herein shall not constitute an admission that such document evidences or is prior art under 35 U.S.C. § 102;

(b) All documents evidencing the conception, reduction to practice, design, and development of each claimed invention, which were created on or before the date of application for the patent in suit or the priority date identified pursuant to Patent L.R. 3-1(f), whichever is earlier;

(c) A copy of the file history for each patent in suit; and

(d) All documents evidencing ownership of the patent rights by the party asserting patent infringement.

(e) If a party identifies instrumentalities pursuant to Patent L.R. 3-1(g), documents sufficient to show the operation of any aspects or elements of such instrumentalities the patent claimant relies upon as embodying any asserted claims.

The producing party shall separately identify by production number which documents correspond to each category.

3-3. Invalidity Contentions

Not later than 45 days after service upon it of the "Disclosure of Asserted Claims and Infringement Contentions," each party opposing a claim of patent infringement, shall serve on all parties its "Invalidity Contentions" which shall contain the following information:

(a) The identity of each item of prior art that allegedly anticipates each asserted claim or renders it obvious. Each prior art patent shall be identified by its number, country of origin, and date of issue. Each prior art publication shall be identified by its title, date of publication, and where feasible, author and publisher. Prior art under 35 U.S.C. § 102(b) shall be identified by specifying the item offered for sale or publicly used or known, the date the offer or use took place or the information became known, and the identity of the person or entity which made the use or which made and received the offer, or the person or entity which made the information known or to whom it was made known. Prior art under 35 U.S.C. § 102(f) shall be identified by providing the name of the person(s) from whom and the circumstances under which the invention or any part of it was derived. Prior art under 35 U.S.C. § 102(g) shall be identified by providing the identities of the person(s) or entities involved in and the circumstances surrounding the making of the invention before the patent applicant(s);

(b) Whether each item of prior art anticipates each asserted claim or renders it obvious. If obviousness is alleged, an explanation of why the prior art renders the asserted claim obvious, including an identification of any combinations of prior art showing obviousness;

(c) A chart identifying where specifically in each alleged item of prior art each limitation of each asserted claim is found, including for each limitation that such party contends is governed by 35 U.S.C. § 112(6), the identity of the structure(s), act(s), or material(s) in each item of prior art that performs the claimed function; and

(d) Any grounds of invalidity based on 35 U.S.C. § 101, indefiniteness under 35 U.S.C. § 112(2) or enablement or written description under 35 U.S.C. § 112(1) of any of the asserted claims.

3-4. Document Production Accompanying Invalidity Contentions

With the "Invalidity Contentions," the party opposing a claim of patent infringement shall produce or make available for inspection and copying:

(a) Source code, specifications, schematics, flow charts, artwork, formulas, or other documentation sufficient to show the operation of any aspects or elements of an Accused Instrumentality identified by the patent claimant in its Patent L.R. 3-1(c) chart; and

(b) A copy or sample of the prior art identified pursuant to Patent L.R. 3-3(a) which does not appear in the file history of the patent(s) at issue. To the extent any such item is not in English, an English translation of the portion(s) relied upon shall be produced.

The producing party shall separately identify by production number which documents correspond to each category.

3-5. Disclosure Requirement in Patent Cases for Declaratory Judgment of Invalidity

(a) **Invalidity Contentions If No Claim of Infringement**. In all cases in which a party files a complaint or other pleading seeking a declaratory judgment that a patent is invalid Patent L.R. 3-1 and 3-2 shall not apply unless and until a claim for patent infringement is made by a party. If the defendant does not assert a claim for patent infringement in its answer to the complaint, no later than 14 days after the defendant serves its answer, or 14 days after the Initial Case Management Conference, whichever is later, the party seeking a declaratory judgment of invalidity shall serve upon each opposing party its Invalidity Contentions that conform to Patent L.R. 3-3 and produce or make available for inspection and copying the documents described in Patent L.R. 3-4.

(b) **Inapplicability of Rule**. This Patent L.R. 3-5 shall not apply to cases in which a request for a declaratory judgment that a patent is invalid is filed in response to a complaint for infringement of the same patent.

3-6. Amendment to Contentions

Amendment of the Infringement Contentions or the Invalidity Contentions may be made only by order of the Court upon a timely showing of good cause. Non-exhaustive examples of circumstances that may, absent undue prejudice to the non-moving party, support a finding of good cause include:

(a) A claim construction by the Court different from that proposed by the party seeking amendment;

(b) Recent discovery of material, prior art despite earlier diligent search; and

(c) Recent discovery of nonpublic information about the Accused Instrumentality which was not discovered, despite diligent efforts, before the service of the Infringement Contentions.

The duty to supplement discovery responses does not excuse the need to obtain leave of court to amend contentions.

3-7. Advice of Counsel

Not later than 50 days after service by the Court of its Claim Construction Ruling, each party relying upon advice of counsel as part of a patent-related claim or defense for any reason shall:

(a) Produce or make available for inspection and copying any written advice and documents related thereto for which the attorney-client and work product protection have been waived;

(b) Provide a written summary of any oral advice and produce or make available for inspection and copying that summary and documents related thereto for which the attorney-client and work product protection have been waived; and

(c) Serve a privilege log identifying any other documents, except those authored by counsel acting solely as trial counsel, relating to the subject matter of the advice which the party is withholding on the grounds of attorney-client privilege or work product protection.

A party who does not comply with the requirements of this Patent L.R. 3-7 shall not be permitted to rely on advice of counsel for any purpose absent a stipulation of all parties or by order of the Court.

4. CLAIM CONSTRUCTION PROCEEDINGS

4-1. Exchange of Proposed Terms for Construction

(a) Not later than 14 days after service of the "Invalidity Contentions" pursuant to Patent L.R. 3-3, not later than 42 days after service upon it of the "Disclosure of Asserted Claims and Infringement Contentions" in those actions where validity is not at issue (and Patent L.R. 3-3 does not apply), or, in all cases in which a party files a complaint or other pleading seeking a declaratory judgment not based on validity, not later than 14 days after the defendant serves an answer that does not assert a claim for patent infringement (and Patent L.R. 3-1 does not apply), each party shall serve on each other party a list of claim terms which that party contends should be construed by the Court, and identify any claim term which that party contends should be governed by 35 U.S.C. § 112(6).

(b) The parties shall thereafter meet and confer for the purposes of limiting the terms in dispute by narrowing or resolving differences and facilitating the ultimate preparation of a Joint Claim Construction and Prehearing Statement. The parties shall also jointly identify the 10 terms likely to be most significant to resolving the parties' dispute, including those terms for which construction may be case or claim dispositive.

4-2. Exchange of Preliminary Claim Constructions and Extrinsic Evidence

(a) Not later than 21 days after the exchange of the lists pursuant to Patent L.R. 4-1, the parties shall simultaneously exchange proposed constructions of each term identified by either party for claim construction. Each such "Preliminary Claim Construction" shall also, for each term which any party contends is governed by 35 U.S.C. § 112(6), identify the structure(s), act(s), or material(s) corresponding to that term's function.

(b) At the same time the parties exchange their respective "Preliminary Claim Constructions," each party shall also identify all references from the specification or prosecution history that support its proposed construction and designate any supporting extrinsic evidence including, without limitation, dictionary definitions, citations to learned treatises and prior art, and testimony of percipient and expert witnesses. Extrinsic evidence shall be identified by production number or by producing a copy if not previously produced. With respect to any supporting witness, percipient or expert, the identifying party shall also provide a description of the substance of that witness' proposed testimony that includes a listing of any opinions to be rendered in connection with claim construction.

(c) The parties shall thereafter meet and confer for the purposes of narrowing the issues and finalizing preparation of a Joint Claim Construction and Prehearing Statement.

4-3. Joint Claim Construction and Prehearing Statement

Not later than 60 days after service of the "Invalidity Contentions," the parties shall complete and file a Joint Claim Construction and Prehearing Statement, which shall contain the following information:

(a) The construction of those terms on which the parties agree;

(b) Each party's proposed construction of each disputed term, together with an identification of all references from the specification or prosecution history that support that construction, and an identification of any extrinsic evidence known to the party on which it intends to rely either to support its proposed construction or to oppose any other party's proposed construction, including, but not limited to, as permitted by law, dictionary definitions, citations to learned treatises and prior art, and testimony of percipient and expert witnesses;

(c) An identification of the terms whose construction will be most significant to the resolution of the case up to a maximum of 10. The parties shall also identify any term among the 10 whose construction will be case or claim dispositive. If the parties cannot agree on the 10 most significant terms, the parties shall identify the ones which they do agree are most significant and then they may evenly divide the remainder with each party identifying what it believes are the remaining most significant terms. However, the total terms identified by all parties as most significant cannot exceed 10. For example, in a case involving two parties, if the parties agree upon the identification of five terms as most significant, each may only identify two additional terms as most significant; if the parties agree upon eight such terms, each party may only identify only one additional term as most significant.

(d) The anticipated length of time necessary for the Claim Construction Hearing;

(e) Whether any party proposes to call one or more witnesses at the Claim Construction Hearing, the identity of each such witness, and for each witness, a summary of his or her testimony including, for any expert, each opinion to be offered related to claim construction.

4-4. Completion of Claim Construction Discovery

Not later than 30 days after service and filing of the Joint Claim Construction and Prehearing Statement, the parties shall complete all discovery relating to claim construction, including any depositions with respect to claim construction of any witnesses, including experts, identified in the Preliminary Claim Construction statement (Patent L.R. 4-2) or Joint Claim Construction and Prehearing Statement (Patent L.R. 4-3).

4-5. Claim Construction Briefs

(a) Not later than 45 days after serving and filing the Joint Claim Construction and Prehearing Statement, the party claiming patent infringement, or the party asserting invalidity if there is no infringement issue present in the case, shall serve and file an opening brief and any evidence supporting its claim construction.

(b) Not later than 14 days after service upon it of an opening brief, each opposing party shall serve and file its responsive brief and supporting evidence.

(c) Not later than 7 days after service upon it of a responsive brief, the party claiming patent infringement, or the party asserting invalidity if there is no infringement issue present in the case, shall serve and file any reply brief and any evidence directly rebutting the supporting evidence contained in an opposing party's response.

4-6. Claim Construction Hearing

Subject to the convenience of the Court's calendar, two weeks following submission of the reply brief specified in Patent L.R. 4-5(c), the Court shall conduct a Claim Construction Hearing, to the extent the parties or the Court believe a hearing is necessary for construction of the claims at issue.

4-7. Good Faith Participation

A failure to make a good faith effort to narrow the instances of disputed terms or otherwise participate in the meet and confer process of any of the provisions of section 4 may expose counsel to sanctions, including under 28 U.S.C. § 1927.

LOCAL CIVIL AND CRIMINAL RULES

OF THE

UNITED STATES DISTRICT COURT

FOR THE

DISTRICT OF NEW JERSEY

With Revisions as of
April 3, 2014

L. Civ. R. 9.3 — LOCAL PATENT RULES

TABLE OF CONTENTS EXPLANATORY NOTES FOR 2011 AMENDMENTS

UNITED STATES DISTRICT COURT
DISTRICT OF NEW JERSEY

REPORT OF THE LOCAL PATENT RULES COMMITTEE
Explanatory Notes for 2011 Amendments

In September 2010, almost two years after the Local Patent Rules had been adopted, the Committee reconvened to assess the impact and effectiveness of the Local Patent Rules. Based on the experiences of members of the Committee from the Judiciary and the Bar, there was an unanimous view that the Local Patent Rules have served to benefit the Court and the parties in patent litigation.

Notwithstanding those positive experiences, the Committee also believed that certain amendments might be warranted. Those areas of proposed changes include: (a) design patents; (b) certain disclosure obligations; (c) clarifying disclosure of evidence in connection with a *Markman* hearing; (d) need for responses to infringement and invalidity contentions; (e) specific modifications for disclosures exclusive to Hatch-Waxman cases; (f) amendments to required submissions or filings; and clarification in the language of rules.

Subcommittees were appointed for each of the subject areas and shortly thereafter recommendations were proposed to the full Committee, which discussed them at length.

With regard to design patents, shortly after the Committee had submitted its proposed patent rules in 2008, the Court of Appeals for the Federal Circuit issued its en banc ruling in Egyptian Goddess v. Swisa, 543 F.3d 665 (2008), which held, in part, that a trial court should not provide a detailed verbal description of the claimed design. This holding is in tension with certain of the Local Patent Rules which call for a narrative claims chart, claim construction contentions and a claim construction hearing. The Committee determined that in light of the Federal Circuit authority modifications were appropriate to better suit the needs of design patents. See L. Pat. R. 3.1(c) and (e); 3.3(c); 3.4A(c); 4.1(c); 4.2(e); 4.3(g); 4.4; and 4.5(d).

While the Local Patent Rules expressly reference obligations regarding infringement and invalidity, the Committee noted that in cases outside of Hatch-Waxman matters, no provision presently exists that requires the allegedly infringing party to provide its non-infringement contentions. Accordingly, the Committee proposed disclosure obligations for non-infringement similar to those required for assertion of infringement and invalidity. See L. Pat. R. 3.2A(a) and (b); and 3.4(c).

As to invalidity contentions, while there are disclosure obligations by a party asserting invalidity, the Committee determined that a requirement that mandates that the patent holder respond in kind to invalidity contentions will provide parity between the parties and serve to focus the invalidity challenge. See L. Pat. R. 3.4A(a),(b) and (c); and 3.5 (a).

To help ensure that the spirit of the disclosure obligations is fully appreciated, the Committee recommended various rules requiring parties to disclose all materials that they intend to rely upon in connection with infringement, non-infringement, and invalidity contentions and or responses thereto. See L. Pat. R. 3.2(f); 3.2A(c); 3.4(c); and 3.4A(d).

In the area of Hatch-Waxman actions under L. Pat. R. 3.6, the Committee concluded that in order to help narrow the focus of a generic's invalidity contentions, the patent holder should be required to provide early disclosure of each patent and patent claim for infringement to which its infringement contentions would be limited. This eliminates speculation and added work by the generics in formulating their non-infringement and invalidity contentions. Changes recommended to disclosure obligations in non-Hatch-Waxman cases as they would apply in the Hatch-Waxman context were also proposed. In addition, the Committee determined that the ANDA filer should produce its Abbreviated New Drug Application or New Drug Application shortly after filing an answer or motion as this is a fundamental element of the Hatch-Waxman action. It was also recommended that the ANDA filer be required to advise the Food and Drug Administration ("FDA") of any motion for injunctive relief and supply the parties with relevant communications with the FDA which concern the subject matter filed in the District Court. This is intended to keep the FDA and parties apprised of any proceedings that may impact the ongoing litigation. See L. Pat. R. 3.6(a), (b), (c), (i) and (j).

In an effort to avoid potential misunderstandings as to the scope of permitted amendments to obligations under the Local Patent Rules, the Committee sought to clarify that amendments apply to all filings with the Court or exchanges between the parties as may be required by the Local Patent Rules. The proposed rule also makes plain that any amendments require the approval of the Court, notwithstanding consent by the parties. See L. Pat. R. 3.7.

Finally, as to claim construction and claim construction proceedings, the Committee proposed adding language to clarify that evidence to be used must be disclosed in a timely fashion. See L. Pat. R. 4.2(b) and (c); and 4.3(f).

In December 2010, the Committee submitted the proposed amendments to the Board of Judges for their consideration.

Local Patent Rules Committee

Hon. Jerome B. Simandle, U.S.D.J., Chair
Hon. Stanley R. Chesler, U.S.D.J.
Hon. Mary L. Cooper, U.S.D.J.
Hon. Faith S. Hochberg, U.S.D.J.
Hon. Peter G. Sheridan, U.S.D.J.
Hon. Tonianne J. Bongiovanni, U.S.M.J.
Hon. Joel Schneider, U.S.M.J.
Hon. Mark Falk, U.S.M.J.
Hon. Patty Shwartz, U.S.M.J.
John T. O'Brien, Legal Coordinator
Arnold B. Calmann, Esq.
Thomas Curtin, Esq.
David De Lorenzi, Esq.
Marc S. Friedman, Esq.
Dennis F. Gleason, Esq.
Mary Sue Henifin, Esq.
Norman E. Lehrer, Esq.
Peter Menell, Prof. of Law, Univ. of Calif., Berkeley School of Law
William L. Mentlik, Esq.
George F. Pappas, Esq.
Matthew D. Powers, Esq.
Donald Robinson, Esq.
Robert G. Shepherd Esq.

December 2, 2010

1.1. Title.

L. Civ. R. 9.3 -- LOCAL PATENT RULES

1. SCOPE OF RULES These are the Local Patent Rules for the United States District Court for the District of New Jersey. They should be cited as "L. Pat. R. _____."

1.2. Scope and Construction.

These rules apply to all civil actions filed in or transferred to this Court which allege infringement of a patent in a complaint, counterclaim, cross-claim or third party claim, or which seek a declaratory judgment that a patent is not infringed, is invalid or is unenforceable. The Local Civil Rules of this Court shall also apply to such actions, except to the extent that they are inconsistent with these Local Patent Rules. If the filings or actions in a case do not trigger the application of these Local Patent Rules under the terms set forth herein, the parties shall, as soon as such circumstances become known, meet and confer for the purpose of agreeing on the application of these Local Patent Rules to the case and promptly report the results of the meet and confer to the Court.

1.3. Modification of these Rules.

The Court may modify the obligations or deadlines set forth in these Local Patent Rules based on the circumstances of any particular case, including, without limitation, the simplicity or complexity of the case as shown by the patents, claims, products, or parties involved. Such modifications shall, in most cases, be made at the initial Scheduling Conference, but may be made at other times by the Court sua sponte or upon a showing of good cause. In advance of submission of any request for a modification, the parties shall meet and confer for purposes of reaching an agreement, if possible, upon any modification.

1.4. Effective Date.

These Local Patent Rules take effect on January 1, 2009. They govern patent cases filed, transferred or removed on or after that date. For actions pending prior to the effective date, the Court will confer with the parties and apply these rules as the Court deems practicable.

1.5. Patent Pilot Project.

Procedures for allocation and assignment of patent cases under the Patent Pilot Project pursuant to Pub. L. No. 111-349, § 1, are provided in L. Civ. R. 40.1(f) and Appendix T to the Local Civil Rules.

2. GENERAL PROVISIONS

2.1. Governing Procedure.

(a) Initial Scheduling Conference. When the parties confer pursuant to Fed. R. Civ. P. 26(f), the parties shall discuss and address in the Discovery Plan submitted pursuant to Fed. R. Civ. P. 26(f) and L. Civ. R. 26.1(b)(2) the topics set forth in those rules and the following topics:

(1) Proposed modification of the obligations or deadlines set forth in these Local Patent Rules to ensure that they are suitable for the circumstances of the particular case (see L. Pat. R. 1.3);

(2) The scope and timing of any claim construction discovery including disclosure of and discovery from any expert witness permitted by the court;

(3) The format of the Claim Construction Hearing, including whether the Court will hear live testimony, the order of presentation, and the estimated length of the hearing;

(4) How the parties intend to educate the Court on the patent(s) at issue; and

(5) The need for any discovery confidentiality order and a schedule for presenting certification(s) required by L. Civ. R. 5.3(b)(2).

2.2. Confidentiality.

Discovery cannot be withheld or delayed on the basis of confidentiality absent Court order. Pending entry of a discovery confidentiality order, discovery and disclosures deemed confidential by a party shall be produced to the adverse party for outside counsel's Attorney's Eyes Only, solely for purposes of the pending case and shall not be disclosed to the client or any other person.

Within 30 days after the initial Scheduling Conference, (a) the parties shall present a consent discovery confidentiality order, supported by a sufficient certification (or statement complying with 28 U.S.C. § 1746) under L. Civ. R. 5.3(b)(2), or (b) in the absence of consent, a party shall, supported by a sufficient certification, apply for entry of a discovery confidentiality order under L. Civ. R. 5.3(b)(5) and L. Civ. R. 37.1(a)(1). The Court will decide those issues and enter the appropriate order, or the Court may enter the District's approved Discovery Confidentiality Order as set forth in Appendix S to these Rules if appropriate, in whole or in part.

With respect to all issues of discovery confidentiality, the parties shall comply with all terms of L. Civ. R. 5.3.

2.3. Relationship to Federal Rules of Civil Procedure.

Except as provided in this paragraph or as otherwise ordered, it shall not be a ground for objecting to an opposing party's discovery request (e.g., interrogatory, document request, request for admission, deposition question) or declining to provide information otherwise required to be disclosed pursuant to Fed. R. Civ. P.

26(a)(1) that the discovery request or disclosure requirement is premature in light of, or otherwise conflicts with, these Local Patent Rules, absent other legitimate objection. A party may object, however, to responding to the following categories of discovery requests (or decline to provide information in its initial disclosures under Fed. R. Civ. P. 26(a)(1)) on the ground that they are premature in light of the timetable provided in the Local Patent Rules:

(a) Requests seeking to elicit a party's claim construction position;

(b) Requests seeking to elicit a comparison of the asserted claims and the accused apparatus, product, device, process, method, act, or other instrumentality;

(c) Requests seeking to elicit a comparison of the asserted claims and the prior art; and

(d) Requests seeking to elicit the identification of any advice of counsel, and related documents.

Where a party properly objects to a discovery request (or declines to provide information in its initial disclosures under Fed. R. Civ. P. 26(a)(1)) as set forth above, that party shall provide the requested information on the date on which it is required to be provided to an opposing party under these Local Patent Rules or as set by the Court, unless there exists another legitimate ground for objection.

2.4. Exchange of Expert Materials.

(a) Disclosures of claim construction expert materials and depositions of such experts are governed by L. Pat. R. 4.1, et seq., unless otherwise ordered by the Court.

(b) Upon a sufficient showing that expert reports related to issues other than claim construction cannot be rendered until after a claim construction ruling has been entered by the Court, the disclosure of expert materials related to issues other than claim construction will not be required until claim construction issues have been decided.

3. PATENT DISCLOSURES

3.1. Disclosure of Asserted Claims and Infringement Contentions.

Not later than 14 days after the initial Scheduling Conference, a party asserting patent infringement shall serve on all parties a "Disclosure of Asserted Claims and Infringement Contentions." Separately for each opposing party, the "Disclosure of Asserted Claims and Infringement Contentions" shall contain the following information:

(a) Each claim of each patent in suit that is allegedly infringed by each opposing party, including for each claim the applicable statutory subsections of 35 U.S.C. § 271 asserted;

(b) Separately for each asserted claim, each accused apparatus, product, device, process, method, act, or other instrumentality ("Accused Instrumentality") of each opposing party of which the party is aware. This identification shall be as specific as possible. Each product, device, and apparatus shall be identified by name or model number, if known. Each method or process shall be identified by name, if known, or by any product, device, or apparatus which, when used, allegedly results in the practice of the claimed method or process;

(c) Other than for design patents, a chart identifying specifically where each limitation of each asserted claim is found within each Accused Instrumentality, including for each limitation that such party contends is governed by 35 U.S.C. § 112(6), the identity of the structure(s), act(s), or material(s) in the Accused Instrumentality that performs the claimed function;

(d) For each claim which is alleged to have been indirectly infringed, an identification of any direct infringement and a description of the acts of the alleged indirect infringer that contribute to or are inducing that direct infringement. Insofar as alleged direct infringement is based on joint acts of multiple parties, the role of each such party in the direct infringement must be described;

(e) Other than for design patents, whether each limitation of each asserted claim is alleged to be literally present or present under the doctrine of equivalents in the Accused Instrumentality;

(f) For any patent that claims priority to an earlier application, the priority date to which each asserted claim allegedly is entitled;

(g) If a party asserting patent infringement wishes to preserve the right to rely, for any purpose, on the assertion that its own apparatus, product, device, process, method, act, or other instrumentality practices the claimed invention, the party shall identify, separately for each asserted claim, each such apparatus, product, device, process, method, act, or other instrumentality that incorporates or reflects that particular claim; and

(h) If a party asserting patent infringement alleges willful infringement, the basis for such allegation.

3.2. Document Production Accompanying Disclosure.

With the "Disclosure of Asserted Claims and Infringement Contentions," the party asserting patent infringement shall produce to each opposing party or make available for inspection and copying:

(a) Documents (e.g., contracts, purchase orders, invoices, advertisements, marketing materials, offer letters, beta site testing agreements, and third party or joint development agreements) sufficient to evidence each discussion with, disclosure to, or other manner of providing to a third party, or sale of or offer to sell, or any public use of, the claimed invention prior to the date of application for the patent in suit. A party's production of a document as required herein shall not constitute an admission that such document evidences or is prior art under 35 U.S.C. § 102;

(b) All documents evidencing the conception, reduction to practice, design, and development of each claimed invention, which were created on or before the date of application for the patent in suit or the priority date identified pursuant to L. Pat. R. 3.1(f), whichever is earlier;

(c) A copy of the file history for each patent in suit (or so much thereof as is in the possession of the party asserting patent infringement);

(d) All documents evidencing ownership of the patent rights by the party asserting patent infringement;

(e) If a party identifies instrumentalities pursuant to L. Pat. R. 3.1(g), documents sufficient to show the operation of any aspects or elements of such instrumentalities the party asserting patent infringement relies upon as embodying any asserted claims; and

(f) All documents or things that a party asserting patent infringement intends to rely on in support of any of its infringement contentions under these Rules.

(g) With respect to each of the above document productions, the producing party shall separately identify by production number which documents correspond to each category.

3.2A. Non-Infringement Contentions and Responses.

Not later than 45 days after service upon it of the "Disclosure of Asserted Claims and Infringement Contentions," each party opposing an assertion of patent infringement shall serve on all parties its "Non-infringement Contentions and Responses" to Infringement Contentions which shall include the following:

(a) The written basis for its Non-Infringement Contentions and responses;

(b) The party's responses shall follow the order of the infringement claims chart that is required under L. Pat. R. 3.1(c), and shall set forth the party's agreement or disagreement with each allegation therein, including any additional or different claims at issue;

(c) The production or the making available for inspection of any document or thing that it intends to rely on in defense against any such Infringement Contentions.

3.3. Invalidity Contentions.

Not later than 45 days after service upon it of the "Disclosure of Asserted Claims and Infringement Contentions," each party opposing an assertion of patent infringement, shall serve on all parties its "Invalidity Contentions" which shall contain the following information:

(a) The identity of each item of prior art that allegedly anticipates each asserted claim or renders it obvious. Each prior art patent shall be identified by its number, country of origin, and date of issue. Each prior art publication shall be identified by its title, date of publication, and where feasible, author and publisher. Prior art under 35 U.S.C. § 102(b) shall be identified by specifying the item offered for sale or publicly used or known, the date the offer or use took place or the information became known, and the identity of the person or entity which made the use or which made and received the offer, or the person or entity which made the information known or to whom it was made known. Prior art under 35 U.S.C. § 102(f) shall be identified by providing the name of the person(s) from whom and the circumstances under which the invention or any part of it was derived. Prior art under 35 U.S.C. § 102(g) shall be identified by providing the identities of the person(s) or entities involved in and the circumstances surrounding the making of the invention before the patent applicant(s);

(b) Whether each item of prior art anticipates each asserted claim or renders it obvious. If obviousness is alleged, an explanation of why the prior art renders the asserted claim obvious, including an identification of any combinations of prior art showing obviousness;

(c) Other than for design patents, a chart identifying where specifically in each alleged item of prior art each limitation of each asserted claim is found, including for each limitation that such party contends is governed by 35 U.S.C. § 112(6), the identity of the structure(s), act(s), or material(s) in each item of prior art that performs the claimed function; and

(d) Any grounds of invalidity based on 35 U.S.C. § 101, indefiniteness under 35 U.S.C. § 112(2) or enablement or written description under 35 U.S.C. § 112(1) of any of the asserted claims.

3.4. Document Production Accompanying Invalidity Contentions.

With the "Invalidity Contentions," the party opposing an assertion of patent infringement shall produce or make available for inspection and copying:

(a) Source code, specifications, schematics, flow charts, artwork, formulas, or other documentation sufficient to show the operation, composition, or structure of any aspects or elements of an Accused Instrumentality identified by the party asserting patent infringement in its L. Pat. R. 3.1(c) chart; and

(b) A copy or sample of the prior art identified pursuant to L. Pat. R. 3.3(a) which does not appear in the file history of the patent(s) at issue. To the extent any such item is not in English, an English translation of the portion(s) relied upon shall be produced.

(c) A party asserting invalidity shall also produce any other document or thing on which it intends to rely in support of its assertion.

(d) With respect to each of the above document productions, the producing party shall separately identify by production number which documents correspond to each category.

3.4A. Responses to Invalidity Contentions.

Not later than 14 days after service upon it of the "Invalidity Contentions," each party defending the validity of the patent shall serve on all parties its "Responses to Invalidity Contentions" which shall include the following:

(a) For each item of asserted prior art, the identification of each limitation of each asserted claim that the party believes is absent from the prior art, except for design patents, where the party shall supply an explanation why the prior art does not anticipate the claim;

(b) If obviousness is alleged, an explanation of why the prior art does not render the asserted claim obvious;

(c) The party's responses shall follow the order of the invalidity chart required under L. Pat. R. 3.3(c), and shall set forth the party's agreement or disagreement with each allegation therein and the written basis thereof; and

(d) The production or the making available for inspection and copying of any document or thing that the party intends to rely on in support of its Responses herein.

3.5. Disclosure Requirement in Patent Cases for Declaratory Judgment of Invalidity.

(a) Invalidity Contentions If No Claim of Infringement. In all cases in which a party files a complaint or other pleading seeking a declaratory judgment that a patent is invalid, L. Pat. R. 3.1 and 3.2 shall not apply unless and until a claim for patent infringement is made by a party. If the declaratory defendant does not assert a claim for patent infringement in its answer to the complaint, or within 14 days after the Initial Scheduling Conference, whichever is later, the party seeking a declaratory judgment of invalidity shall serve upon each opposing party its Invalidity Contentions that conform to L. Pat. R. 3.3 and produce or make available for inspection and copying the documents described in L. Pat. R. 3.4. Each party opposing the declaratory plaintiff's complaint seeking a declaratory judgment of invalidity shall serve its "Responses to Invalidity Contentions" as required under L. Pat. R. 3.4A.

(b) Inapplicability of Rule. This L. Pat. R. 3.5 shall not apply to cases in which a request for a declaratory judgment that a patent is invalid is filed in response to a complaint for infringement of the same patent, in which case the provisions of L. Pat. R. 3.3 and 3.4 shall govern.

3.6. Disclosure Requirements for Patent Cases Arising Under 21 U.S.C. § 355 (commonly referred to as "the Hatch-Waxman Act").

The following applies to all patents subject to a Paragraph IV certification in cases arising under 21 U.S.C. § 355 (commonly referred to as "the Hatch-Waxman Act"). This rule takes precedence over any conflicting provisions in L. Pat. R. 3.1 to 3.5 for all cases arising under 21 U.S.C. § 355.

(a) On the date a party answers, moves, or otherwise responds, each party who is an ANDA filer shall produce to each party asserting patent infringement the entire Abbreviated New Drug Application or New Drug Application that is the basis of the case in question.

(b) Not more than seven days after the initial Scheduling Conference, each party asserting patent infringement shall serve on all parties a "Disclosure of Asserted Claims" that lists each claim of each patent that is allegedly infringed by each opposing party, including for each claim the applicable statutory subsections of 35 U.S.C. § 271 asserted.

(c) Not more than 14 days after the initial Scheduling Conference, each party opposing an assertion of patent infringement shall provide to each party asserting patent infringement the written basis for its "Invalidity Contentions," for any patents referred to in the opposing party's Paragraph IV Certification, which shall contain all disclosures required by L. Pat. R. 3.3.

(d) Any "Invalidity Contentions" disclosed under L. Pat. R. 3.6(c), shall be accompanied by the production of documents required under L. Pat. R. 3.4(b) and (c).

(e) Not more than 14 days after the initial Scheduling Conference, each party opposing an assertion of patent infringement shall provide to each party asserting patent infringement the written basis for its "Non-Infringement Contentions," for any patents referred to in the opposing party's Paragraph IV Certification which shall include a claim chart identifying each claim at issue in the case and each limitation of each claim at issue. The claim chart shall specifically identify for each claim which claim limitation(s) is/(are) literally absent from each opposing party's allegedly infringing Abbreviated New Drug Application or New Drug Application.

(f) Any "Non-Infringement Contentions" disclosed under L. Pat. R. 3.6(e), shall be accompanied by the production of any document or thing that each party who is an ANDA filer intends to rely on in defense against any infringement contentions by each party asserting patent infringement.

(g) Not more than 45 days after the disclosure of the "Non-Infringement Contentions" as required by L. Pat. R. 3.6(e), each party asserting patent infringement shall provide each opposing party with a "Disclosure of Infringement Contentions," for all patents referred to in each opposing party's Paragraph IV Certification, which shall contain all disclosures required by L. Pat. R. 3.1. The infringement contentions shall be limited to the claims identified in L. Pat. R. 3.6(b).

(h) Any "Disclosure of Asserted Claims and Infringement Contentions" disclosed under L. Pat. R. 3.6(g), shall be accompanied by the production of documents required under L. Pat. R. 3.2.

(i) Not more than 45 days after the disclosure of "Invalidity Contentions" as required by L. Pat. R. 3.6(c), the party defending the validity of the patent shall serve on each other party its "Responses to Invalidity Contentions" as required under L. Pat. R. 3.4A.

(j) Each party that has an ANDA application pending with the Food and Drug Administration ("FDA") that is the basis of the pending case shall: (1) notify the FDA of any and all motions for injunctive relief no later than three business days after the date on which such a motion is filed; and (2) provide a copy of all correspondence between itself and the FDA pertaining to the ANDA application to each party asserting infringement, or set forth the basis of any claim of privilege for such correspondence pursuant to L. Civ. R. 34.1, no later than seven days after the date it sends same to the FDA or receives same from the FDA.

3.7. Amendments.

Amendment of any contentions, disclosures, or other documents required to be filed or exchanged pursuant to these Local Patent Rules may be made only by order of the Court upon a timely application and showing of good cause. The application shall disclose whether parties consent or object. Non-exhaustive examples of circumstances that may, absent undue prejudice to the adverse party, support a finding of good cause include: (a) a claim construction by the Court different from that proposed by the party seeking amendment; (b) recent discovery of material prior art despite earlier diligent search; (c) recent discovery of nonpublic information about the Accused Instrumentality which was not discovered, despite diligent efforts, before the service of the Infringement Contention; (d) disclosure of an infringement contention by a Hatch- Waxman Act party asserting infringement under L. Pat. R. 3.6(g) that requires response by the adverse party because it was not previously presented or reasonably anticipated; and (e) consent by the parties in interest to the amendment and a showing that it will not lead to an enlargement of time or impact other scheduled deadlines. The duty to supplement discovery responses under Fed. R. Civ. P. 26(e) does not excuse the need to obtain leave of Court to amend contentions, disclosures, or other documents required to be filed or exchanged pursuant to these Local Patent Rules.

3.8. Advice of Counsel.

Unless otherwise ordered by the Court, not later than 30 days after entry of the Court's claim construction order, or upon such other date as set by the Court, each party relying upon advice of counsel as part of a patent-related claim or defense for any reason shall:

(a) Produce or make available for inspection and copying any written advice and documents related thereto for which the attorney-client and work product protection have been waived;

(b) Provide a written summary of any oral advice and produce or make available for inspection and copying that summary and documents related thereto for which the attorney-client and work product protection have been waived; and

(c) Serve a privilege log identifying any documents other than those identified in subpart (a) above, except those authored by counsel acting solely as trial counsel, relating to the subject matter of the advice which the party is withholding on the grounds of attorney-client privilege or work product protection.

A party who does not comply with the requirements of this L. Pat. R. 3.8 shall not be permitted to rely on advice of counsel for any purpose absent a stipulation of all parties or by order of the Court.

4. CLAIM CONSTRUCTION PROCEEDINGS

4.1. Exchange of Proposed Terms for Construction.

(a) Not later than 14 days after service of the "Responses to Invalidity Contentions" pursuant to L. Pat. R. 3.4A, not later than 45 days after service upon it of the "Non-Infringement Contentions and Responses" pursuant to L. Pat. R. 3.2A in those actions where validity is not at issue (and L. Pat. R. 3.3 does not apply), or, in all cases in which a party files a complaint or other pleading seeking a declaratory judgment not based on validity, not later than 14 days after the defendant serves an answer that does not assert a claim for patent infringement (and L. Pat. R. 3.1 does not apply), each party shall serve on each other party a list of claim terms which that party contends should be construed by the Court, and identify any claim term which that party contends should be governed by 35 U.S.C. § 112(6).

(b) The parties shall thereafter meet and confer for the purposes of limiting the terms in dispute by narrowing or resolving differences and facilitating the ultimate preparation of a Joint Claim Construction and Prehearing Statement.

(c) This rule does not apply to design patents.

4.2. Exchange of Preliminary Claim Constructions and Extrinsic Evidence.

(a) Not later than 21 days after the exchange of the lists pursuant to L. Pat. R. 4.1, the parties shall simultaneously exchange preliminary proposed constructions of each term identified by any party for claim construction. Each such "Preliminary Claim Construction" shall also, for each term which any party contends is governed by 35 U.S.C. § 112(6), identify the structure(s), act(s), or material(s) corresponding to that term's function.

(b) At the same time the parties exchange their respective "Preliminary Claim Constructions," each party shall also identify all intrinsic evidence, all references from the specification or prosecution history that support its preliminary proposed construction and designate any supporting extrinsic evidence including, without limitation, dictionary definitions, citations to learned treatises and prior art and testimony of all witnesses including expert witnesses. Extrinsic evidence shall be identified by production number or by producing a copy if not previously produced. With respect to all witnesses including experts, the identifying party shall also provide a description of the substance of that witness' proposed testimony that includes a listing of any opinions to be rendered in connection with claim construction.

(c) Not later than 14 days after the parties exchange the "Preliminary Claim Constructions" under this rule, the parties shall exchange an identification of all intrinsic evidence and extrinsic evidence that each party intends to rely upon to oppose any other party's proposed construction, including without limitation, the evidence referenced in L. Pat. R. 4.2(b).

(d) The parties shall thereafter meet and confer for the purposes of narrowing the issues and finalizing preparation of a Joint Claim Construction and Prehearing Statement.

(e) This rule does not apply to design patents.

4.3. Joint Claim Construction and Prehearing Statement.

Not later than 30 days after the exchange of "Preliminary Claim Constructions" under L. Pat. R. 4.2(a), the parties shall complete and file a Joint Claim Construction and Prehearing Statement, which shall contain the following information:

(a) The construction of those terms on which the parties agree;

(b) Each party's proposed construction of each disputed term, together with an identification of all references from the intrinsic evidence that support that construction, and an identification of any extrinsic evidence known to the party on which it intends to rely either to support its proposed construction or to oppose any other party's proposed construction, including, but not limited to, as permitted by law, dictionary definitions, citations to learned treatises and prior art, and testimony of all witnesses including experts;

(c) An identification of the terms whose construction will be most significant to the resolution of the case. The parties shall also identify any term whose construction will be case or claim dispositive or substantially conducive to promoting settlement, and the reasons therefor;

(d) The anticipated length of time necessary for the Claim Construction Hearing; and (e) Whether any party proposes to call one or more witnesses at the Claim Construction Hearing, the identity of each such witness, and for each witness, a summary of his or her testimony including, for any expert, each opinion to be offered related to claim construction.

(f) Any evidence that is not identified under L. Pat. R. 4.2(a) through 4.2(c) inclusive shall not be included in the Joint Claim Construction and Prehearing Statement.

(g) This rule does not apply to design patents.

4.4. Completion of Claim Construction Discovery.

Not later than 30 days after service and filing of the Joint Claim Construction and Prehearing Statement, the parties shall complete all discovery relating to claim construction, including any depositions with respect to claim construction of any witnesses, other than experts, identified in the Preliminary Claim Construction statement (L. Pat. R. 4.2) or Joint Claim Construction and Prehearing Statement (L. Pat. R. 4.3). This rule does not apply to design patents.

4.5. Claim Construction Submissions.

(a) Not later than 45 days after serving and filing the Joint Claim Construction and Prehearing Statement, the parties shall contemporaneously file and serve their opening Markman briefs and any evidence supporting claim construction, including experts' certifications or declarations ("Opening Markman Submissions").

(b) Unless otherwise ordered by the Court, any discovery from an expert witness who submitted a certification or declaration under L. Pat. R. 4.5(a) shall be concluded within 30 days after filing the Opening Markman Submissions.

(c) Not later than 60 days after the filing of the Opening Markman Submissions, the parties shall contemporaneously file and serve responding Markman briefs and any evidence supporting claim construction, including any responding experts' certifications or declarations.

(d) With regard to design patents only, subsections (a), (b), and (c) shall not apply. Where a design patent is at issue, not later than 45 days after the submission of "Non- Infringement Contentions and Responses" under L. Pat. R. 3.2A and/or "Responses to Invalidity Contentions" under L. Pat. R. 3.4A, the parties shall contemporaneously file and serve opening Markman briefs and any evidence supporting claim construction. Not more than 30 days after the filing of the opening Markman briefs, the parties shall contemporaneously file and serve responding Markman briefs and any evidence supporting claim construction.

4.6. Claim Construction Hearing.

Within two weeks following submission of the briefs and evidence specified in L. Pat. R. 4.5(c) and (d), counsel shall confer and propose to the Court a schedule for a Claim Construction Hearing, to the extent the parties or the Court believe a hearing is necessary for construction of the claims at issue.

Adopted December 11, 2008, Effective January 1, 2009, Amended March 18, 2011, October 4, 2011, June 9, 2013.

- Current as of May 6, 2015
(General Order 15-12)

APPENDIX B PATENT RULES

1. SCOPE OF RULES

1-1. Title.

These are the Rules of Practice for Patent Cases before the Eastern District of Texas. They should be cited as "P. R. __."

1-2. Scope and Construction.

These rules apply to all civil actions filed in or transferred to this Court which allege infringement of a utility patent in a complaint, counterclaim, cross-claim or third party claim, or which seek a declaratory judgment that a utility patent is not infringed, is invalid or is unenforceable. The Court may accelerate, extend, eliminate, or modify the obligations or deadlines set forth in these Patent Rules based on the circumstances of any particular case, including, without limitation, the complexity of the case or the number of patents, claims, products, or parties involved. If any motion filed prior to the Claim Construction Hearing provided for in P. R. 4-6 raises claim construction issues, the Court may, for good cause shown, defer the motion until after completion of the disclosures, filings, or ruling following the Claim Construction Hearing. The Civil Local Rules of this Court shall also apply to these actions, except to the extent that they are inconsistent with these Patent Rules. The deadlines set forth in these rules may be modified by Docket Control Order issued in specific cases.

1-3. Effective Date.

These Patent Rules shall take effect on February 22, 2005 and shall apply to any case filed thereafter and to any pending case in which more than 9 days remain before the Initial Disclosure of Asserted Claims is made. The parties to any other pending civil action shall meet and confer promptly after February 22, 2005, for the purpose of determining whether any provision in these Patent Rules should be made applicable to that case. No later than 7 days after the parties meet and confer, the parties shall file a stipulation setting forth a proposed order that relates to the application of these Patent Rules. Unless and until an order is entered applying these Patent Local Rules to any pending case, the Rules previously applicable to pending patent cases shall govern.

2. GENERAL PROVISIONS

2-1. Governing Procedure.

(a) Initial Case Management Conference. Prior to the Initial Case Management Conference with the Court, when the parties confer with each other pursuant to Fed. R. Civ. P. 26(f), in addition to the matters covered by Fed. R. Civ. P. 26, the parties must discuss and address in the Case Management Statement filed pursuant to Fed. R. Civ. P. 26(f), the following topics:

> **(1)** Proposed modification of the deadlines provided for in the Patent Rules, and the effect of any such modification on the date and time of the Claim Construction Hearing, if any;
>
> **(2)** Whether the Court will hear live testimony at the Claim Construction Hearing;
>
> **(3)** The need for and any specific limits on discovery relating to claim construction, including depositions of witnesses, including expert witnesses;
>
> **(4)** The order of presentation at the Claim Construction Hearing; and
>
> **(5)** The scheduling of a Claim Construction Prehearing Conference to be held after the Joint Claim Construction and Prehearing Statement provided for in P. R. 4-3 has been filed.
>
> **(6)** Whether the court should authorize the filing under seal of any documents containing confidential information.

(b) Further Case Management Conferences. To the extent that some or all of the matters provided for in P. R. 2-1 (a)(1)-(5) are not resolved or decided at the Initial Case Management Conference, the parties shall propose dates for further Case Management Conferences at which such matters shall be decided.

(c) Electronic Filings. All patents attached as exhibits to any filing submitted electronically shall be in searchable PDF format. Any other documents attached as exhibits to any filing submitted electronically should be in searchable PDF format whenever possible.

2-2. Confidentiality.

If any document or information produced under these Patent Local Rules is deemed confidential by the producing party and if the Court has not entered a protective order, until a protective order is issued by the Court, the document shall be marked "confidential." or with some other confidential designation (such as "Confidential B Outside Attorneys Eyes Only") by the disclosing party and disclosure of the confidential document or information shall be limited to each party's outside attorney(s) of record and the employees of such outside attorney(s).

If a party is not represented by an outside attorney, disclosure of the confidential document or information shall be limited to one designated "in house" attorney, whose identity and job functions shall be disclosed to the producing party 5 days prior to any such disclosure, in order to permit any motion for protective order or other relief regarding such disclosure. The person(s) to whom disclosure of a confidential document or information is made under this local rule shall keep it confidential and use it only for purposes of litigating the case.

2-3. Certification of Initial Disclosures.

All statements, disclosures, or charts filed or served in accordance with these Patent Rules must be dated and signed by counsel of record. Counsel's signature shall constitute a certification that to the best of his or her knowledge, information, and belief, formed after an inquiry that is reasonable under the circumstances, the information contained in the statement, disclosure, or chart is complete and correct at the time it is made.

2-4. Admissibility of Disclosures.

Statements, disclosures, or charts governed by these Patent Rules are admissible to the extent permitted by the Federal Rules of Evidence or Procedure. However, the statements or disclosures provided for in P. R. 4-1 and 4-2 are not admissible for any purpose other than in connection with motions seeking an extension or modification of the time periods within which actions contemplated by these Patent Rules must be taken.

2-5. Relationship to Federal Rules of Civil Procedure.

Except as provided in this paragraph or as otherwise ordered, it shall not be a legitimate ground for objecting to an opposing party's discovery request (e.g., interrogatory, document request, request for admission, deposition question) or declining to provide information otherwise required to be disclosed pursuant to Fed. R. Civ. P. 26(a)(1) that the discovery request or disclosure requirement is premature in light of, or otherwise conflicts with, these Patent Rules. A party may object, however, to responding to the following categories of discovery requests (or decline to provide information in its initial disclosures under Fed. R. Civ. P. 26(a)(1)) on the ground that they are premature in light of the timetable provided in the Patent Rules:

(a) Requests seeking to elicit a party's claim construction position;

(b) Requests seeking to elicit from the patent claimant a comparison of the asserted claims and the accused apparatus, product, device, process, method, act, or other instrumentality;

(c) Requests seeking to elicit from an accused infringer a comparison of the asserted claims and the prior art; and

(d) Requests seeking to elicit from an accused infringer the identification of any opinions of counsel, and related documents, that it intends to rely upon as a defense to an allegation of willful infringement.

Where a party properly objects to a discovery request (or declines to provide information in its initial disclosures under Fed. R. Civ. P. 26(a)(1)) as set forth above, that party shall provide the requested information on the date on which it is required to provide the requested information to an opposing party under these Patent Rules, unless there exists another legitimate ground for objection.

2-6. Assignment of Related Cases. Separately filed cases related to the same patent shall be assigned to the same judge, i.e., the judge assigned to the first related case.

3. PATENT INITIAL DISCLOSURES

3-1. Disclosure of Asserted Claims and Infringement Contentions.

Not later than 10 days before the Initial Case Management Conference with the Court, a party claiming patent infringement must serve on all parties a "Disclosure of Asserted Claims and Infringement Contentions." Separately for each opposing party, the "Disclosure of Asserted Claims and Infringement Contentions" shall contain the following information:

(a) Each claim of each patent in suit that is allegedly infringed by each opposing party;

(b) Separately for each asserted claim, each accused apparatus, product, device, process, method, act, or other instrumentality ("Accused Instrumentality") of each opposing party of which the party is aware. This identification shall be as specific as possible. Each product, device, and apparatus must be identified by name or model number, if known. Each method or process must be identified by name, if known, or by any product, device, or apparatus which, when used, allegedly results in the practice of the claimed method or process;

(c) A chart identifying specifically where each element of each asserted claim is found within each Accused Instrumentality, including for each element that such party contends is governed by 35 U.S.C. § 112(6), the identity of the structure(s), act(s), or material(s) in the Accused Instrumentality that performs the claimed function;

(d) Whether each element of each asserted claim is claimed to be literally present or present under the doctrine of equivalents in the Accused Instrumentality;

(e) For any patent that claims priority to an earlier application, the priority date to which each asserted claim allegedly is entitled; and

(f) If a party claiming patent infringement wishes to preserve the right to rely, for any purpose, on the assertion that its own apparatus, product, device, process, method, act, or other instrumentality practices the claimed invention, the party must identify, separately for each asserted claim, each such apparatus, product, device, process, method, act, or other instrumentality that incorporates or reflects that particular claim.

3-2. Document Production Accompanying Disclosure.

With the "Disclosure of Asserted Claims and Infringement Contentions," the party claiming patent infringement must produce to each opposing party or make available for inspection and copying:

(a) Documents (e.g., contracts, purchase orders, invoices, advertisements, marketing materials, offer letters, beta site testing agreements, and third party or joint development agreements) sufficient to evidence each discussion with, disclosure to, or other manner of providing to a third party, or sale of or offer to sell, the claimed invention prior to the date of application for the patent in suit. A party's production of a document as required herein shall not constitute an admission that such document evidences or is prior art under 35 U.S.C. § 102;

(b) All documents evidencing the conception, reduction to practice, design, and development of each claimed invention, which were created on or before the date of application for the patent in suit or the priority date identified pursuant to P. R. 3-1(e), whichever is earlier; and

(c) A copy of the file history for each patent in suit.

The producing party shall separately identify by production number which documents correspond to each category.

3-3. Invalidity Contentions.

Not later than 45 days after service upon it of the "Disclosure of Asserted Claims and Infringement Contentions," each party opposing a claim of patent infringement, shall serve on all parties its "Invalidity Contentions" which must contain the following information:

(a) The identity of each item of prior art that allegedly anticipates each asserted claim or renders it obvious. Each prior art patent shall be identified by its number, country of origin, and date of issue. Each prior art publication must be identified by its title, date of publication, and where feasible, author and publisher. Prior art under 35 U.S.C. § 102(b) shall be identified by specifying the item offered for sale or publicly used or known, the date the offer or use took place or the information became known, and the identity of the person or entity which made the use or which made and received the offer, or the person or entity which made the information known or to whom it was made known. Prior art under 35 U.S.C. § 102(f) shall be identified by providing the name of the person(s) from whom and the circumstances under which the invention or any part of it was derived. Prior art under 35 U.S.C. § 102(g) shall be identified by providing the identities of the person(s) or entities involved in and the circumstances surrounding the making of the invention before the patent applicant(s);

(b) Whether each item of prior art anticipates each asserted claim or renders it obvious. If a combination of items of prior art makes a claim obvious, each such combination, and the motivation to combine such items, must be identified;

(c) A chart identifying where specifically in each alleged item of prior art each element of each asserted claim is found, including for each element that such party contends is governed by 35 U.S.C. § 112(6), the identity of the structure(s), act(s), or material(s) in each item of prior art that performs the claimed function; and

(d) Any grounds of invalidity based on indefiniteness under 35 U.S.C. § 112(2) or enablement or written description under 35 U.S.C. § 112(1) of any of the asserted claims.

3-4. Document Production Accompanying Invalidity Contentions.

With the "Invalidity Contentions," the party opposing a claim of patent infringement must produce or make available for inspection and copying:

(a) Source code, specifications, schematics, flow charts, artwork, formulas, or other documentation sufficient to show the operation of any aspects or elements of an Accused Instrumentality identified by the patent claimant in its P. R. 3-1(c) chart; and

(b) A copy of each item of prior art identified pursuant to P. R. 3-3(a) which does not appear in the file history of the patent(s) at issue. To the extent any such item is not in English, an English translation of the portion(s) relied upon must be produced.

3-5. Disclosure Requirement in Patent Cases for Declaratory Judgment.

(a) Invalidity Contentions If No Claim of Infringement. In all cases in which a party files a complaint or other pleading seeking a declaratory judgment that a patent is not infringed, is invalid, or is unenforceable, P. R. 3-1 and 3-2 shall not apply unless and until a claim for patent infringement is made by a party. If the defendant does not assert a claim for patent infringement in its answer to the complaint, no later than 10 days after the defendant serves its answer, or 10 days after the Initial Case Management Conference, whichever is later, the party seeking a declaratory judgment must serve upon each opposing party its Invalidity Contentions that conform to P. R. 3-3 and produce or make available for inspection and copying the documents described in P. R. 3-4. The parties shall meet and confer within 10 days of the service of the Invalidity Contentions for the purpose of determining the date on which the plaintiff will file its Final Invalidity Contentions which shall be no later than 50 days after service by the Court of its Claim Construction Ruling.

(b) Applications of Rules When No Specified Triggering Event. If the filings or actions in a case do not trigger the application of these Patent Rules under the terms set forth herein, the parties shall, as soon as such circumstances become known, meet and confer for the purpose of agreeing on the application of these Patent Rules to the case.

(c) Inapplicability of Rule. This P. R. 3-5 shall not apply to cases in which a request for a declaratory judgment that a patent is not infringed, is invalid, or is unenforceable is filed in response to a complaint for infringement of the same patent.

3-6. Amending Contentions.

(a) Leave not required. Each party's "Infringement Contentions" and "Invalidity Contentions" shall be deemed to be that party's final contentions, except as set forth below.

> **(1)** If a party claiming patent infringement believes in good faith that the Court's Claim Construction Ruling so requires, not later than 30 days after service by the Court of its Claim Construction Ruling, that party may serve "Amended Infringement Contentions" without leave of court that amend its "Infringement Contentions" with respect to the information required by Patent R. 3-1(c) and (d).
>
> **(2)** Not later than 50 days after service by the Court of its Claim Construction Ruling, each party opposing a claim of patent infringement may serve "Amended Invalidity Contentions" without leave of court that amend its "Invalidity Contentions" with respect to the information required by P. R. 3-3 if:

(A) a party claiming patent infringement has served "Infringement Contentions" pursuant to P. R. 3-6(a), or

(B) the party opposing a claim of patent infringement believes in good faith that the Court's Claim Construction Ruling so requires.

(b) Leave required. Amendment or supplementation any Infringement Contentions or Invalidity Contentions, other than as expressly permitted in P. R. 3-6(a), may be made only by order of the Court, which shall be entered only upon a showing of good cause.

3-7 Opinion of Counsel Defenses.

By the date set forth in the Docket Control Order, each party opposing a claim of patent infringement that will rely on an opinion of counsel as part of a defense shall:

(a) Produce or make available for inspection and copying the opinion(s) and any other documents relating to the opinion(s) as to which that party agrees the attorney-client or work product protection has been waived; and

(b) Serve a privilege log identifying any other documents, except those authored by counsel acting solely as trial counsel, relating to the subject matter of the opinion(s) which the party is withholding on the grounds of attorney-client privilege or work product protection.

A party opposing a claim of patent infringement who does not comply with the requirements of this P. R. 3-7 shall not be permitted to rely on an opinion of counsel as part of a defense absent a stipulation of all parties or by order of the Court, which shall be entered only upon a showing of good cause.

3-8. Disclosure Requirements for Patent Cases Arising Under 21 U.S.C. § 355 (Hatch-Waxman Act).

The following provision applies to all patents subject to a Paragraph IV certification in cases arising under 21 U.S.C. § 355 (commonly referred to as " the Hatch-Waxman Act"). This provision takes precedence over any conflicting provisions in P.R. 3-1 to 3-5 for all cases arising under 21 U.S.C. § 355.

(a) Upon the filing of a responsive pleading to the complaint, the Defendant(s) shall produce to Plaintiff(s) the entire Abbreviated New Drug Application or New Drug Application that is the basis of the case in question.

(b) Not more than 7 days after the Initial Case Management Conference, Plaintiff(s) must identify the asserted claims.

(c) Not more than 14 days after the Initial Case Management Conference, the Defendant(s) shall provide to Plaintiff(s) the written basis for their "Invalidity Contentions" for any patents referred to in Defendant(s) Paragraph IV Certification. This written basis shall contain all disclosures required by P.R. 3-3 and shall be accompanied by the production of documents required by P.R. 3-4.

(d) Not more than 14 days after the Initial Case Management Conference, the Defendant(s) shall provide to Plaintiff(s) the written basis for any defense of non-infringement for any patent referred to in Defendant(s) Paragraph IV Certification. This written basis shall include a claim chart identifying each claim at issue in the case and each limitation of each claim at issue. The claim chart shall specifically identify for each claim those claim limitation(s) that are literally absent from the Defendant(s) allegedly infringing Abbreviated New Drug Application or New Drug Application. The written basis for any defense of non-infringement shall also be accompanied by the production of any document or thing that the Defendant(s) intend to rely upon in defense of any infringement allegations by Plaintiff(s).

(e) Not more than 45 days after the disclosure of the written basis for any defense of non-infringement as required by P.R. 3-8(c), Plaintiff(s) shall provide Defendant(s) with a "Disclosure of Asserted Claims and Infringement Contentions," for all patents referred to in Defendant(s) Paragraph IV Certification, which shall contain all disclosures required by P.R. 3-1 and shall be accompanied by the production of documents required by P.R. 3-2.

(f) Each party that has an ANDA application pending with the Food and Drug Administration ("FDA") that is the basis of the pending case shall: (1) notify the FDA of any and all motions for injunctive relief no later than three business days after the date on which such a motion is filed; and (2) provide a copy of all correspondence between itself and the FDA pertaining to the ANDA application to each party asserting infringement, or set forth the basis of any claim of privilege for such correspondence, no later than seven days after the date it sends or receives any such correspondence.

(g) Unless informed of special circumstances, the Court intends to set all Hatch-Waxman cases for final pretrial hearing at or near 24 months from the date of the filing of the complaint.

4. CLAIM CONSTRUCTION PROCEEDINGS

4-1. Exchange of Proposed Terms and Claim Elements for Construction.

(a) Not later than 10 days after service of the "Invalidity Contentions" pursuant to P. R. 3-3, each party shall simultaneously exchange a list of claim terms, phrases, or clauses which that party contends should be construed by the Court, and identify any claim element which that party contends should be governed by 35 U.S.C. § 112(6).

(b) The parties shall thereafter meet and confer for the purposes of finalizing this list, narrowing or resolving differences, and facilitating the ultimate preparation of a Joint Claim Construction and Prehearing Statement.

4-2. Exchange of Preliminary Claim Constructions and Extrinsic Evidence.

(a) Not later than 20 days after the exchange of "Proposed Terms and Claim Elements for Construction" pursuant to P. R. 4-1, the parties shall simultaneously exchange a preliminary proposed construction of each claim term, phrase, or clause which the parties collectively have identified for claim construction purposes. Each such "Preliminary Claim Construction" shall also, for each element which any party contends is governed by 35 U.S.C. § 112(6), identify the structure(s), act(s), or material(s) corresponding to that element.

(b) At the same time the parties exchange their respective "Preliminary Claim Constructions," they shall each also provide a preliminary identification of extrinsic evidence, including without limitation, dictionary definitions, citations to learned treatises and prior art, and testimony of percipient and expert witnesses they contend support their respective claim constructions. The parties shall identify each such item of extrinsic evidence by production number or produce a copy of any such item not previously produced. With respect to any such witness, percipient or expert, the parties shall also provide a brief description of the substance of that witness' proposed testimony.

(c) The parties shall thereafter meet and confer for the purposes of narrowing the issues and finalizing preparation of a Joint Claim Construction and Prehearing Statement.

4-3. Joint Claim Construction and Prehearing Statement.

Not later than 60 days after service of the "Invalidity Contentions," the parties shall complete and file a Joint Claim Construction and Prehearing Statement, which shall contain the following information:

(a) The construction of those claim terms, phrases, or clauses on which the parties agree;

(b) Each party's proposed construction of each disputed claim term, phrase, or clause, together with an identification of all references from the specification or prosecution history that support that construction, and an identification of any extrinsic evidence known to the party on which it intends to rely either to support its proposed construction of the claim or to oppose any other party's proposed construction of the claim, including, but not limited to, as permitted by law, dictionary definitions, citations to learned treatises and prior art, and testimony of percipient and expert witnesses;

(c) The anticipated length of time necessary for the Claim Construction Hearing;

(d) Whether any party proposes to call one or more witnesses, including experts, at the Claim Construction Hearing, the identity of each such witness, and for each expert, a summary of each opinion to be offered in sufficient detail to permit a meaningful deposition of that expert; and

(e) A list of any other issues which might appropriately be taken up at a prehearing conference prior to the Claim Construction Hearing, and proposed dates, if not previously set, for any such prehearing conference.

4-4. Completion of Claim Construction Discovery.

Not later than 30 days after service and filing of the Joint Claim Construction and Prehearing Statement, the parties shall complete all discovery relating to claim construction, including any depositions with respect to claim construction of any witnesses, including experts, identified in the Joint Claim Construction and Prehearing Statement.

4-5. Claim Construction Briefs.

(a) Not later than 45 days after serving and filing the Joint Claim Construction and Prehearing Statement, the party claiming patent infringement shall serve and file an opening brief and any evidence supporting its claim construction. All asserted patents shall be attached as exhibits to the opening claim construction brief in searchable PDF form.

(b) Not later than 14 days after service upon it of an opening brief, each opposing party shall serve and file its responsive brief and supporting evidence.

(c) Not later than 7 days after service upon it of a responsive brief, the party claiming patent infringement shall serve and file any reply brief and any evidence directly rebutting the supporting evidence contained in an opposing party's response.

(d) At least 10 days before the Claim Construction Hearing held pursuant to P.R. 4-6, the parties shall jointly file a claim construction chart.

> **(1)** Said chart shall have a column listing complete language of disputed claims with disputed terms in bold type and separate columns for each party's proposed construction of each disputed term. The chart shall also include a fourth column entitled "Court's Construction" and otherwise left blank. Additionally, the chart shall also direct the Court's attention to the patent and claim number(s) where the disputed term(s) appear(s).
>
> **(2)** The parties may also include constructions for claim terms to which they have agreed. If the parties choose to include agreed constructions, each party's proposed construction columns shall state "[**AGREED**]" and the agreed construction shall be inserted in the "Court's Construction" column.
>
> **(3)** The purpose of this claim construction chart is to assist the Court and the parties in tracking and resolving disputed terms. Accordingly, aside from the requirements set forth in this rule, the parties are afforded substantial latitude in the chart's format so that they may fashion a chart that most clearly and efficiently outlines the disputed terms and proposed constructions. Appendices to the Court's prior published and unpublished claim construction opinions may provide helpful guidelines for parties fashioning claim construction charts.

(e) Unless otherwise ordered by the Court, the page limitations governing dispositive motions pursuant to Local Rule CV-7(a) shall apply to claim construction briefing.

4-6. Claim Construction Hearing.

Subject to the convenience of the Court's calendar, two weeks following submission of the reply brief specified in P.R. 4-5(c), the Court shall conduct a Claim Construction Hearing, to the extent the parties or the Court believe a hearing is necessary for construction of the claims at issue.

Appendix E
Model Patent Jury Instructions

FEDERAL CIRCUIT BAR ASSOCIATION

MODEL PATENT JURY INSTRUCTIONS

Last Edited: January 2016

Acknowledgement

The Association thanks the Patent Litigation Committee and in particular the Jury Instruction Subcommittee for their efforts in creating these Model Patent Jury Instructions.

TABLE OF CONTENTS

TABLE OF AUTHORITIES

Page(s)

Cases

Statutes

Preliminary Instructions

A.1 Preliminary Instructions

WHAT A PATENT IS AND HOW ONE IS OBTAINED

This case involves a dispute relating to a United States patent. Before summarizing the positions of the parties and the issues involved in the dispute, let me take a moment to explain what a patent is and how one is obtained.

Patents are granted by the United States Patent and Trademark Office (sometimes called "the PTO"). A valid United States patent gives the patent holder the right [for up to 20 years from the date the patent application was filed] [for 17 years from the date the patent issued] to prevent others from making, using, offering to sell, or selling the patented invention within the United States, or from importing it into the United States, without the patent holder's permission. A violation of the patent holder's rights is called infringement. The patent holder may try to enforce a patent against persons believed to be infringers by a lawsuit filed in federal court.

The process of obtaining a patent is called patent prosecution. To obtain a patent, one must first file an application with the PTO. The PTO is an agency of the Federal Government and employs trained Examiners who review applications for patents. The application includes what is called a "specification," which contains a written description of the claimed invention telling what the invention is, how it works, how to make it, and how to use it. The specification concludes with one or more numbered sentences. These are the patent "claims." When the patent is eventually granted by the PTO, the claims define the boundaries of its protection and give notice to the public of those boundaries.

After the applicant files the application, an Examiner reviews the application to determine whether or not the claims are patentable (appropriate for patent protection) and whether or not the specification adequately describes the invention claimed. In examining a patent application, the Examiner reviews certain information about the state of the technology at the time the application was filed. The PTO searches for and reviews information that is publicly available or that is submitted by the applicant. This information is called "prior art." The Examiner reviews this prior art to determine whether or not the invention is truly an advance over the state of the art at the time. Prior art is defined by law, and I will give you, at a later time during these instructions, specific instructions as to what constitutes prior art. However, in general, prior art includes information that demonstrates the state of technology that existed before the claimed invention was made or before the application was filed. A patent lists the prior art that the Examiner considered; this list is called the "cited references."

After the prior art search and examination of the application, the Examiner informs the applicant in writing of what the Examiner has found and whether the Examiner considers any claim to be patentable and, thus, would be "allowed." This writing from the Examiner is called an "Office Action." If the Examiner rejects the claims, the applicant has an opportunity to respond to the Examiner to try to persuade the Examiner to allow the claims, and to change the claims or to submit new claims. This process may go back and forth for some time until the Examiner is satisfied that the application meets the requirements for a patent and the application issues as a patent, or that the application should be rejected and no patent should issue. Sometimes, patents are issued after appeals within the PTO or to a court. The papers generated during these communications between the Examiner and the applicant are called the "prosecution history."

The fact that the PTO grants a patent does not necessarily mean that any invention claimed in the patent, in fact, deserves the protection of a patent. For example, the PTO may not have had available to it all other prior art that will be presented to you. A person accused of infringement has the right to argue here in federal court that a claimed invention in the patent is invalid because it does not meet the requirements for a patent. It is your job to consider the evidence presented by the parties and determine independently whether or not [alleged infringer] has proven that the patent is invalid.

A.2 Preliminary Instructions

SUMMARY OF CONTENTIONS

To help you follow the evidence, I will now give you a summary of the positions of the parties.

The parties in this case are [patent holder] and [alleged infringer]. The case involves United States Patent No(s). [ ], obtained by [inventor], and transferred by [inventor] to [patent holder]. For your convenience, the parties and I will often refer to this patent number [full patent number] by the last three numbers of the patent number, namely, as the "[last three numbers of the patent] patent."

[Patent holder] filed suit in this court seeking money damages from [alleged infringer] for allegedly infringing the [ ] patent by [making], [importing], [using], [selling], [offering for sale], [supplying or causing to be supplied in or from the United States all or a substantial portion of the components of a patented invention] [in/into/within] the United States [products] [methods] [products which are made by a process patented in the United States] that [patent holder] argues are covered by claims [ ] of the [ ] patent. [[Patent holder] also argues that [alleged infringer] has [actively induced infringement of these claims of the [ ] patent by others] [and/or] [contributed to the infringement of claims [ ] of the [ ] patent by others].]

The [products] [methods] that are alleged to infringe are [list of accused products or methods].

[Alleged infringer] denies that it has infringed claims [ ] of the [ ] patent. [Alleged infringer] also argues that claims [ ] are invalid. I will instruct you later as to the ways in which a patent may be invalid. In general, however, a patent is invalid if it is not new or is obvious in view of the state of the art at the relevant time, or if the description in the patent does not meet certain requirements. [Add other defenses, if applicable.]

Your job will be to decide whether or not claims [ ] of the [ ] patent have been infringed and whether or not those claims are invalid. If you decide that any claim of the [ ] patent has been infringed and is not invalid, you will then need to decide any money damages to be awarded to [patent holder] to compensate it for the infringement. [You will also need to make a finding as to whether the infringement was willful. If you decide that any infringement was willful, that decision should not affect any damages award you give. I will take willfulness into account later.]

A.3 Preliminary Instructions

PATENT AT ISSUE

[The Court should show the jury the patent at issue and point out the parts, which include the specification, drawings, and claims, including the claims at issue. The Court may wish to include a joint, nonargumentative statement of the patented subject matter at this point in the instructions.

The Court may wish to hand out its claim constructions (if the claims have been construed at this point) and the glossary at this time. If the claim constructions are handed out, the following instruction should be read:]

I have already determined the meaning of the claims of the [ ] patent. You have been given a document reflecting those meanings. For a claim term for which I have not provided you with a definition, you should apply the ordinary meaning. You are to apply my definitions of these terms throughout this case. However, my interpretation of the language of the claims should not be taken as an indication that I have a view regarding issues such as infringement and invalidity. Those issues are yours to decide. I will provide you with more detailed instructions on the meaning of the claims before you retire to deliberate your verdict.

A.4 Preliminary Instructions

OVERVIEW OF APPLICABLE LAW

[The Court may wish to give preliminary instructions that are applicable to the specific issues in the case. This may help focus the jury on the facts that are relevant to the issues it will have to decide. Even if preliminary instructions are given, the Court would, nonetheless, give complete instructions at the close of evidence.]

In deciding the issues I just discussed, you will be asked to consider specific legal standards. I will give you an overview of those standards now and will review them in more detail before the case is submitted to you for your verdict.

The first issue you will be asked to decide is whether [alleged infringer] has infringed the claims of the [ ] patent. Infringement is assessed on a claim-by-claim basis. Therefore, there may be infringement as to one claim but not infringement as to another. There are a few different ways that a patent may be infringed. I will explain the requirements for each of these types of infringement to you in detail at the conclusion of the case. In general, however, [alleged infringer] may infringe the [ ] patent by making, using, selling, or offering for sale in the United States, or by importing into the United States, a product or by using a method meeting all the requirements of a claim of the [ ] patent. [Alleged infringer] may also indirectly infringe the [ ] patent by contributing to infringement by another entity, or by inducing another person or entity to infringe. I will provide you with more detailed instructions on the requirements for each of these types of infringement at the conclusion of the case.

Another issue you will be asked to decide is whether the [ ] patent is invalid. A patent may be invalid for a number of reasons, including because it claims subject matter that is not new or is obvious. For a claim to be invalid because it is not new, [alleged infringer] must show, by clear and convincing evidence, that all of the elements of a claim are present in a single previous device or method, or sufficiently described in a single previous printed publication or patent. We call these "prior art." If a claim is not new, it is said to be anticipated.

Another way that a claim may be invalid is that it may have been obvious. Even though every element of a claim is not shown or sufficiently described in a single piece of "prior art," the claim may still be invalid if it would have been obvious to a person of ordinary skill in the field of technology of the patent at the relevant time. You will need to consider a number of questions in deciding whether the invention(s) claimed in the [ ] patent are obvious. I will provide you detailed instructions on these questions at the conclusion of the case.

[Where a written description or enablement defense is presented: A patent may also be invalid if its description in the specification does not meet certain requirements. To be valid, a patent must meet the "written description" requirement. In order to meet this written description requirement, the description of the invention in the specification portion of the patent must be detailed enough to demonstrate that the applicant actually possessed the invention as broadly as claimed in the claims of the issued patent. The disclosure of a patent must also meet the "enablement" requirement. To meet this requirement, the description in the patent has to be sufficiently full and clear to have allowed persons of ordinary skill in the field of technology of the patent to make and use the invention without undue experimentation, at the time the patent application was originally filed.]

If you decide that any claim of the [ ] patent has been infringed and is not invalid, you will then need to decide any money damages to be awarded to [patent holder] to compensate it for the infringement. A damages award should put [patent holder] in approximately the same financial position that it would have been in had the infringement not occurred, but in no event may the damages award be less than what [patent holder] would have received had it been paid a reasonable royalty. I will instruct you later on the meaning of a reasonable royalty. The damages you award are meant to compensate [patent holder] and not to punish [alleged infringer]. You may not include in your award any additional amount as a fine or penalty, above what is necessary to compensate [patent holder] for the infringement, in order to punish [alleged infringer]. I will give you more detailed instructions on the calculation of damages at the conclusion of the case.

A.5 Preliminary Instructions

OUTLINE OF TRIAL

The trial will now begin. First, each side may make an opening statement. An opening statement is not evidence. It is simply an opportunity for the lawyers to explain what they expect the evidence will show.

There are two standards of proof that you will apply to the evidence, depending on the issue you are deciding. On some issues, you must decide whether certain facts have been proven by a preponderance of the evidence. A preponderance of the evidence means that the fact that is to be proven is more likely true than not, i.e., that the evidence in favor of that fact being true is sufficient to tip the scale, even if slightly, in its favor. On other issues that I will identify for you, you must use a higher standard and decide whether the fact has been proven by clear and convincing evidence, i.e., that you have been left with a clear conviction that the fact has been proven.

These standards are different from what you may have heard about in criminal proceedings where a fact must be proven beyond a reasonable doubt. On a scale of these various standards of proof, as you move from preponderance of the evidence, where the proof need only be sufficient to tip the scale in favor of the party proving the fact, to beyond a reasonable doubt, where the fact must be proven to a very high degree of certainty, you may think of clear and convincing evidence as being between the two standards.

After the opening statements, [patent holder] will present its evidence in support of its contention that [some of the] [the] claims of the [ ] patent have been [and continue to be] infringed by [alleged infringer] [and that the infringement has been [and continues to be] willful]. To prove infringement of any claim, [patent holder] must persuade you that it is more likely than not that [alleged infringer] has infringed that claim. [To persuade you that any infringement was willful, [patent holder] must prove that the infringement was willful by clear and convincing evidence.]

[Alleged infringer] will then present its evidence that the claims of the [ ] patent are invalid [and/or unenforceable]. To prove invalidity [and/or unenforceability] of any claim, [alleged infringer] must persuade you by clear and convincing evidence that the claim is invalid [and/or unenforceable]. In addition to presenting its evidence of invalidity [and/or unenforceability], [alleged infringer] will put on evidence responding to [patent holder]'s proof of infringement [and willfulness].

[Patent holder] may then put on additional evidence responding to [alleged infringer]'s evidence that the claims of the [ ] patent are invalid [and/or unenforceable], and to offer any additional evidence of infringement [and willfulness]. This is referred to as "rebuttal" evidence. [Patent holder]'s "rebuttal" evidence may respond to any evidence offered by [alleged infringer].

Finally, [alleged infringer] may have the option to put on its "rebuttal" evidence to support its contentions as to the validity [and/or enforceability] of [some of the] [the] claims of the [ ] patent by responding to any evidence offered by [patent holder] on that issue.

[During the presentation of the evidence, the attorneys will be allowed brief opportunities to explain what they believe the evidence has shown or what they believe upcoming evidence will show. The attorneys' comments are not evidence and the attorneys are being allowed to comment solely for the purpose of helping you to understand the evidence.]

After the evidence has been presented, [the attorneys will make closing arguments and I will give you final instructions on the law that applies to the case] [I will give you final instructions on the law that applies to the case and the attorneys will make closing arguments]. These closing arguments by the attorneys are not evidence. After the closing arguments and instructions, you will then decide the case.

Instructions at the Close of Evidence

B.1 Summary of Contentions

SUMMARY OF CONTENTIONS

As I did at the start of the case, I will first give you a summary of each side's contentions in this case. I will then provide you with detailed instructions on what each side must prove to win on each of its contentions.

As I previously told you, [patent holder] seeks money damages from [alleged infringer] for allegedly infringing the [ ] patent by [making], [importing], [using], [selling], and [offering for sale] [products] [methods] that [patent holder] argues are covered by claims [ ] of the [ ] patent. These are the asserted claims of the [ ] patent. [Patent holder] also argues that [alleged infringer] has [actively induced infringement of these claims of the [ ] patent by others] [contributed to the infringement of these claims of the [ ] patent by others]. The [products] [methods] that are alleged to infringe are [list of accused products or methods].

[Alleged infringer] denies that it has infringed the asserted claims of the [ ] patent [and argues that, in addition, claims [ ] are invalid.] [Add other defenses if applicable.]

Your job is to decide whether [alleged infringer] has infringed the asserted claims of the [ ] patent and whether any of the asserted claims of the [ ] patent are invalid. If you decide that any claim of the [ ] patent has been infringed and is not invalid, you will then need to decide any money damages to be awarded to [patent holder] to compensate it for the infringement. [You will also need to make a finding as to whether the infringement was willful. If you decide that any infringement was willful, that decision should not affect any damages award you make. I will take willfulness into account later.]

B.2 Claim Construction

2.1 THE ROLE OF THE CLAIMS OF A PATENT

Before you can decide many of the issues in this case, you will need to understand the role of patent "claims." The patent claims are the numbered sentences at the end of each patent. The claims are important because it is the words of the claims that define what a patent covers. The figures and text in the rest of the patent provide a description and/or examples of the invention and provide a context for the claims, but it is the claims that define the breadth of the patent's coverage. Each claim is effectively treated as if it were a separate patent, and each claim may cover more or less than another claim. Therefore, what a patent covers depends, in turn, on what each of its claims covers.

You will first need to understand what each claim covers in order to decide whether or not there is infringement of the claim and to decide whether or not the claim is invalid. The law says that it is my role to define the terms of the claims and it is your role to apply my definitions to the issues that you are asked to decide in this case. Therefore, as I explained to you at the start of the case, I have determined the meaning of the claims and I will provide to you my definitions of certain claim terms. You must accept my definitions of these words in the claims as being correct. It is your job to take these definitions and apply them to the issues that you are deciding, including the issues of infringement and validity.

B.2 Claim Construction

2.2 HOW A CLAIM DEFINES WHAT IT COVERS

I will now explain how a claim defines what it covers.

A claim sets forth, in words, a set of requirements. Each claim sets forth its requirements in a single sentence. If a device or a method satisfies each of these requirements, then it is covered by the claim.

There can be several claims in a patent. Each claim may be narrower or broader than another claim by setting forth more or fewer requirements. The coverage of a patent is assessed claim-by-claim. In patent law, the requirements of a claim are often referred to as "claim elements" or "claim limitations." When a thing (such as a product or a process) meets all of the requirements of a claim, the claim is said to "cover" that thing, and that thing is said to "fall" within the scope of that claim. In other words, a claim covers a product or process where each of the claim elements or limitations is present in that product or process.

Sometimes the words in a patent claim are difficult to understand, and therefore it is difficult to understand what requirements these words impose. It is my job to explain to you the meaning of the words in the claims and the requirements these words impose.

As I just instructed you, there are certain specific terms that I have defined and you are to apply the definitions that I provide to you.

By understanding the meaning of the words in a claim and by understanding that the words in a claim set forth the requirements that a product or process must meet in order to be covered by that claim, you will be able to understand the scope of coverage for each claim. Once you understand what each claim covers, then you are prepared to decide the issues that you will be asked to decide, such as infringement and invalidity.

<u>Authorities</u>

For "comprising," *see, e.g.*, *Cook Biotech Inc. v. ACell, Inc.*, 460 F.3d 1365, 1373-78 (Fed. Cir. 2006); *Invitrogen Corp. v. Biocrest Mfg., L.P.*, 327 F.3d 1364, 1368 (Fed. Cir. 2003) ("The transition 'comprising' in a method claim . . . is open-ended and allows for additional steps."); for "consisting of," *see, e.g.*, *Conoco, Inc. v. Energy & Envtl. Int'l, L.C.*, 460 F.3d 1349, 1358-61 (Fed. Cir. 2006); *Vehicular Techs. Corp. v. Titan Wheel Int'l, Inc.*, 212 F.3d 1377, 1383 (Fed. Cir. 2000) ("In simple terms, a drafter uses the phrase 'consisting of' to mean 'I claim what follows and nothing else.'"); for "consisting essentially of," *see, e.g.*, *CIAS, Inc. v. Alliance Gaming Corp.*, 504 F.3d 1356, 1361 (Fed. Cir. 2007); *AK Steel Corp. v. Sollac & Ugine*, 344 F.3d 1234, 1239 (Fed. Cir. 2003) ("consisting essentially of" is a middle ground between open-ended term "comprising" and closed-ended phrase "consisting of").

B.2 Claim Construction

2.2a INDEPENDENT AND DEPENDENT CLAIMS

[This instruction should only be given where both dependent and independent claims are at issue.]

This case involves two types of patent claims: independent claims and dependent claims.

An "independent claim" sets forth all of the requirements that must be met in order to be covered by that claim. Thus, it is not necessary to look at any other claim to determine what an independent claim covers. In this case, claim(s) [ ] of the [ ] patent are each independent claims.

The remainder of the claims in the [ ] patent are "dependent claims." A dependent claim does not itself recite all of the requirements of the claim but refers to another claim for some of its requirements. In this way, the claim "depends" on another claim. A dependent claim incorporates all of the requirements of the claim(s) to which it refers. The dependent claim then adds its own additional requirements. To determine what a dependent claim covers, it is necessary to look at both the dependent claim and any other claim(s) to which it refers. A product [or process] that meets all of the requirements of both the dependent claim and the claim(s) to which it refers is covered by that dependent claim.

[Note: It may be helpful to submit to the jury a chart setting forth all dependencies for each dependent claim.]

B.2 Claim Construction

2.3 CLAIM INTERPRETATION

I will now explain to you the meaning of some of the words of the claims in this case. In doing so, I will explain some of the requirements of the claims. As I have previously instructed you, you must accept my definition of these words in the claims as correct. For any words in the claim for which I have not provided you with a definition, you should apply their common meaning. You should not take my definition of the language of the claims as an indication that I have a view regarding how you should decide the issues that you are being asked to decide, such as infringement and invalidity. These issues are yours to decide.

[Court gives its claim interpretation. This instruction may be divided up into claim-by-claim sub-instructions if the Court believes it would be helpful.]

Authorities

Markman v. Westview Instruments, Inc., 517 U.S. 370 (1996) (claim construction of a patent, including claim terms, is exclusively within the province of the court); *O2 Micro Int'l Ltd. v. Beyond Innovation Tech. Co.*, 521 F.3d 1351, 1360-63 (Fed. Cir. 2008) (remanding to the district court to determine the construction of "only if" when the "ordinary" meaning did not resolve the parties' dispute); *Phillips v. AWH Corp.*, 415 F.3d 1303, 1312-13 (Fed. Cir. 2005) (en banc) ("ordinary and customary meaning" is based on the understanding of a person of ordinary skill in the art in question at the time of the invention); *Pitney Bowes, Inc. v. Hewlett-Packard Co.*, 182 F.3d 1298, 1304 (Fed. Cir. 1999) (claim construction is a question of law reviewed de novo); *Cybor Corp. v. FAS Techs.*, 138 F.3d 1448, 1456 (Fed. Cir. 1998) (same); *Markman v. Westview Instruments, Inc.*, 52 F.3d 967, 977 (Fed. Cir. 1995) (in jury cases, court has obligation to construe claim terms).

B.2 Claim Construction

2.3a SECTION 112, PARAGRAPH 6

[This instruction should only be given where the asserted claims include means-plus-function or step-plus-function requirements.]

Where claims include means-plus-function requirements:

Claim [ ] uses the phrase "means for [function]." This "means for" phrase has a special meaning in patent law. It is called a "means-plus-function" requirement. It does not cover all of the structures that could perform the function set forth in the claim, namely, "[function]." Instead, it covers a structure or a set of structures that performs that function and that is either identical or "equivalent" to [at least one of] the [set(s) of] structure(s) described in the [ ] patent for performing that function. The issue of whether two structures are identical or equivalent is for you to decide. I will explain to you later how to determine whether two structures or two sets of structures are "equivalent" to one another. For purposes of this case, I have identified the [set(s) of] structure(s) described in the [ ] patent that perform(s) the function of "[function]." [Claims [ ] also include similar means-plus-function requirements.] When I read you my definitions for certain claim terms a few moments ago, I identified the structures described in the [ ] patent for performing the relevant functions. You should apply my definition of the function and the structures described in the [ ] patent for performing it as you would apply my definition of any other claim term.

Where claims include step-plus-function requirements:

Claim [ ] uses the phrase "step for [function]." It does not cover all of the acts that could perform the function set forth in the claim. Instead, it covers acts that perform that function and are either identical or "equivalent" to [at least one of] the [set(s) of] act(s) described in the [ ] patent for performing that function. The issue of whether two structures are identical or equivalent is for you to decide. I will explain to you later how to determine whether two acts or two sets of acts are "equivalent" to one another. For purposes of this case, I have identified the [set(s) of] act(s) described in the [ ] patent that perform(s) the function of "[function]." [Claims [ ] also include similar step-plus-function requirements.] When I read you my definitions for certain claim terms a few moments ago, I identified the acts described in the [ ] patent for performing the relevant functions. You should apply my definition of the function and the acts described in the [ ] patent for performing it as you would apply my definition of any other claim term.

<u>Authorities</u>

35 U.S.C. § 112, ¶ 6; *Allvoice Computing PLC v. Nuance Commc'ns, Inc.*, 504 F.3d 1236, 1240-41 (Fed. Cir. 2007); *Applied Med. Res. Corp. v. U.S. Surgical Corp.*, 448 F.3d 1324, 1332-34 (Fed. Cir. 2006) (explaining that an object meeting a means-plus-function limitation with two functions must perform both claimed functions and be an equivalent structure. Equivalence of structure can be shown here if the objects perform both identical functions in substantially the same way to achieve substantially the same result.); *Al-Site Corp. v. VSI Int'l Inc.*, 174 F.3d 1308, 1318-21 (Fed. Cir. 1999) (distinguishing between means- or step-plus-function to

equivalents available at time of issuance and application of doctrine of equivalents to after-arising inventions); *WMS Gaming Inc. v. Int'l Game Tech.*, 184 F.3d 1339, 1351 (Fed. Cir. 1999) ("The proper test for determining whether the structure in an accused device is equivalent to the structure recited in a section 112, ¶ 6, claim is whether the differences between the structure in the accused device and any disclosed in the specification are insubstantial."); *Odetics, Inc. v. Storage Tech. Corp.*, 185 F.3d 1259, 1266-67 (Fed. Cir. 1999); *Chiuminatta Concrete Concepts, Inc. v. Cardinal Indus., Inc.*, 145 F.3d 1303, 1307-08 (Fed. Cir. 1998).

B.3 Infringement

3.1 INFRINGEMENT GENERALLY

I will now instruct you how to decide whether or not [alleged infringer] has infringed the [ ] patent. Infringement is assessed on a claim-by-claim basis. Therefore, there may be infringement as to one claim but no infringement as to another.

In this case, there are five possible ways that a claim may be infringed. The five types of infringement are called: (1) direct infringement; (2) active inducement; (3) contributory infringement; (4) infringement through the supply of components from the United States to another country; and (5) infringement through importation of a product made abroad by a patented process. Active inducement and contributory infringement are referred to as indirect infringement. There cannot be indirect infringement without someone else engaging in direct infringement. To prove indirect infringement, [patent holder] must also prove that [alleged infringer]'s indirect infringement caused direct infringement.

In this case, [patent holder] has alleged that [alleged infringer] directly infringes the [ ] patent. [[In addition,] [patent holder] has alleged that [alleged direct infringer] directly infringes the [ ] patent, and [alleged infringer] is liable for [actively inducing or contributing to] that direct infringement by [alleged direct infringer]. [Patent holder] has also alleged that [alleged infringer] is liable for [infringement through the supply of components from the United States for combination outside of the United States] [and/or] [infringement through importation into the United States of a product made by the patented process].]

In order to prove infringement, [patent holder] must prove that the requirements for one or more of these types of infringement are met by a preponderance of the evidence, i.e., that it is more likely than not that all of the requirements of one or more of each of these types of infringement have been proved.

I will now explain each of these types of infringement in more detail.

Authorities

Warner-Lambert Co. v. Teva Pharms. USA, Inc., 418 F.3d 1326, 1341 n.15 (Fed. Cir. 2005) (infringement must be proven by a preponderance of the evidence); *Seal-Flex, Inc. v. Athletic Track & Court Constr.*, 172 F.3d 836, 842 (Fed. Cir. 1999) (a patentee must "prove that the accused product or process contains, either literally or under the doctrine of equivalents, every limitation of the properly construed claim"); *Morton Int'l, Inc. v. Cardinal Chem. Co.*, 5 F.3d 1464, 1468-69 (Fed. Cir. 1993) (upholding lower court's finding of noninfringement based on plaintiff's failure to prove that the accused product met all of the claimed requirements).

B.3 Infringement

3.1a DIRECT INFRINGEMENT BY "LITERAL INFRINGEMENT"

There are two types of "direct infringement": (1) "literal infringement" and (2) "infringement under the doctrine of equivalents." In order to prove direct infringement by literal infringement, [patent holder] must prove by a preponderance of the evidence, i.e., that it is more likely than not, that [alleged infringer] made, used, sold, offered for sale within, or imported into the United States a [product or process] that meets all of the requirements of a claim and did so without the permission of [patent holder] during the time the [ ] patent was in force. You must compare the [product or process] with each and every one of the requirements of a claim to determine whether all of the requirements of that claim are met.

You must determine, separately for each asserted claim, whether or not there is infringement. There is one exception to this rule. If you find that a claim on which other claims depend is not infringed, there cannot be infringement of any dependent claim that refers directly or indirectly to that independent claim. On the other hand, if you find that an independent claim has been infringed, you must still decide, separately, whether the [product or process] meets additional requirements of any claims that depend from the independent claim, thus, whether those claims have also been infringed. A dependent claim includes all the requirements of any of the claims to which it refers plus additional requirements of its own.

<u>Authorities</u>

Kim v. ConAgra Foods, Inc., 465 F.3d 1312, 1316, n.1 (Fed. Cir. 2006) (dependent claims not infringed when independent claim not infringed); *MicroStrategy Inc. v. Bus. Objects, S.A.*, 429 F.3d 1344, 1352-53 (Fed. Cir. 2005) (no literal infringement where accused product did not contain every element of the claim); *Cross Med. Prods. v. Medtronic Sofamor Danek*, 424 F.3d 1293, 1309-11 (Fed. Cir. 2005) (no direct infringement where accused product did not include each claim limitation); *Netword, LLC v. Centraal Corp.*, 242 F.3d 1347, 1353-54 (Fed. Cir. 2001) (no literal infringement where all of the elements of the claim not present in the accused system); *Moleculon Research Corp. v. CBS, Inc.*, 793 F.2d 1261 (Fed. Cir. 1986) (affirming finding of direct infringement based on circumstantial evidence).

B.3 Infringement

3.1b DIRECT INFRINGEMENT BY "LITERAL INFRINGEMENT" OF SECTION 112, PARAGRAPH 6 CLAIM REQUIREMENTS

[This instruction should only be given where the asserted claims include means-plus-function or step-plus-function requirements.]

Where claims include means/step-plus-function requirements:

As I have previously explained, claims [ ] include requirements that are in [means/step-plus-function] form.

A product or a process meets a means/step-plus-function requirement of a claim if: (1) it has [a structure or a set of structures/an action or a set of actions] that perform(s) the identical function recited in the claim, and (2) that [structure or set of structures/action or set of actions] is either identical or "equivalent" to [one or more of] the described [set(s) of] [structure(s)/ action(s)] that I defined earlier as performing the function of [functional limitation]. If the [product] does not perform the specific function recited in the claim, the "means-plus-function" requirement is not met, and the [product] does not literally infringe the claim. Alternatively, even if the [product] has [a structure or a set of structures] that performs the function recited in the claim but the [structure or set of structures] is not either identical or "equivalent" to [one or more of] the [set(s) of] [structure(s)/action(s)] that I defined to you as being described in the [ ] patent and performing this function, the [product] does not literally infringe the asserted claim.

[A structure or a set of structures/An action or a set of actions] may be found to be "equivalent" to [one of] [the/a] [set(s) of] [structure(s)/action(s)] I have defined as being described in the [ ] patent if a person having ordinary skill in the field of technology of the [ ] patent either would have considered the differences between them to be insubstantial at the time the [ ] patent issued or if that person would have found the [structure(s)/actions(s)] performed the function in substantially the same way to accomplish substantially the same result. In deciding whether the differences would be "insubstantial," you may consider whether a person having an ordinary level of skill in the field of technology of the patent would have known of the interchangeability of the two structures or sets of structures. Interchangeability itself is not sufficient; in order for the structures to be considered to be interchangeable, the interchangeability of the two structures must have been known to persons of ordinary skill in that art at the time the patent issued. The fact that [a structure or a set of structures/an act or a set of acts] is known now and is "equivalent" is not enough. The [structure or set of structures/act or set of acts] must also have been available at the time the [ ] patent issued.

[In this case, the parties have agreed that the relevant field of technology is [field of technology] and that a person having an ordinary level of skill would [qualifications].] [In this case, you will have to decide [issues regarding field of technology and level of ordinary skill in the art]. I will instruct you later how to decide this.]

In order to prove direct infringement by literal infringement of a means-plus/step-plus-function limitation, [patent holder] must prove the above requirements are met by a preponderance of the evidence.

Authorities

35 U.S.C. § 112, ¶ 6; *Allvoice Computing PLC v. Nuance Commc'ns, Inc.*, 504 F.3d 1236, 1240-41 (Fed. Cir. 2007); *Cross Med. Prods., Inc. v. Medtronic Sofamor Danek, Inc.*, 424 F.3d 1293, 1315-17 (Fed. Cir. 2005); *Applied Med. Res. Corp. v. U.S. Surgical Corp.*, 448 F.3d 1324, 1333-34 (Fed. Cir. 2006); *Omega Eng'g, Inc. v. Raytek Corp.*, 334 F.3d 1314, 1328 (Fed. Cir. 2003) (holding that the structure in an accused device meets a § 112, ¶ 6, limitation if the structure performs the identical function recited in the claim and is identical or equivalent to the structure in the specification corresponding to that limitation); *Al-Site Corp. v. VSI Int'l Inc.*, 174 F.3d 1308, 1320 (Fed. Cir. 1999) (holding that an equivalent structure or act under § 112 cannot embrace technology developed after the patent issued because the literal meaning of a claim is fixed upon issuance); *WMS Gaming, Inc. v. Int'l Game Tech.*, 184 F.3d 1339, 1350 (Fed. Cir. 1999); *Odetics, Inc. v. Storage Tech. Corp.*, 185 F.3d 1259, 1266-68 (Fed. Cir. 1999); *Chiuminatta Concrete Concepts, Inc. v. Cardinal Indus., Inc.*, 145 F.3d 1303, 1307-11 (Fed. Cir. 1998); *Micro Chem., Inc. v. Great Plains Chem. Co.*, 103 F.3d 1538, 1547 (Fed. Cir. 1997); *Valmont Indus., Inc. v. Reinke Mfg. Co.*, 983 F.2d 1039, 1042 (Fed. Cir. 1993).

B.3 Infringement

3.1c DIRECT INFRINGEMENT UNDER THE DOCTRINE OF EQUIVALENTS

[This instruction should only be given where the patentee asserts infringement under the doctrine of equivalents.]

If a [person] [company] makes, uses, sells, offers to sell within, or imports into the United States a [product] [process] that does not meet all of the requirements of a claim and thus does not literally infringe that claim, there can still be direct infringement if that [product or process] satisfies that claim "under the doctrine of equivalents."

Under the doctrine of equivalents, a [product or process] infringes a claim if the accused [product or process] [contains elements or performs steps] corresponding to each and every requirement of the claim that is equivalent to, even though not literally met by, the accused [product or process]. You may find that an element or step is equivalent to a requirement of a claim that is not met literally if a person having ordinary skill in the field of technology of the patent would have considered the differences between them to be "insubstantial" or would have found that the [structure or action]: (1) performs substantially the same function and (2) works in substantially the same way (3) to achieve substantially the same result as the requirement of the claim. In order for the [structure or action] to be considered interchangeable, the [structure or action] must have been known at the time of the alleged infringement to a person having ordinary skill in the field of technology of the patent. Interchangeability at the present time is not sufficient. In order to prove infringement by "equivalents," [patent holder] must prove the equivalency of the [structure or actions] to a claim element by a preponderance of the evidence.

If claims with means-plus-function clauses are at issue:

When the claim requirement that is not met by the [product or process] is a ["means-plus-function" or "step-plus-function"] requirement, and if you determined that there is no "literal infringement" because there is no [structure or set of structures/action or set of actions] in the [product or process] that performs the specific function of the means-plus-function requirement,, you may decide that the [structure or action] nonetheless corresponds to the requirements of the claim under the doctrine of equivalents if it performs an "equivalent" function and has an "equivalent" [structure or action].

On the other hand, if you find that the accused [product or process] has no corresponding [structure or set of structures/action or set of actions] to [any of] the [set(s) of] [structure(s) or action(s)] that I defined as performing that function, then you must find that there is no infringement under the doctrine of equivalents. This is the case even if you find that the accused [product or process] has some other [structure or set of structures/action or set of actions] that performs the specific function of the means-plus-function requirement. In other words, for a means-plus-function requirement, a determination that there is no "equivalent" structure for purposes of "literal infringement" precludes you from finding infringement under the "doctrine of equivalents."

Authorities

Festo Corp. v. Shoketsu Kinzoku Kogyo Kabushiki Co., 535 U.S. 722 (2002); *Warner-Jenkinson Co. v. Hilton Davis Chem. Co.*, 520 U.S. 17 (1997); *Graver Tank & Mfg. Co. v. Linde Air Prods. Co.*, 339 U.S. 605, 609 (1950) (explaining what constitutes an "equivalent"); *Interactive Pictures Corp. v. Infinite Pictures Inc.*, 274 F.3d 1371, 1381-82 (Fed. Cir. 2001); *Johnson & Johnston Assocs. v. R.E. Serv. Co.*, 285 F.3d 1046 (Fed. Cir. 2002) (no infringement under the doctrine of equivalents); *Al-Site Corp. v. VSI Int'l, Inc.*, 174 F.3d 1308, 1320 (Fed. Cir. 1999) (distinguishing between the doctrine of equivalents and the statutory term "equivalents"); *Hughes Aircraft Co. v. United States*, 140 F.3d 1470, 1475 (Fed. Cir. 1998); *Multiform Desiccants, Inc. v. Medzam, Ltd.*, 133 F.3d 1473, 1480 (Fed. Cir. 1998); *Dolly, Inc. v. Spalding & Evenflo Cos.*, 16 F.3d 394, 397 (Fed. Cir. 1994).

B.3 Infringement

3.1d LIMITATIONS ON DIRECT INFRINGEMENT UNDER THE DOCTRINE OF EQUIVALENTS

[Although the applicability of these limitations is ultimately decided by the Court, this instruction is provided for the case in which the Court decides to submit these issues to the jury for advisory findings.]

[If there is a question as to whether the prior art limits the doctrine of equivalents:

The prior art may preclude a finding of infringement under the doctrine of equivalents. I will explain what "prior art" is, but, generally speaking, "prior art" is things that were already known or done before the invention. In reaching your decisions in this case, you must use the definition of "prior art" that I provide to you.]

[Statement of the law not using "hypothetical claim":

To determine whether the prior art precludes a finding of infringement under the doctrine of equivalents for a particular [product or process] that is accused of infringing a particular claim, you must determine what [products or processes] are in the "prior art" as well as what [products or processes] would have been obvious from the "prior art" to a person having an ordinary level of skill in the field of technology of the patent at the time of the invention.

If [alleged infringer] establishes that a [product or process] that (1) meets the same claim requirements as the [product or process] that is accused of infringing and (2) has the same allegedly "equivalent" alternative feature(s) as the [product or process] that is accused of infringing is in the prior art or would have been obvious from the prior art to a person having ordinary skill in the field of technology of the invention at the time of the invention, you must find that the claim has not been infringed.

[Alleged infringer] has the burden of proving that this hypothetical, equivalent claim was within the prior art at the time of the alleged infringement, by a preponderance of the evidence.]

[Alternative statement of the law using "hypothetical claim":

To determine whether the prior art precludes a finding of infringement under the doctrine of equivalents, you must first have in mind a "hypothetical claim" that would cover the accused, allegedly equivalent [product or process] literally. The hypothetical claim is exactly the same as the claim at issue, except that the unmet claim requirements are broadened so that they would be met by the allegedly "equivalent" hypothetical claim.

Once you have this equivalent "hypothetical claim" in mind, you must decide whether this hypothetical claim would have been invalid for either anticipation or obviousness. I will instruct you later on how to determine if a claim is invalid for anticipation or obviousness. You should use these same rules to determine whether or not the "hypothetical claim" would be invalid for anticipation or obviousness. If you determine that the "hypothetical claim" would have been invalid for anticipation or obviousness, then you must find that there is no infringement of this particular claim under the doctrine of equivalents.]

[If there is a question as to whether a disclosure in the patent precludes equivalence:

You may not find that a [product or process] infringes a claim under the doctrine of equivalents if you find that: (1) the allegedly "equivalent" alternative feature(s) of that [product or process] was/were described somewhere in the patent and (2) that [product or process] is not covered literally by any of the claims of the patent.]

[If there is a question as to argument-based prosecution history estoppel:

You may not find that a [product or process] infringes a claim under the doctrine of equivalents if you find that, during the patent application process, the applicant for the patent distinguished an unmet requirement from the allegedly "equivalent" alternative aspect of that [product or process].]

[If there is a question as to amendment-based prosecution history estoppel:

[Alleged infringer] has argued that [patent holder] cannot assert infringement under the doctrine of equivalents due to statements [patent holder] made to the PTO in order to get the claim allowed in the first place. In order to find [accused product] to be equivalent, you must also make certain findings regarding the statements [patent holder] made to the PTO in order to get the [ ] patent. Specifically, in order to find equivalents, you must first also find one or more of the following: (1) the amendment that is asserted by [alleged infringer] to limit the scope of equivalents substituted a broader requirement for a narrower requirement or replaced a requirement of equal scope; (2) the reason for making this amendment was not related to patentability; (3) a person having ordinary skill in the field of technology of the patent at the time of the amendment would not have foreseen the potential substitution of the allegedly "equivalent" alternative for the unmet claim requirement; (4) the reason for the amendment is tangential or relates to some issue other than the assertion of equivalence at issue; or (5) some other reason, such as the shortcomings of language, prevented the applicant from using claim language that included the allegedly "equivalent" alternative. You may not find that the alternative feature of the [accused product or process] is an equivalent to an unmet requirement of a claim if that requirement was added to the claim (or to any claim of the [ ] patent) by amendment during the prosecution of the applications that led to issuance of the [ ] patent, unless you also find that at least one of these factors that I have identified to you.]

[If there is a question as to vitiation:

You may not determine that an alternative aspect of a [product or process] is equivalent to an unmet requirement of a claim if a finding of infringement under the doctrine of equivalents would effectively eliminate that requirement. Specifically, the alleged equivalent cannot eliminate or ignore an element or requirement of the claim.]

Authorities

Honeywell Int'l v. Hamilton Sundstrand Corp., 370 F.3d 1131 (Fed. Cir. 2004); *Festo Corp. v. Shoketsu Kinzoku Kogyo Kabushiki Co.*, 344 F.3d 1359 (Fed. Cir. 2003) (en banc); *Interactive Pictures Corp. v. Infinite Pictures, Inc.*, 274 F.3d 1371, 1380 (Fed. Cir. 2001); *Al-Site Corp. v. VSI Int'l, Inc.*, 174 F.3d 1308, 1320 (Fed. Cir. 1999); *Wilson Sporting Goods Co. v. David Geoffrey & Assocs.*, 904 F.2d 676, 684 (Fed. Cir. 1990).

B.3 Infringement

3.2 INDIRECT INFRINGEMENT—ACTIVE INDUCEMENT

[Patent holder] alleges that [alleged infringer] is liable for infringement by actively inducing [someone else] [some other company] to directly infringe the [ ] patent literally or under the doctrine of equivalents. As with direct infringement, you must determine whether there has been active inducement on a claim-by-claim basis.

[Alleged infringer] is liable for active inducement of a claim only if [patent holder] proves by a preponderance of the evidence:

(1) that the acts are actually carried out by [insert name or other description of alleged direct infringer] and directly infringe that claim;

(2) that [alleged infringer] took action during the time the [ ] patent was in force intending to cause the infringing acts by [insert name or other description of alleged direct infringer]; and

(3) that [alleged infringer] was aware of the [ ] patent and knew that the acts, if taken, would constitute infringement of that patent.

> [addition to the end of (3) above when willful blindness concerning the [ ] patent's existence is at issue:]
>
> > or that [alleged infringer] believed there was a high probability that the acts by [insert name or other description of alleged direct infringer] would infringe a patent [by patent holder] and [alleged infringer] took deliberate steps to avoid learning of that infringement.
>
> [alternative addition to the end of (3) above when knowledge of the patent is undisputed but willful blindness concerning infringement of that patent is at issue:]
>
> > or that [alleged infringer] believed there was a high probability that the acts by [insert name or other description of alleged direct infringer] infringed the [ ] patent and took deliberate steps to avoid learning of that infringement.

If you find that [alleged infringer] was aware of the patent, but believed that the acts it encouraged did not infringe that patent, [alleged infringer] cannot be liable for inducement.

In order to establish active inducement of infringement, it is not sufficient that [insert name or other description of alleged direct infringer] itself directly infringes the claim. Nor is it sufficient that [alleged infringer] was aware of the act(s) by [insert name or other description of alleged direct infringer] that allegedly constitute the direct infringement. Rather, in order to find active inducement of infringement, you must find either that [accused infringer] specifically intended [insert name or other description of alleged direct infringer] to infringe the [ ] patent or that [accused infringer] believed there was a high probability that [insert name or other description of alleged direct infringer] would infringe the [ ] patent, but deliberately avoided learning the infringing nature of [insert name or other description of alleged direct infringer]'s acts. The mere fact, if true, that [alleged infringer] knew or should have known that there was a substantial risk that [insert name or description of alleged direct infringer]'s acts would infringe the [] patent would not be sufficient for active inducement of infringement.

Authorities

35 U.S.C. § 271(b); *Commil USA, LLC v. Cisco Sys.*, __ U.S. __, __; 135 S. Ct. 1920, __ (U.S. 2015); *Global-Tech Appliances, Inc. v. SEB S. A.*, 563 U.S. 754, __; 131 S.Ct. 2060, 2068-2071; 179 L.Ed. 1167, 1177-1180 (2012); *Muniauction Inc. v. Thomson Corp.*, 532 F.3d 1318, 1329-30 (Fed. Cir. 2008); *Lucent Technologies, Inc. v. Gateway, Inc.*, 580 F.3d 1301, 1340 (Fed. Cir. 2009); *DSU Med. Corp. v. JMS Co.*, 471 F.3d 1293, 1306 (Fed. Cir. 2006) ("[I]nducement requires that the alleged infringer knowingly induced infringement and possessed specific intent to encourage another's infringement.") (citation and internal quotation marks omitted); *MGM Studios Inc. v. Grokster*, 419 F.3d 1005 (Fed. Cir. 2005); *Insituform Techs., Inc. v. CAT Contracting, Inc.*, 385 F.3d 1360, 1377-78 (Fed. Cir. 2004) (inducer must have actual or constructive knowledge of the patent); *Ferguson Beauregard/Logic Controls, Div. of Dover Res., Inc. v. Mega Sys., LLC*, 350 F.3d 1327, 1342 (Fed. Cir. 2003) (no inducement where evidence did not show defendant knew or should have known that his actions were encouraging infringement); *Warner-Lambert Co. v. Apotex Corp.*, 316 F.3d 1348, 1363-66 (Fed. Cir. 2003) (no infringement where lack of intent to induce).

Committee Comments: The underlined language in the instruction incorporates the "willful blindness" standard addressed by the Supreme Court in *Global-Tech Appliances, Inc. v. SEB S. A.*, 563 U.S. 754, __; 131 S.Ct. 2060, 2068-2071 (2012). The Committee is of the opinion that in cases where willful blindness is not an issue, the underlined language should be omitted to reduce the possibility of juror confusion.

An earlier version of this instruction included a belief in invalidity as a ground for finding no induced infringement. That instruction was based on *Commil USA, LLC v. Cisco Sys.*, 720 F.3d 1361 (Fed. Cir. 2013), in which a divided panel of the Federal Circuit held that an accused infringer's "evidence of a good-faith belief of invalidity may negate the requisite intent for induced infringement."

In June of 2015, however, the Supreme Court reversed, holding that "a belief as to invalidity cannot negate the scienter required for induced infringement." *Commil USA, LLC v. Cisco Sys.*, __ U.S. __, __; 135 S. Ct. 1920, __ (U.S. 2015).

B.3 Infringement

3.3 INDIRECT INFRINGEMENT—CONTRIBUTORY INFRINGEMENT

[Patent holder] argues that [alleged infringer] is liable for contributory infringement by contributing to the direct infringement of the [ ] patent by [insert name or other description of direct infringer]. As with direct infringement, you must determine contributory infringement on a claim-by-claim basis.

[Alleged infringer] is liable for contributory infringement of a claim if [patent holder] proves by a preponderance of the evidence:

(1) [alleged infringer] sells, offers to sell, or imports within the United States a component of a product, or apparatus for use in a process, during the time the [ ] patent is in force;

(2) the component or apparatus has no substantial, noninfringing use;

(3) the component or apparatus constitutes a material part of the invention;

(4) [alleged infringer] is aware of the [ ] patent and knows that the [products or processes] for which the [component or apparatus] has no other substantial use may be covered by a claim of the [ ] patent or may satisfy a claim of the [ ] patent under the doctrine of equivalents; and

(5) that use directly infringes the claim.

In order to prove contributory infringement, [patent holder] must prove that each of the above requirements is met. This proof of each requirement must be by a preponderance of the evidence, i.e., that it is more likely than not that each of the above requirements is met.

<u>Authorities</u>

35 U.S.C. § 271(c) ("not a staple article"); *Aro Mfg. Co. v. Convertible Top Replacement Co.*, 377 U.S. 476 (1964) (knowledge of plaintiff's patent and that the part supplied is significant); *Ricoh Co. v. Quanta Computer Inc.*, 550 F.3d 1325, 1327 (Fed. Cir. 2008), *cert denied*, 129 S. Ct. 2864 (2009); *Alloc, Inc. v. ITC*, 342 F.3d 1361, 1374 (Fed. Cir. 2003) (affirming determination of no contributory infringement); *Mentor H/S, Inc. v. Med. Device Alliance, Inc.*, 244 F.3d 1365 (Fed. Cir. 2001) (reversing district court's finding of no contributory infringement and inducement); *Hewlett-Packard Co. v. Bausch & Lomb, Inc.*, 909 F.2d 1464, 1469 (Fed. Cir. 1990) (differentiating contributory infringement from inducement); *Preemption Devices, Inc. v. Minn. Mining & Mfg. Co.*, 803 F.2d 1170, 1174 (Fed. Cir. 1986) (direct infringement findings supported contributory infringement findings).

B.3 Infringement

3.4 INFRINGEMENT THROUGH THE SUPPLY OF COMPONENTS FROM UNITED STATES FOR COMBINATION ABROAD

[This instruction should be given if patentee asserts infringement under 35 U.S.C. § 271(f)(1) or § 271(f)(2).]

[If § 271(f)(1)—active inducement—is at issue:

[Alleged infringer] is liable for § 271(f)(1) infringement of a claim (active inducement of foreign combination of components supplied from the United States) if patentee proves by a preponderance of the evidence that:

(1) [alleged infringer] supplies [or causes to be supplied] components from the United States to a place outside the United States, which make up all or a substantial portion of the invention of any one of the claims of the [ ] patent;

(2) [alleged infringer] takes action intentionally to cause another to act by [insert name or other description of alleged direct infringer] outside of the United States to assemble the components;

(3) [alleged infringer] knows of the [ ] patent, and knows that the encouraged acts constitute infringement of that patent; and

(4) the encouraged acts would constitute direct infringement of the claim if they had been carried out in the United States.

If you find that [alleged infringer] was aware of the patent, but believed that the acts it encouraged would not constitute infringement of the patent if carried out in the United States, [alleged infringer] cannot be liable for inducement.

In order to establish active inducement of infringement, it is not sufficient that [insert name or other description of alleged direct infringer] itself allegedly directly infringes the claim. Nor is it sufficient that [alleged infringer] was aware of the act(s) that allegedly constitute the direct infringement. Rather, you must find that [alleged infringer] specifically intended for [insert name or other description of alleged direct infringer] to infringe the [ ] patent, in order to find inducement of infringement. If you do not find that [alleged infringer] specifically intended to infringe, then you must find that [alleged infringer] has not actively induced the alleged infringement under § 271(f)(1).]

[If § 271(f)(2)—contributory foreign infringement—is at issue:

[Alleged infringer] is [also] liable for § 271(f)(2) infringement of a claim if [patent holder] proves by a preponderance of the evidence that:

(1) [alleged infringer] supplies a component, or causes a component to be supplied, from the United States to a place outside of the United States;

(2) the only substantial use for the component is in a product that [product or process] would infringe if the combination had occurred in the United States;

(3) [alleged infringer] is aware of the [ ] patent and knows that the [component or apparatus] has no other substantial use and may be covered by a claim of the patent [literally or under the doctrine of equivalents]; and

(4) intends for the component to be used in a product that would directly infringe the claim if it had been used in the United States.

Authorities

35 U.S.C. § 271(f); *Cardiac Pacemakers, Inc. v. St. Jude Med.*, 576 F.3d 1348, 1365 (Fed. Cir. 2009) (§ 271(f) does not cover method claims); *Microsoft Corp. v. AT&T Corp.*, 550 U.S. 437 (2007); *Liquid Dynamics Corp. v. Vaughan Co.*, 449 F.3d 1209, 1222-23 (Fed. Cir. 2006); *Pellegrini v. Analog Devices, Inc.*, 375 F.3d 1113, 1117-18 (Fed. Cir. 2004); *NTP, Inc. v. Research in Motion, Ltd.*, 418 F.3d 1282, 1366 (Fed. Cir. 2005); *Union Carbide Chems. & Plastics Tech. Corp. v. Shell Oil Co.*, 425 F.3d 1366 (Fed. Cir. 2005); *Waymark Corp. v. Porta Sys., Corp.*, 245 F.3d 1364, 1368 (Fed. Cir. 2001) ("[T]he statutory language in this section [271(f)(2)] does not require an actual combination of the components, but only a showing that the infringer shipped them with the intent that they be combined.").

Committee Comments: For simplicity's sake, this instruction does not incorporate the "willful blindness" standard for induced infringement addressed by the Supreme Court in *Global-Tech Appliances, Inc. v. SEB S. A.*, 563 U.S. 754, __; 131 S.Ct. 2060, 2068-2071 (2012). If the patentee is proceeding on a theory of willful blindness, however, that standard should be addressed in this instruction. *See* Instruction 3.2.

B.3 Infringement

3.5 INFRINGEMENT BY SALE, OFFER FOR SALE, USE, OR IMPORTATION OF A PRODUCT MADE OUTSIDE THE UNITED STATES BY PATENTED PROCESS

[Alleged infringer] is liable for direct infringement of a claim if [patent holder] proves by a preponderance of the evidence that [alleged infringer], without [patent holder]'s authorization, imports, offers to sell, sells, or uses within the United States a product which was made outside of the United States during the time the [ ] patent is in force by a process that, if performed in the United States, would infringe the claim literally or under the doctrine of equivalents. However, if the product has been materially changed by an additional process or the product has become a trivial and nonessential component of another product, you must find [alleged infringer] did not infringe the [ ] patent.

Authorities

35 U.S.C. § 271(g); *Bayer AG v. Housey Pharms., Inc.*, 340 F.3d 1367 (Fed. Cir. 2003) (finding infringement under this section); *Ajinomoto Co. v. Archer-Daniels-Midland Co.*, 228 F.3d 1338, 1347 (Fed. Cir. 2000) (same).

B.3 Infringement

3.6 DIRECT INFRINGEMENT: ONE OR MORE SYSTEM COMPONENTS LOCATED OUTSIDE THE UNITED STATES

[This instruction should only be given where one or more components of an accused system are located outside of the United States.]

Direct infringement requires that the accused system include every element recited in the claim.

[Patent holder] claims that infringement occurred within the United States even though some (but not all) of the elements of the claim were located outside of the United States. For infringement to occur within the United States, [patent holder] must prove by a preponderance of the evidence that the control of the system was exercised and the benefit of the system was enjoyed in the United States.

Authorities

35 U.S.C. § 271(a); *NTP, Inc. v. Research in Motion Ltd.*, 418 F.3d 1282, 1313-21 (Fed. Cir. 2005); *id.* 1317 ("The use of a claimed system under section 271(a) is the place at which the system as a whole is put into service, i.e., the place where control of the system is exercised and beneficial use of the system obtained.").

B.3 Infringement

3.7 DIRECT INFRINGEMENT: ACTS OF MULTIPLE PARTIES MUST BE COMBINED TO MEET ALL CLAIM LIMITATIONS

[This instruction should only be given where the patentee alleges direct infringement by the combined acts of multiple persons or companies.]

Direct infringement occurs where all steps of a claimed method are performed by or are attributable to a single party. Where more than one party is involved in practicing the steps, you must determine whether the acts of one are attributable to the other such that a single party is responsible for the infringement. There are two situations where there may be direct infringement if no single party performs all of the steps of a claimed process but more than one party performs every step of the process: (1) the parties have formed a joint enterprise or (2) one party directs or controls other party's performance of the claim steps.

[Patent holder] alleges that [alleged infringer A] and [alleged infringer B, etc.] collectively infringe claim(s) [ ] of the [ ] patent.

For infringement to be proved, [patent holder] must prove by a preponderance of the evidence (1) that all the steps of the claimed process were performed in the United States and (2) that the acts of [alleged infringer B] are attributable to [alleged infringer A], either because [alleged infringer A] and [alleged infringer B] have formed a joint enterprise or because [alleged infringer A] directs or controls the acts of [alleged infringer B].

To prove that [alleged infringer A] and [alleged infringer B] have formed a joint enterprise, [Patent holder] must prove four elements:

(1) there was an agreement, either express or implied, between [alleged infringer A] and [alleged infringer B];

(2) they shared a common purpose;

(3) each had a financial interest in that purpose; and

(4) each had an equal right of control in the enterprise.

To prove that [alleged infringer A] directed or controlled the acts of [alleged infringer B], [Patent holder] must prove that [alleged infringer B] performed the claim step(s) in order to receive a benefit from [alleged infringer A] and that [alleged infringer A] established how or when the claim step(s) were performed.

Authorities

35 U.S.C. § 271(a); *Limelight Networks, Inc. v. Akamai Technologies, Inc.*, 797 F.3d 1020, 1022-24 (Fed. Cir. 2015) (en banc).

B.3 Infringement

3.8 [DELETED] INDIRECT INFRINGEMENT: ACCUSED INFRINGER PRACTICES SOME CLAIMED STEPS AND ANOTHER PRACTICES THE REMAINING STEPS

This instruction has been removed. *See Limelight Networks, Inc. v. Akamai Technologies, Inc.*, __ U.S. __, 134 S.Ct. 2111 (2014), No. 12-786, 2014 U.S. LEXIS 3817, 2014 WL 2440535 (U.S. June 2, 2014) (finding there can be no induced-infringement liability where no single entity is liable for direct infringement of the patent under §271(a) because "where there has been no direct infringement, there can be no inducement of infringement under §271(b)").

B.3 Infringement

3.9 [DELETED] INDIRECT INFRINGEMENT: ACCUSED INFRINGER ALLEGEDLY INDUCES OTHERS TO COLLECTIVELY PRACTICE ALL CLAIMED STEPS

This instruction has been removed. *See Limelight Networks, Inc. v. Akamai Technologies, Inc.*, __ U.S. __, 134 S.Ct. 2111 (2014), No. 12-786, 2014 U.S. LEXIS 3817, 2014 WL 2440535 (U.S. June 2, 2014) (finding there can be no induced-infringement liability where no single entity is liable for direct infringement of the patent under §271(a) because "where there has been no direct infringement, there can be no inducement of infringement under §271(b)").

B.3 Infringement

3.10 WILLFUL INFRINGEMENT

[This instruction should be given only if willfulness is in issue.]

In this case, [patent holder] argues both that [alleged infringer] infringed and, further, that [alleged infringer] infringed willfully. If you have decided that [alleged infringer] has infringed, you must go on and address the additional issue of whether or not this infringement was willful. Willfulness requires you to determine by clear and convincing evidence that [alleged infringer] acted recklessly.

To prove that [alleged infringer] acted recklessly, [patent holder] must prove two things by clear and convincing evidence:

The first part of the test is objective: the patent holder must persuade you that [alleged infringer] acted despite a high likelihood that [alleged infringer]'s actions infringed a valid and enforceable patent. In making this determination, you may not consider [alleged infringer]'s state of mind. Legitimate or credible defenses to infringement, even if not ultimately successful, demonstrate a lack of recklessness.[1]

Only if you conclude that the [alleged infringer]'s conduct was reckless do you need to consider the second part of the test. The second part of the test does depend on the state of mind of the [alleged infringer]. The patent holder must persuade you that [alleged infringer] actually knew or should have known that its actions constituted an unjustifiably high risk of infringement of a valid and enforceable patent. To determine whether [alleged infringer] had this state of mind, consider all facts which may include, but are not limited, to:

(1) Whether or not [alleged infringer] acted in accordance with the standards of commerce for its industry;

(2) Whether or not [alleged infringer] intentionally copied a product of [patent holder] that is covered by the [ ] patent;

(3) Whether or not there is a reasonable basis to believe that [alleged infringer] did not infringe or had a reasonable defense to infringement;

---

[1] In determining whether to present this instruction to the jury, the parties and the Court should recognize that "the objective determination of recklessness, even though predicated on underlying mixed questions of law and fact, is best decided by the judge as a question of law subject to de novo review." *Bard Peripheral Vascular, Inc. v. W.L. Gore & Assocs., Inc.*, 682 F.3d 1003, 1007 (Fed. Cir. 2012). *See also id.* ("When the objective prong turns on fact questions, as related, for example, to anticipation, or on legal questions dependent on the underlying facts, as related, for example, to questions of obviousness, the judge remains the final arbiter of whether the defense was reasonable, even when the underlying fact question is sent to a jury.").

(4) Whether or not [alleged infringer] made a good-faith effort to avoid infringing the [ ] patent, for example, whether [alleged infringer] attempted to design around the [ ] patent; [and]

(5) Whether or not [alleged infringer] tried to cover up its infringement[./; and]

(6) [Give this instruction only if [alleged infringer] relies upon an opinion of counsel as a defense to an allegation of willful infringement:

[Alleged infringer] argues it did not act recklessly because it relied on a legal opinion that advised [alleged infringer] either (1) that the [product] [method] did not infringe the [ ] patent or (2) that the [ ] patent was invalid [or unenforceable]. You must evaluate whether the opinion was of a quality that reliance on its conclusions was reasonable.]

Authorities

35 U.S.C. § 284; *In re Seagate Tech., LLC*, 497 F.3d 1360 (Fed. Cir. 2007) (standard for finding willfulness); *Knorr-Bremse v. Dana Corp.*, 383 F.3d 1337 (Fed. Cir. 2004) (en banc) (opinion of counsel defense); *Crystal Semiconductor Corp. v. Tritech Microelectronics Int'l, Inc.*, 246 F.3d 1336, 1346 (Fed. Cir. 2001) (burden of proof for willfulness); *WMS Gaming Inc. v. Int'l Game Tech.*, 184 F.3d 1339, 1354 (Fed. Cir. 1999) (knowledge of the patent necessary to show willfulness); *Read Corp. v. Portec, Inc.*, 970 F.2d 816 (Fed. Cir. 1992) (identifying factors that may show willfulness); *Gustafson, Inc. v. Intersystems Indus. Prods., Inc.*, 897 F.2d 508, 510 (Fed. Cir. 1990) (history of Federal Circuit decisions on willfulness).

Committee Comments: The National Patent Jury Instructions include whether the alleged infringer acted in a manner consistent with the standards of commerce for its industry in the subjective part of the test. (www.nationaljuryinstructions.org.) Some other pattern jury instructions decline to provide a list of nonexhaustive considerations, *see, e.g.*, Seventh Circuit, 2008 Patent Jury Instructions, at 11.2.14, on the theory that the factors are better left to attorney argument or may mislead a jury to believe other factors should not be considered. (www.ca7.uscourts.gov/Pattern-Jury-Instr.) Appropriate factors for the jury's consideration may be tailored to each case, or may be omitted.

B.4 Validity

4.1 INVALIDITY—BURDEN OF PROOF

I will now instruct you on the rules you must follow in deciding whether or not [alleged infringer] has proven that claims [ ] of the [ ] patent are invalid. To prove that any claim of a patent is invalid, [alleged infringer] must persuade you by clear and convincing evidence, i.e., you must be left with a clear conviction that the claim is invalid.

<u>Authorities</u>

35 U.S.C. § 282 (patents presumed valid); *Microsoft Corp. v. i4i Limited Partnerhsip,* 131 S.Ct. 2238 (2011). Invalidity may be asserted for failure to comply with any requirement of 35 U.S.C. § 101, 102, 103, 112, or 251, as a defense to alleged infringement. *Schumer v. Lab. Computer Sys., Inc.*, 308 F.3d 1304, 1315 (Fed. Cir. 2002) (to overcome presumption of validity, challenging party must present clear and convincing evidence of invalidity); *Buildex, Inc. v. Kason Indus., Inc.*, 849 F.2d 1461, 1463 (Fed. Cir. 1988) (clear and convincing evidence is that "which produces in the mind of the trier of fact an abiding conviction that the truth of [the] factual contentions are highly probable") (alteration in original) (citation and internal quotation marks omitted); *Hybritech Inc. v. Monoclonal Antibodies, Inc.*, 802 F.2d 1367, 1375 (Fed. Cir. 1986) ("Notwithstanding that the introduction of prior art not before the examiner may facilitate the challenger's meeting the burden of proof on invalidity, the presumption remains intact and on the challenger throughout the litigation, and the clear and convincing standard does not change.").

B.4.2 Validity—Adequacy of Patent Specification

4.2a WRITTEN DESCRIPTION REQUIREMENT

The patent law contains certain requirements for the part of the patent called the specification. [Alleged infringer] contends that claim(s) [ ] of [patent holder]'s [ ] patent [is/are] invalid because the specification of the [ ] patent does not contain an adequate written description of the invention. To succeed, [alleged infringer] must show by clear and convincing evidence that the specification fails to meet the law's requirements for written description of the invention. In the patent application process, the applicant may keep the originally filed claims, or change the claims between the time the patent application is first filed and the time a patent is issued. An applicant may amend the claims or add new claims. These changes may narrow or broaden the scope of the claims. The written description requirement ensures that the issued claims correspond to the scope of the written description that was provided in the original application.

In deciding whether the patent satisfies this written description requirement, you must consider the description from the viewpoint of a person having ordinary skill in the field of technology of the patent when the application was filed. The written description requirement is satisfied if a person having ordinary skill reading the original patent application would have recognized that it describes the full scope of the claimed invention as it is finally claimed in the issued patent and that the inventor actually possessed that full scope by the filing date of the original application.

The written description requirement may be satisfied by any combination of the words, structures, figures, diagrams, formulas, etc., contained in the patent application. The full scope of a claim or any particular requirement in a claim need not be expressly disclosed in the original patent application if a person having ordinary skill in the field of technology of the patent at the time of filing would have understood that the full scope or missing requirement is in the written description in the patent application.

Authorities

35 U.S.C. § 112, ¶¶ 1, 2; *Ariad Pharmaceuticals, Inc. v. Eli Lilly & Co.*, 598 F.3d 1336 (Fed. Cir. 2010) (en banc); *Lizard Tech., Inc. v. Earth Res. Mapping Inc.*, 424 F.3d 1336, 1344-45 (Fed. Cir. 2005); *Univ. of Rochester v. G.D. Searle & Co.*, 358 F.3d 916, 929 (Fed. Cir. 2004); *Chiron Corp. v. Genentech, Inc.*, 363 F.3d 1247, 1253-55 (Fed. Cir. 2004); *Purdue Pharma L.P. v. Faulding, Inc.*, 230 F.3d 1320, 1323 (Fed. Cir. 2000) (patent's specification must include an adequate written description; however, it need not include the exact words of the claim); *Lampi Corp. v. Am. Power Prods., Inc.*, 228 F.3d 1365, 1377-78 (Fed. Cir. 2000); *Gentry Gallery, Inc. v. Berkline Corp.*, 134 F.3d 1473, 1478-80 (Fed. Cir. 1998); *Regents of the Univ. of Cal. v. Eli Lilly & Co.*, 119 F.3d 1559, 1568 (Fed. Cir. 1997); *In re Alton*, 76 F.3d 1168, 1172 (Fed. Cir. 1996).

B.4.2 Validity—Adequacy of Patent Specification

4.2b ENABLEMENT

The patent law contains certain requirements for the part of the patent called the specification. [Alleged infringer] contends that claim(s) [ ] of [patent holder]'s [ ] patent [is/are] invalid because the specification does not contain a sufficiently full and clear description of how to make and use the full scope of the claimed invention. To succeed, [alleged infringer] must show by clear and convincing evidence that the [ ] patent does not contain a sufficiently full and clear description of the claimed invention. To be sufficiently full and clear, the description must contain enough information to have allowed a person having ordinary skill in the field of technology of the patent to make and use the full scope of the claimed invention at the time the [original] patent application was filed. This is known as the "enablement" requirement. If a patent claim is not enabled, it is invalid.

In order to be enabling, the patent must permit persons having ordinary skill in the field of technology of the patent to make and use the full scope of the claimed invention at the time of [original] filing without having to conduct undue experimentation. However, some amount of experimentation to make and use the invention is allowable. In deciding whether a person having ordinary skill would have to experiment unduly in order to make and use the invention, you may consider several factors:

(1) the time and cost of any necessary experimentation;

(2) how routine any necessary experimentation is in the field of [identify field];

(3) whether the patent discloses specific working examples of the claimed invention;

(4) the amount of guidance presented in the patent;

(5) the nature and predictability of the field of [identify field];

(6) the level of ordinary skill in the field of [identify field]; and

(7) the scope of the claimed invention.

No one or more of these factors is alone dispositive. Rather, you must make your decision whether or not the degree of experimentation required is undue based upon all of the evidence presented to you. You should weigh these factors and determine whether or not, in the context of this invention and the state of the art at the time of the [original] application, a person having ordinary skill would need to experiment unduly to make and use the full scope of the claimed invention.

<u>Authorities</u>

35 U.S.C. § 112, ¶ 1; *Sitrick v. Dreamworks, LLC*, 516 F.3d 993, 999 (Fed. Cir. 2008) ("'The scope of the claims must be less than or equal to the scope of the enablement' to 'ensure[ ] that

the public knowledge is enriched by the patent specification to a degree at least commensurate with the scope of the claims.'") (quoting *Nat'l Recovery Techs., Inc. v. Magnetic Separation Sys., Inc.*, 166 F.3d 1190, 1195-96 (Fed. Cir. 1999)); *Auto. Techs. Int'l, Inc. v. BMW of N. Am., Inc.*, 501 F.3d 1274, 1285 (Fed. Cir. 2007) (full scope of claimed invention must be enabled); *AK Steel Corp. v. Sollac*, 344 F.3d 1234, 1244 (Fed. Cir. 2003) (enabling the full scope of each claim is "part of the *quid pro quo* of the patent bargain"); *Union Pac. Res. Co. v. Chesapeake Energy Corp.*, 236 F.3d 684, 690-92 (Fed. Cir. 2001); *Ajinomoto Co. v. Archer-Daniels-Midland Co.*, 228 F.3d 1338, 1345-46 (Fed. Cir. 2000); *In re Wands*, 858 F.2d 731, 737 (Fed. Cir. 1988) (factors for determining undue experimentation).

B.4.2 Validity—Adequacy of Patent Specification

4.2c [DELETED] BEST MODE

This instruction has been removed because under section 15 of the America Invents Act, enacted on September 16, 2011, failure to disclose the best mode is no longer a basis for invalidity or unenforceability.

B.4.3 Validity—The Claims

4.3a-1 PRIOR ART
(For Patents Having an Effective Filing Date Before March 16, 2013)

Prior art may include items that were publicly known or that have been used or offered for sale, or references, such as publications or patents, that disclose the claimed invention or elements of the claimed invention. To be prior art, the item or reference must have been made, known, used, published, or patented either before the invention was made or [insert date if undisputed] or more than one year before the filing date of the patent application. However, prior art does not include a publication that describes the inventor's own work and was published less than one year before the date of invention. [Where appropriate, add limitation that subject matter developed by another which qualifies as prior art only under one or more of subsections (e), (f), and (g) of 35 U.S.C. § 102 where the subject matter and the claimed invention were, at the time the claimed invention was made, owned by the same person, or subject to an obligation of assignment to the same person.]

[For anticipation:

For the claim to be invalid because it is not new, [alleged infringer] must show by clear and convincing evidence that all of the requirements of that claim were present in a single previous device or method that was known of, used, or described in a single previous printed publication or patent. We call these things "anticipating prior art." To anticipate the invention, the prior art does not have to use the same words as the claim, but all of the requirements of the claim must have been disclosed, either stated expressly or implied to a person having ordinary skill in the art in the technology of the invention, so that looking at that one reference, that person could make and use the claimed invention.]

[If invention date is disputed: In this case, you must determine the date of invention [or conception] [and/or] [reduction to practice] for the [claimed invention or alleged prior art].

The date of invention is either when the invention was reduced to practice or when conceived, provided the inventor(s) were diligent in reducing the invention to practice. Diligence means working continuously, though not necessarily every day. Conception is the mental part of an inventive act, i.e., the formation in the mind of the inventor of a definite and permanent idea of the complete and operative invention as it is thereafter to be applied in practice, even if the inventor did not know at the time that the invention would work. Conception of an invention is complete when the idea is so clearly defined in the inventor's mind that, if the idea were communicated to a person having ordinary skill in the field of the technology, he or she would be able to reduce the invention to practice without undue research or experimentation. This requirement does not mean that the inventor has to have a prototype built, or actually explained her or his invention to another person. But, there must be some evidence beyond the inventor's own testimony that confirms the date on which the inventor had the complete idea. Conception may be proven when the invention is shown in its complete form by drawings, disclosure to another person, or other forms of evidence presented at trial.

A claimed invention is "reduced to practice" when it has been constructed/used/tested sufficiently to show that it will work for its intended purpose or when the inventor files a patent application. An invention may also be reduced to practice even if the inventor has not made or tested a prototype of the invention if it has been fully described in a filed patent application.]

B.4.3 Validity—The Claims

4.3b-1 ANTICIPATION
(For Patents Having an Effective Filing Date Before March 16, 2013)

In order for someone to be entitled to a patent, the invention must actually be "new" and the inventor must not have lost her or his rights by delaying the filing of an application claiming the invention. In general, inventions are new when the identical [product or process] has not been made, used, or disclosed before. Anticipation must be determined on a claim-by-claim basis.

[Alleged infringer] contends that claim(s) [ ] of the [ ] patent is/are invalid because the claimed invention(s) is/are anticipated or because [patent holder] lost the right to obtain a patent. [Alleged infringer] must convince you of this by clear and convincing evidence, i.e., that the evidence highly probably demonstrates that the claim(s) is/are invalid.

Here is a list of ways that [alleged infringer] can show that a patent claim was not new or that the patentee lost the right to patent the claim(s) [choose those that apply based on alleged infringer's contentions]:

(1) An invention is not new if it was known to or used by others in the United States before the [insert date of invention]. An invention is known when the information about it was reasonably accessible to the public on that date.

(2) An invention is not new if it was already patented or described in a printed publication, anywhere in the world before the [insert date of invention]. [A description is a "printed publication" only if it was publicly accessible.]

(3) [Patent holder] has lost her or his rights if the claimed invention was already patented or described in a printed publication, anywhere in the world by [patent holder] or anyone else, more than a year before [insert date], which is the effective filing date of the application for the [ ] patent. An invention was patented by another if the other patent describes the same invention claimed by [patent holder] to a person having ordinary skill in the technology.

(4) [Patent holder] has lost her or his rights if the claimed invention was publicly used, sold, or offered for sale in the United States more than one year before [insert date], which is the effective filing date of the application for the [ ] patent. An invention was publicly used when it was either accessible to the public or commercially exploited. An invention was sold or offered for sale when it was offered commercially and what was offered was ready to be patented, i.e., a description to one having ordinary skill in the field of the technology could have made and used the claimed invention, even if it was not yet reduced to practice.

(5) [Patent holder] has lost his or her rights if he or she abandoned the invention.

(6) [Patent holder] has lost her or his rights if she or he had already obtained a patent for the invention in a foreign country before the filing date of the application in the United States or the patent application was filed in a foreign country more than a year before the filing date of the application for the patent in the United States.

(7) An invention is not new if it was described in a published patent application filed by another in the United States [or under the PCT system and designated the United States, and was published in English] before [insert date of invention].

(8) An invention is not new if the claimed invention was described in a patent granted on an application for patent by another filed in the United States [or under the PCT system and designated the United States, and was published in English] and the application was filed before [insert date of reduction to practice or the filing date of the application for the [ ] patent].

(9) [Patent holder] is not entitled to the [ ] patent if [named inventor] did not himself invent the invention.

(10) An invention is not new if the invention was made by someone else in the United States before the invention was made by [patent holder] and the other person did not abandon, suppress, or conceal the invention.

If an interference proceeding has been declared, additional instructions should be given on this issue.

Authorities

35 U.S.C. § 102(a)-(g); *Flex-Rest, LLC v. Steelcase, Inc.*, 455 F.3d 1351, 1358-60 (Fed. Cir. 2006); *Invitrogen Corp. v. Biocrest Mfg., L.P.*, 424 F.3d 1374, 1379-82 (Fed. Cir. 2005); *In re Klopfenstein*, 380 F.3d 1345, 1348-51 (Fed. Cir. 2004); *Toro Co. v. Deere & Co.*, 355 F.3d 1313, 1320-21 (Fed. Cir. 2004); *Schering Corp. v. Geneva Pharms., Inc.*, 339 F.3d 1373, 1377-80 (Fed. Cir. 2003); *Apotex U.S.A., Inc. v. Merck & Co.*, 254 F.3d 1031, 1035 (Fed. Cir. 2001); *Mycogen Plant Sci., Inc. v. Monsanto Co.*, 243 F.3d 1316, 1330-31 (Fed. Cir. 2001); *Ecolochem, Inc. v. S. Cal. Edison Co.*, 227 F.3d 1361, 1367-70 (Fed. Cir. 2000); *Singh v. Brake*, 222 F.3d 1362, 1366-70 (Fed. Cir. 2000); *Pannu v. Iolab Corp.*, 155 F.3d 1344, 1349 (Fed. Cir. 1998); *Gambro Lundia AB v. Baxter Healthcare Corp.*, 110 F.3d 1573, 1576-78 (Fed. Cir. 1997); *Lamb-Weston, Inc. v. McCain Foods, Ltd.*, 78 F.3d 540, 545 (Fed. Cir. 1996); *In re Bartfeld*, 925 F.2d 1450, 1452-53 (Fed. Cir. 1991); *Ralston Purina Co. v. Far-Mar-Co, Inc.*, 772 F.2d 1570, 1574 (Fed. Cir. 1985); *Am. Stock Exch., LLC v. Mopex, Inc.*, 250 F. Supp. 2d 323, 328-32 (S.D.N.Y. 2003); *In re Wyer*, 655 F.2d 221, 226 (C.C.P.A. 1981); *Pfaff v. Wells Elecs. Inc.*, 525 U.S. 55 (1998); *Helifix Ltd. v. Blok-Lok, Ltd.*, 208 F.3d 1339, 1346 (Fed. Cir. 2000); *Abbott Labs. v. Geneva Pharms., Inc.*, 182 F.3d 1315, 1318 (Fed. Cir. 1999); *Finnigan Corp. v. ITC*, 180 F.3d 1354, 1365 (Fed. Cir. 1999); *J.A. LaPorte, Inc. v. Norfolk Dredging Co.*, 787 F.2d 1577, 1581 (Fed. Cir. 1986); *In re Hall*, 781 F.2d 897, 898-99 (Fed. Cir. 1986); *D.L. Auld Co. v. Chroma Graphics Corp.*, 714 F.2d 1144, 1147-50 (Fed. Cir. 1983).

4.3a-2 PRIOR ART
(For Patents Having an Effective Filing Date on or After March 16, 2013)

Prior art to a patent may include:

> (1) items that were publicly known or that have been used, on sale, or otherwise made available to the public before the filing date of the patent,
>
> (2) publications that were published or otherwise made available to the public before the filing date of the patent, and
>
> (3) patents and published patent applications naming another inventor that were filed before the filing date of the patent.

However, prior art does not include:

> an item or publication that (a) is the inventor's own work or (b) describes the inventor's own work or (c) was directly or indirectly obtained from the inventor, unless it was made public more than one year before the filing date of the patent's application, or
>
> a patent or patent application that (a) discloses the inventor's own work or (b) was directly or indirectly obtained from the inventor or (c) was owned by the same person or subject to an obligation of assignment to the same person.

[For anticipation:

For the claim to be invalid because it is not new, [alleged infringer] must show by clear and convincing evidence that all of the requirements of that claim were present in a single previous device or method that was known of, used, or described in a single previous printed publication or patent. We call these things "anticipating prior art." To anticipate the invention, the prior art does not have to use the same words as the claim, but all of the requirements of the claim must have been disclosed, either stated expressly or implied to a person having ordinary skill in the art in the technology of the invention, so that looking at that one reference, that person could make and use the claimed invention.]

<u>Authorities</u>

35 U.S.C. § 102(a)(1)-(2); 35 U.S.C. § 102(b)(1)-(2).

B.4.3 Validity—The Claims

4.3c OBVIOUSNESS

Even though an invention may not have been identically disclosed or described before it was made by an inventor, in order to be patentable, the invention must also not have been obvious to a person of ordinary skill in the field of technology of the patent [at the time the invention was made] or [before the filing date of the patent].[2]

[Alleged infringer] may establish that a patent claim is invalid by showing, by clear and convincing evidence, that the claimed invention would have been obvious to persons having ordinary skill in the art at the time the [invention was made] or [patent was filed] in the field of [insert the field of the invention].

In determining whether a claimed invention is obvious, you must consider the level of ordinary skill in the field [of the invention] that someone would have had at the time the [invention was made] or [patent was filed], the scope and content of the prior art, and any differences between the prior art and the claimed invention.

Keep in mind that the existence of each and every element of the claimed invention in the prior art does not necessarily prove obviousness. Most, if not all, inventions rely on building blocks of prior art. In considering whether a claimed invention is obvious, you may but are not required to find obviousness if you find that at the time of the claimed invention [or the patent's filing date] there was a reason that would have prompted a person having ordinary skill in the field of [the invention] to combine the known elements in a way the claimed invention does, taking into account such factors as (1) whether the claimed invention was merely the predictable result of using prior art elements according to their known function(s); (2) whether the claimed invention provides an obvious solution to a known problem in the relevant field; (3) whether the prior art teaches or suggests the desirability of combining elements claimed in the invention; (4) whether the prior art teaches away from combining elements in the claimed invention; (5) whether it would have been obvious to try the combinations of elements, such as when there is a design need or market pressure to solve a problem and there are a finite number of identified, predictable solutions; and (6) whether the change resulted more from design incentives or other market forces. To find it rendered the invention obvious, you must find that the prior art provided a reasonable expectation of success. Obvious to try is not sufficient in unpredictable technologies.

In determining whether the claimed invention was obvious, consider each claim separately. Do not use hindsight, i.e., consider only what was known at the time of the invention [or the patent's filing date].

---

[2] The "at the time invention was made" standard is used for patents that were filed before March 16, 2013. For patents filed on or after March 16, 2013, the appropriate standard is "before the effective filing date of the claimed invention."

In making these assessments, you should take into account any objective evidence (sometimes called "secondary considerations") that may shed light on the obviousness or not of the claimed invention, such as:

a. Whether the invention was commercially successful as a result of the merits of the claimed invention (rather than the result of design needs or market-pressure advertising or similar activities);

b. Whether the invention satisfied a long-felt need;

c. Whether others had tried and failed to make the invention;

d. Whether others invented the invention at roughly the same time;

e. Whether others copied the invention;

f. Whether there were changes or related technologies or market needs contemporaneous with the invention;

g. Whether the invention achieved unexpected results;

h. Whether others in the field praised the invention;

i. Whether persons having ordinary skill in the art of the invention expressed surprise or disbelief regarding the invention;

j. Whether others sought or obtained rights to the patent from the patent holder; and

k. Whether the inventor proceeded contrary to accepted wisdom in the field.

B.4.3 Validity—The Claims

4.3c(i) LEVEL OF ORDINARY SKILL

In deciding what the level of ordinary skill in the field of [invention] is, you should consider all the evidence introduced at trial, including but not limited to: (1) the levels of education and experience of the inventor and other persons actively working in the field; (2) the types of problems encountered in the field; (3) prior art solutions to those problems; (4) rapidity with which innovations are made; and (5) the sophistication of the technology.

4.3c(ii) SCOPE AND CONTENT OF THE PRIOR ART

[Option 1: parties stipulate to prior art.]

In considering whether the claimed invention was obvious at the time it was made, you should consider the scope and content of the following prior art: [Insert art as stipulated].

[Option 2: parties dispute the prior art.]

In considering whether the claimed invention was obvious, you must first determine the scope and content of the prior art.

The scope and content of prior art for deciding whether the invention was obvious includes at least prior art in the same field as the claimed invention. It also includes prior art from different fields that a person of ordinary skill in the art would have considered when trying to solve the problem that is addressed by the invention.

Where the party challenging the validity of the patent is relying on prior art that was not considered by the PTO during examination, you may consider whether that prior art is significantly different and more relevant than the prior art that the PTO did consider. If you decide it was different and more relevant, you may weigh that prior art more heavily when considering whether the challenger has carried its clear-and-convincing burden of proving invalidity.

<u>Authorities</u>

35 U.S.C. § 103. The four-factor test, including articulation of the objective factors, is found in *Graham v. John Deere Co.*, 383 U.S. 1, 17-18 (1966); *see also Ruiz v. A.B. Chance Co.*, 234 F.3d 654, 662-63 (Fed. Cir. 2000). The test was reaffirmed in *KSR International Co. v. Teleflex Inc.*, 550 U.S. 398, 407 (2007) ("While the sequence of these questions might be reordered in any particular case, the factors continue to define the inquiry that controls."). *See also Cordis Corp. v. Medtronic Ave., Inc.*, 511 F.3d 1157, 1172 (Fed. Cir. 2008).

In cases where the invalidity defense is based on a combination of prior art, the proper inquiry is a flexible analysis considering whether, among other factors, the prior art teaches, suggests, or motivates the claimed invention. *KSR*, 550 U.S. at 419-20; *Esai Co. v. Dr. Reddy's Labs. Ltd.*,

533 F.3d 1353, 1356-57 (Fed. Cir. 2008); *Takeda Chem. Indus., Ltd. v. Alphapharm Pty., Ltd.*, 492 F.3d 1350, 1356-57 (Fed. Cir. 2007); *Hybritech Inc. v. Monoclonal Antibodies, Inc.*, 802 F.2d 1367, 1380-81 (Fed. Cir. 1986).

For patents having filing dates before March 16, 2013, obviousness should be assessed at the time of the invention. For patents having filing dates on or after March 16, 2013, obviousness should be assessed at the time just before the patent's effective filing date. In either case, fact-finders should be made aware "of the distortion caused by hindsight bias and must be cautious of arguments reliant upon *ex post* reasoning." *KSR*, 550 U.S. at 421.

For recent authority that invalidity must be shown by clear and convincing evidence, but that this burden can be carried more easily when the challenger is relying on prior art materially different from the art considered during examination, *see Microsoft Corp. v. i4i Limited Partnerhsip,* 131 S.Ct. 2238 (2011). Obviousness should be evaluated on a claim-by-claim basis. *Aventis Pharma Deutschland GmbH v. Lupin, Ltd.*, 499 F.3d 1293, 1303 (Fed. Cir. 2007).

For factors to consider in determining the level of ordinary skill, *see, e.g., Daiichi Sankyo Co. v. Apotex, Inc.*, 501 F.3d 1254, 1256 (Fed. Cir. 2007); *Ruiz*, 234 F.3d at 666-67. For authority on the standards for determining the scope and content of prior art, *see, e.g., KSR*, 550 U.S. at 420; *Circuit Check, Inc. v. QXQ Inc.*, 795 F.3d 1331, 1482 (Fed. Cir. 2015) (stating that when considering whether prior art is analogous, "the question is whether an inventor would look to this particular art to solve the particular problem at hand"); *In re Icon Health & Fitness, Inc.*, 496 F.3d 1374, 1379-80 (Fed. Cir. 2007); *Princeton Biochems., Inc. v. Beckman Coulter, Inc.*, 411 F.3d 1332, 1339 (Fed. Cir. 2005).

B.4.3 Validity—The Claims

4.3d INVENTORSHIP

[This instruction should only be given in the event the alleged infringer has contended that the patent suffers from improper inventorship.]

In this case, [alleged infringer] contends that the [ ] patent is invalid because of improper inventorship. A patent is invalid if it fails to meet the requirement that all of the actual inventors, and only the actual inventors, be named as inventors in the patent. This is known as the "inventorship" requirement.

To be an inventor, one must make a significant contribution to the conception of at least one or more of the claims of the patent [even if that claim has not been alleged to be infringed]. Whether the contribution is significant is measured against the scope of the full invention.

If someone only explains to the actual inventors well-known concepts or the current state of the art, he or she is not an inventor. Merely helping with experimentation, by carrying out the inventor's instructions, also does not make someone an inventor. What is required is some significant contribution to the idea claimed.

Persons may be inventors even if they do not make the same type or amount of contribution, and even if they do not contribute to the subject matter of each claim of the patent. Persons may be joint or co-inventors even though they do not physically work together, but they must have some open line of communication during or at approximately the time of their inventive effort.

Authorities

35 U.S.C. §§ 102, 256; *Pannu v. Iolab Corp.*, 155 F.3d 1344, 1349-50 (Fed. Cir. 1998) ("If a patentee demonstrates that inventorship can be corrected as provided for in section 256, a district court must order correction of the patent, thus saving it from being rendered invalid."); *Eli Lilly & Co. v. Aradigm Corp.*, 376 F.3d 1352, 1358-59 (Fed. Cir. 2004); *Hess v. Advanced Cardiovascular Sys. Inc.*, 106 F.3d 976, 980-81 (Fed. Cir. 1997) (applying "clear and convincing evidence" standard to inventorship claims and finding plaintiff who offered suggestions to named inventors was not an inventor); *Burroughs Wellcome Co. v. Barr Labs., Inc.*, 40 F.3d 1223, 1227-28 (Fed. Cir. 1994); *Shatterproof Glass Corp. v. Libbey-Owens Ford Co.*, 758 F.2d 613, 624 (Fed. Cir. 1985).

B.5 Equitable Defenses

[Although these equitable defenses are ultimately decided by the Court, these instructions are provided for the case in which the Court decides to submit these issues to the jury for advisory findings.]

5.1 INEQUITABLE CONDUCT

Every applicant for a patent has a duty of candor and good faith in its dealing with the United States Patent and Trademark Office. This is important because the PTO has limited resources.

When a person involved in the prosecution of an application fails to supply material information or supplies false information or statements and does so with an intent to deceive the PTO, he or she may commit what is called "inequitable conduct." When inequitable conduct occurs during the examination of an application, any patent that issues from that application is unenforceable as a matter of fairness. This means that despite the existence and validity of the patent, the patent holder may not prevent others from using the invention covered by the patent and may not collect damages from those who use the invention that is covered by the patent.

Because a finding of inequitable conduct completely extinguishes a patent holder's right to prevent others from using an invention, the burden of proving inequitable conduct is high. [Alleged infringer] must prove by clear and convincing evidence both that a person meaningfully involved in the prosecution of the [ ] patent withheld material information or submitted materially false information or statements to the PTO during the examination of the [ ] patent(s), and that the person did so with an intent to deceive the Examiner into issuing the [ ] patent(s).

I will now explain to you what "material" and "intent to deceive" mean.

Material

Information that was withheld from the PTO is material if the PTO would not have allowed the claim had it been aware of the withheld information. A false or misleading statement is material when it convinces the PTO to allow a claim that it would not have allowed if the statement had not been made. You may also find that affirmative, egregious misconduct is material. An example of affirmative, egregious misconduct is the filing of an unmistakably false affidavit.

You may only find information, statements, or misconduct to be material if there is clear and convincing evidence that they are material.

Intent to Deceive

In order for inequitable conduct to have occurred, [alleged infringer] must establish that any [failure to disclose material information/false or misleading statements/misconduct] [was/were] done with an intent to deceive the Examiner. If the [failure to disclose material information/false or misleading statements/misconduct] occurred through negligence, oversight, carelessness, or an error in judgment, even if it was grossly negligent, then there was no intent to deceive and there is no inequitable conduct.

Intent may be shown through direct evidence, such as documents or testimony about one's intent to deceive. Intent also may be shown through indirect evidence or, in other words, it may be inferred from conduct. However, an intent to deceive may be inferred only where it is the single most reasonable inference that can be drawn from the evidence. In other words, if it could be reasonable to conclude that the [failure to disclose material information/false or misleading statements/misconduct] was an honest mistake, intent to deceive cannot be found.

Conclusion of Inequitable Conduct

Materiality and intent to deceive are separate issues: proof of materiality does not give rise to an inference of intent to deceive, and proof of an intent to deceive does not give rise to an inference of materiality. There must be clear and convincing evidence that establishes materiality and there must be clear and convincing evidence that establishes an intent to deceive. If clear and convincing evidence of either, or both, is missing, there can be no inequitable conduct.

If you find, however, that [alleged infringer] has proved by clear and convincing evidence that [material information was withheld/materially misleading statements were made or false information provided/affirmative, egregious misconduct occurred] and, further, that these acts or omissions were done with an intent to deceive the Examiner, you must then determine whether the patent(s) should in fairness be declared unenforceable.

Authorities

35 U.S.C. § 282; *Therasense Inc. v. Becton, Dickinson and Co.*, 649 F.3d 1276 (Fed. Cir. 2011) (en banc).

B.5 Equitable Defenses

5.2 LACHES

[Alleged infringer] contends that [patent holder] is not entitled to recover damages for acts that occurred before it filed a lawsuit because: (1) [patent holder] delayed filing the lawsuit for an unreasonably long and inexcusable period of time, and (2) [alleged infringer] has been or will be prejudiced in a significant way due to [patent holder]'s delay in filing the lawsuit. This is referred to as laches. [Alleged infringer] must prove delay and prejudice by a preponderance of the evidence.

Whether [patent holder]'s delay was unreasonably long and unjustified is a question that must be answered by considering the facts and circumstances as they existed during the period of delay. There is no minimum amount of delay required to establish laches. If suit was delayed for six years, a rebuttable presumption arises that the delay was unreasonable and unjustified, and that material prejudice resulted. This presumption shifts the burden of proof to [patent holder] to come forward with evidence to prove that the delay was justified or that material prejudice did not result, and if [patent holder] presents such evidence, the burden of proving laches remains with [alleged infringer]. Laches may be found for delays of less than six years if there is proof of unreasonably long and unjustifiable delay causing material prejudice to [alleged infringer]. Facts and circumstances that can justify a long delay can include:

(1) being involved in other litigation during the period of delay;

(2) being involved in negotiations with [alleged infringer] during the period of delay;

(3) poverty or illness during the period of delay;

(4) wartime conditions during the period of delay;

(5) being involved in a dispute about ownership of the patent during the period of delay; or

(6) minimal amounts of allegedly infringing activity by [alleged infringer] during the period of delay.

If you find unreasonable and unjustified delay occurred, to find laches, you must also determine if [alleged infringer] suffered material prejudice as a result of the delay. Prejudice to [alleged infringer] can be evidentiary or economic. Whether [alleged infringer] suffered evidentiary prejudice is a question that must be answered by evaluating whether delay in filing this case resulted in [alleged infringer] not being able to present a full and fair defense on the merits to [patent holder]'s infringement claim. Not being able to present a full and fair defense on the merits to an infringement claim can occur due to the loss of important records, the death or impairment of an important witness(es), the unreliability of memories about important events because they occurred in the distant past, or other similar types of things. Economic prejudice is determined by whether or not [alleged infringer] changed its economic position in a significant way during the period of delay resulting in losses beyond merely paying for infringement (such as if [alleged infringer] could have switched to a noninfringing product if sued earlier), and also whether [alleged infringer]'s losses as a result of that change in economic position likely would have been avoided if [patent holder] had filed this lawsuit sooner. In all scenarios though, the ultimate determination of whether laches should apply in this case is a question of fairness, given all the facts and circumstances. Thus, you may find that laches does not apply if there is no evidence establishing each of the three elements noted above (unreasonable delay, lack of excuse or justification, and significant prejudice). You may also find that even though all of the elements of laches have been proved, it should not, in fairness, apply, given all the facts and circumstances in this case.

Authorities

35 U.S.C. § 282; *Gasser Chair Co. v. Infanti Chair Mfg. Corp.*, 60 F.3d 770, 773-74 (Fed. Cir. 1995); *A.C. Aukerman Co. v. R.L. Chaides Constr. Co.*, 960 F.2d 1020, 1039 (Fed. Cir. 1992) (en banc).

B.5 Equitable Defenses

5.3 EQUITABLE ESTOPPEL

The owner of a patent may forfeit its right to any relief from an infringer where: (1) the patent holder communicates something in a misleading way to the infringing party about the lack of infringement or about not being sued, (2) the infringer relies upon the misleading communication from the patent holder, and (3) the infringer will be materially harmed if the patent holder is allowed to assert a claim relating to the issue that is inconsistent with the patent holder's prior misleading communication. This is referred to as an "equitable estoppel" and it is a defense that [alleged infringer] contends precludes any recovery by [patent holder] in this lawsuit. [Alleged infringer] must prove each of these elements by a preponderance of the evidence, but even if all these elements are proven, equitable estoppel need not be found if such a finding would be unfair in light of the conduct of the parties.

[Alleged infringer] contends that [patent holder] made a misleading communication about [ ] before [patent holder] filed this lawsuit. A communication may be made through written or spoken words, conduct, silence, or a combination of words, conduct, and silence. Conduct may include action or inaction. Whether in fact [patent holder] communicated with [alleged infringer] about [ ] prior to the filing of this lawsuit, and whether in fact that communication, if you find there to have been any, was misleading, are questions that must be answered by considering the facts and circumstances as they existed at the time.

Material harm to [alleged infringer] can be evidentiary or economic in form. Whether [alleged infringer] suffered evidentiary harm is a question that must be answered by evaluating whether [alleged infringer] will be unable to present a full and fair defense on the merits of [patent holder]'s claim(s). Not being able to present a full and fair defense on the merits of [patent holder]'s claim(s) can occur due to the loss of important records, the death or impairment of an important witness(es), the unreliability of memories about important events because they occurred in the distant past, or other similar types of things. Whether [alleged infringer] suffered economic prejudice is a question that must be answered by evaluating whether [alleged infringer] changed its economic position as a result of its reliance on any misleading communication from [patent holder] about [ ], resulting in losses beyond merely paying for infringement (such as if [alleged infringer] could have switched to a noninfringing product if sued earlier) and whether losses as a result of any change in economic position could have been avoided.

<u>Authorities</u>

35 U.S.C. § 282; *Gasser Chair Co. v. Infanti Chair Mfg. Corp.*, 60 F.3d 770 (Fed. Cir. 1995) (to establish equitable estoppel, one must show reliance on patentee's misleading conduct); *A.C. Aukerman Co. v. R.L. Chaides Constr. Co.*, 960 F.2d 1020 (Fed. Cir. 1992) (en banc).

B.5 Equitable Defenses

5.4 PROSECUTION LACHES

The owner of a patent may be barred from enforcing claims of a patent against an infringer where: (1) there was an unreasonably long delay in filing the claims of the patent, and (2) the infringer, another private party, or the public will be prejudiced if the patent holder is entitled to enforce the patent despite the unreasonable delay in securing the claims of the patent. This is referred to as prosecution laches, and it is a defense that [alleged infringer] contends precludes any recovery by [patent holder] in this lawsuit.

The delay that must be considered is the period of time beginning when [patent holder or its predecessor(s) in interest] filed the original application for a patent and ending when [patent holder or its predecessor(s) in interest] filed the application for the patent asserted in this lawsuit. [Patent holder] filed the original application for a patent on [ ], and filed the application for the patent asserted in this lawsuit on [ ].

Whether [patent holder]'s delay in securing the patent asserted in this lawsuit was unreasonably long is a question that must be answered, and you should consider the facts and circumstances as they existed during the period of delay. In determining whether [alleged infringer], another private party, or the public will be prejudiced as a result of any unreasonably long delay in filing the claims of the patent(s) asserted in this case, consider whether [alleged infringer] or others invested time, money, and effort in developing, manufacturing, or selling products now covered by the patent(s) asserted in this case during the period of unreasonably long delay, whether other private parties have done so and may be potentially subject to infringement, and whether the time when the public will be able to freely practice the invention(s) now covered by the patent(s) asserted in this case was unduly and unfairly postponed as a result of delay.

You may also consider whether [patent holder] intentionally or deliberately delayed the time when it filed the claim(s) of the patent(s) and whether [alleged infringer] or the public was aware that patent applications were pending that did or potentially could have covered the invention.

<u>Authorities</u>

35 U.S.C. § 282; *Crown Cork & Seal Co. v. Ferdinand Gutmann Co.*, 304 U.S. 159 (1938); *Gen. Talking Pictures Corp. v. W. Elec. Co.*, 304 U.S. 175 (1938); *Webster Elec. Co. v. Splitdorf Elec. Co.*, 264 U.S. 463 (1924); *Woodbridge v. United States*, 263 U.S. 50 (1923); *Kendall v. Winsor*, 62 U.S. 322 (1859); *Symbol Techs., Inc. v. Lemelson Med., Educ. & Research Found., L.P.*, 277 F.3d 1361, 1363 (Fed. Cir. 2002) ("[T]he equitable doctrine of laches may be applied to bar enforcement of patent claims that issued after an unreasonable and unexplained delay in prosecution even though the applicant complied with pertinent statutes and rules."); *Symbol Techs., Inc. v. Lemelson Med., Educ. & Research Found., L.P.*, 301 F. Supp. 2d 1147 (D. Nev. 2004) (patent claims unenforceable because eighteen- to thirty-nine-year delay in prosecuting patents was unreasonable and unjustified), *aff'd*, 422 F.3d 1378 (Fed. Cir. 2005); *see also In re Bogese II*, 303 F.3d 1362 (Fed. Cir. 2002) (affirming patent board's order of forfeiture of patent rights after twelve continuation applications over eight-year period and failure to advance prosecution of application).

B.5. Equitable Defenses

5.5 UNCLEAN HANDS

The owner of a patent may be barred from enforcing the patent against an infringer where the owner of the patent acts or acted inequitably, unfairly, or deceitfully towards the infringer or the Court in a way that has immediate and necessary relation to the relief that the patent holder seeks in a lawsuit. This is referred to as "unclean hands," and it is a defense that [alleged infringer] contends precludes any recovery by [patent holder] in this lawsuit.

You must consider and weigh all the facts and circumstances to determine whether you believe that, on balance, [patent holder] acted in such an unfair way towards [alleged infringer] or the Court in the matters relating to the controversy between [patent holder] and [alleged infringer] that, in fairness, [patent holder] should be denied the relief it seeks in this lawsuit. [Alleged infringer] must prove unclean hands by a preponderance of the evidence.

<u>Authorities</u>

35 U.S.C. § 282; *Keystone Driller Co. v. Gen. Excavator Co.*, 290 U.S. 240 (1933) (affirming dismissal of patent holder's complaints for unclean hands from suppressing evidence of prior use in another litigation); *Aptix Corp. v. Quickturn Design Sys., Inc.*, 269 F.3d 1369 (Fed. Cir. 2001) (affirming district court's finding of unclean hands when inventor added new material to signed and dated pages, but vacating judgment of unenforceability because unclean hands do not nullify grant of personal property).

B.6 Patent Damages

6.1 DAMAGES—INTRODUCTION

If you find that [alleged infringer] infringed any valid claim of the [ ] patent, you must then consider what amount of damages to award to [patent holder]. I will now instruct you about the measure of damages. By instructing you on damages, I am not suggesting which party should win this case, on any issue. If you find that [alleged infringer] has not infringed any valid claim of the patent, then [patent holder] is not entitled to any damages.

The damages you award must be adequate to compensate [patent holder] for the infringement. They are not meant to punish an infringer. Your damages award, if you reach this issue, should put [patent holder] in approximately the same financial position that it would have been in had the infringement not occurred.

[Patent holder] has the burden to establish the amount of its damages by a preponderance of the evidence. In other words, you should award only those damages that [patent holder] establishes that it more likely than not suffered. While [patent holder] is not required to prove the amount of its damages with mathematical precision, it must prove them with reasonable certainty. You may not award damages that are speculative, damages that are only possible, or damages that are based on guesswork.

There are different types of damages that [patent holder] may be entitled to recover. In this case, [patent holder] seeks [insert as appropriate, e.g., lost profits, price erosion, lost convoyed sales, or a reasonable royalty]. Lost profits consist of any actual reduction in business profits [patent holder] suffered as a result of [alleged infringer]'s infringement. A reasonable royalty is defined as the money amount [patent holder] and [alleged infringer] would have agreed upon as a fee for use of the invention at the time prior to when infringement began. But, regardless of the type of damages you may choose to award, you must be careful to ensure that award is no more or no less than the value of the patented invention.

[*Add if patent holder is under a RAND obligation*: Because [patent holder] committed to license the patent on Reasonable and Non-Discriminatory ("RAND") terms, you must ensure that any damages award is consistent with and does not exceed the amount permitted under [patent holder's] RAND obligations.]

I will give more detailed instructions regarding damages shortly. Note, however, that [patent holder] is entitled to recover no less than a reasonable royalty for each infringing [sale; fill in other infringing act].

Committee Comments and Authorities

See 35 U.S.C. § 284; *Ericsson, Inc. v. D-Link Sys.*, 773 F.3d 1201, 1226 (Fed. Cir. 2014) ("What is taken from the owner of a utility patent (for purposes of assessing damages under § 284) is only the patented technology, and so the value to be measured is only the value of the infringing features of an accused product."); *Virnetx, Inc. v. Cisco Sys., Inc.,* 767 F.3d 1308, 1326 (Fed. Cir. 2014) ("No matter what the form of the royalty, a patentee must take care to seek only those damages attributable to the infringing features."); *Calico Brand, Inc. v. Ameritek Imps., Inc.*, 527

Fed. Appx. 987, 996 (Fed. Cir. 2013) ("lost profits must be tied to the intrinsic value of the patented feature"); *ResQNet.com, Inc. v. Lansa, Inc,*, 594 F.3d 860, 869 (Fed. Cir. 2010) ("the trial court must carefully tie proof of damages to the claimed invention's footprint in the market place"); *Dow Chem. Co. v. Mee Indus., Inc.*, 341 F.3d 1370, 1381-82 (Fed. Cir. 2003); *Integra Lifesciences I, Ltd. v. Merck KGaA*, 331 F.3d 860, 870 (Fed. Cir. 2003); *Grain Processing Corp. v. Am. Maize-Prods. Co.*, 185 F.3d 1341, 1349 (Fed. Cir. 1999); *Maxwell v. J. Baker, Inc.*, 86 F.3d 1098, 1108-09 (Fed. Cir. 1996); *Rite-Hite Corp. v. Kelley Co.*, 56 F.3d 1538, 1545 (Fed. Cir. 1995) (en banc); *Lam, Inc. v. Johns-Manville Corp.*, 718 F.2d 1056, 1065 (Fed. Cir. 1983).

A patent holder is not entitled to damages that are remote or speculative. *See, e.g., Lucent Techs., Inc. v. Gateway, Inc.*, 580 F.3d 1301, 1340 (Fed. Cir. 2009) (vacating and remanding jury award as excessive); *Lam*, 718 F.2d at 1067 (holding that lost profits, as well as the harm to the goodwill of the entire market stemming from the infringer's inferior product, were not remote or speculative, and thus recoverable). The Federal Circuit has opined, in *dicta*, that "remote consequences, such as a heart attack of the inventor or loss in value of shares of common stock of a patentee corporation caused indirectly by infringement are not compensable." *Rite-Hite*, 56 F.3d at 1546. While a patent holder is not required to prove its damages with mathematical precision, it must prove them with reasonable certainty. *Standard Havens Prods., Inc. v. Gencor Indus., Inc.*, 953 F.2d 1360 (Fed. Cir. 1991).

When the amount of damages cannot be ascertained with precision, any doubts regarding the amount must be resolved against the alleged infringer. *Lam*, 718 F.2d at 1064. Any such adverse consequences must rest on the alleged infringer when the inability to ascertain lost profits is due to the infringer's own failure to keep accurate records. *Id.*

B.6 Patent Damages

6.2 LOST PROFITS—"BUT FOR" TEST

[This instruction should only be given in the event the patent holder is seeking lost profits damages, in whole or in part.]

In this case, [patent holder] seeks to recover lost profits for some of [alleged infringer]'s sales of [infringing product], and a reasonable royalty on the rest of [alleged infringer]'s sales.

To recover lost profits (as opposed to reasonable royalties), [patent holder] must show a causal relationship between the infringement and [patent holder]'s loss of profit. In other words, [patent holder] must show that, but for the infringement, there is a reasonable probability that [patent holder] would have earned higher profits. To show this, [patent holder] must prove that, if there had been no infringement, [it would have made some portion of the sales that [alleged infringer] made of the infringing product,] [it would have sold more products that are functionally related to those products,] [it would have sold its products at higher prices,] [or it would have had lower costs].

[Patent holder] is entitled to lost profits if it establishes each of the following:

(1) That there was a demand for the patented [product] [method] [product produced by the method].

(2) That there were no available, acceptable, noninfringing substitute products, or, if there were, its market share of the number of the sales made by [alleged infringer] that [patent holder] would have made, despite the availability of other acceptable noninfringing substitutes.

(3) That [patent holder] had the manufacturing and marketing capacity to make any infringing sales actually made by [alleged infringer] and for which [patent holder] seeks an award of lost profits—in other words, that [patent holder] was capable of satisfying the demand.

(4) The amount of profit that [patent holder] would have made if [alleged infringer] had not infringed.

<u>Committee Comments and Authorities</u>

35 U.S.C. § 284; *Aro Mfg. Co. v. Convertible Top Co.*, 377 U.S. 476, 502-07 (1964); *Ericsson, Inc. v. Harris Corp.*, 352 F.3d 1369, 1377-79 (Fed. Cir. 2003); *Micro Chem., Inc. v. Lextron, Inc.*, 318 F.3d 1119, 1123 (Fed. Cir. 2003); *Gargoyles, Inc. v. United States*, 113 F.3d 1572, 1577-78 (Fed. Cir. 1997); *Rite-Hite Corp. v. Kelley Co.*, 56 F.3d 1538, 1545 (Fed. Cir. 1995) (en banc); *BIC Leisure Prods., Inc. v. Windsurfing Int'l, Inc.*, 1 F.3d 1214, 1218-19 (Fed. Cir. 1993); *Carella v. Starlight Archery*, 804 F.2d 135, 141 (Fed. Cir. 1986); *Gyromat Corp. v. Champion Spark Plug Co.*, 735 F.2d 549, 552 (Fed. Cir. 1984); *Panduit Corp. v. Stahlin Bros. Fibre Works, Inc.*, 575 F.2d 1152, 1156 (6th Cir. 1978).

The four-factor "but for" test was first articulated in *Panduit*, 575 F.2d at 1156, and has since been adopted by the Federal Circuit. *See, e.g.*, *Rite-Hite*, 56 F.3d at 1545. It is not, however, the only available method for proving lost profits. *Id.*; *see also BIC*, 1 F.3d at 1218-19.
Once a patent holder has shown the four elements of the *Panduit* test, the burden then shifts to alleged infringer to show that patent holder's "but for" causation analysis is unreasonable under the specific circumstances. *Rite-Hite*, 56 F.3d at 1545.

LOST PROFITS—DEMAND

Demand for the patented product can be proven by significant sales of a patent holder's patented product or significant sales of an infringing product containing the patented features.

Authorities

DePuy Spine, Inc. v. Medtronic Sofamor Danek, Inc., 567 F.3d 1314, 1330 (Fed. Cir. 2009).

LOST PROFITS—NONINFRINGING SUBSTITUTES—ACCEPTABILITY

To be an "acceptable, [noninfringing] substitute," a product must have the advantages of the patented invention that were important to people who purchased an alleged infringer's product. If purchasers of an alleged infringer's product were motivated to buy that product because of features available only from that product and a patent holder's patented product, then some other, alternative product is not an acceptable substitute, even if it otherwise competed with a patent holder's and an alleged infringer's products. On the other hand, if the realities of the marketplace are that competitors other than the patentee would likely have captured the sales made by the infringer, despite a difference in the products, then the patentee is not entitled to lost profits on those sales.

Authorities

Am. Seating Co. v. USSC Group, 514 F.3d 1262, 1270 (Fed. Cir. 2008) ("[B]uyers must view the substitute as equivalent to the patented device."); *Standard Havens Prods., Inc. v. Gencor Indus.*, 953 F.2d 1360, 1373 (Fed. Cir. 1991); *SmithKline Diagnostics, Inc. v. Helena Lab. Corp.*, 926 F.2d 1161, 1166 (Fed. Cir. 1991).

LOST PROFITS—NONINFRINGING SUBSTITUTES—AVAILABILITY

An alternative product may be considered "available" as a potential substitute even if the product was not actually on sale during the infringement period. Factors suggesting the alternative was available include whether the material, experience, and know-how for the alleged substitute were readily available at the time of infringement. Factors suggesting the alternative was not available include whether the material was of such high cost as to render the alternative unavailable and whether an alleged infringer had to design or invent around the patented technology to develop an alleged substitute.

Authorities

Grain Processing Corp. v. Am. Maize-Prods. Co., 185 F.3d 1341, 1349 (Fed. Cir. 1999) (holding that an unused, but available, noninfringing process was an acceptable substitute); *Micro Chem., Inc. v. Lextron, Inc.*, 318 F.3d 1119, 1123 (Fed. Cir. 2003) ("The record shows that Lextron did not have the necessary equipment, know-how, and experience to make the [alternative] machine at the time of infringement.").

LOST PROFITS—CAPACITY

A patent holder is only entitled to lost profits for sales it could have actually made. In other words, [patent holder] must show that it had the manufacturing and marketing capability to make the sales it said it lost. This means [patent holder] must prove it is more probable than not that it could have made and sold, or could have had someone else make or sell for it, the additional products it says it could have sold but for the infringement.

<u>Authorities</u>

Fonar Corp. v. Gen. Elec. Co., 107 F.3d 1543, 1553 (Fed. Cir. 1997) (finding that the patent holder, a young company, would have expanded to meet the increased demand created by the success of the patented product); *Gyromat Corp. v. Champion Spark Plug Co.*, 735 F.2d 549, 554 (Fed. Cir. 1984).

LOST PROFITS—AMOUNT OF PROFIT

A patent holder may calculate its lost profits on lost sales by computing the lost revenue for sales it claims it would have made but for the infringement and subtracting from that figure the amount of additional costs or expenses it would have incurred in making those lost sales, such as cost of goods, sales costs, packaging costs, and shipping costs. Certain fixed costs that do not vary with increases in production or scale, such as taxes, insurance, rent, and administrative overhead, should not be subtracted from a patent holder's lost revenue.

<u>Authorities</u>

Paper Converting Mach. Co. v. Magna-Graphics Corp., 745 F.2d 11 (Fed. Cir. 1984).

LOST PROFITS—MARKET SHARE

If a patent holder establishes it would have made some, but not all, of an alleged infringer's sales but for the infringement, the amount of sales that the patent holder lost may be shown by proving the patent holder's share of the relevant market, excluding infringing products. A patent holder may be awarded a share of profits equal to its market share even if there were noninfringing substitutes available. In determining a patent holder's market share, the market must be established first, which requires determining which products are in that market. Products are considered in the same market if they are considered "sufficiently similar" to compete against each other. Two products are sufficiently similar if one does not have a significantly higher price than, or possess characteristics significantly different from, the other.

Authorities

State Indus., Inc. v. Mor-Flo Indus., Inc., 883 F.2d 1573, 1557 (Fed. Cir. 1989); *BIC Leisure Prods., Inc. v. Windsurfing Int'l, Inc.*, 1 F.3d 1214, 1218-19 (Fed. Cir. 1993); *Micro Chem., Inc. v. Lextron, Inc.*, 318 F.3d 1119, 1124 (Fed. Cir. 2003); *Crystal Semiconductor Corp. v. Tritech Microelectronics Int'l, Inc.*, 246 F.3d 1336, 1354-55 (Fed. Cir. 2001).

B.6 Patent Damages

6.3 LOST PROFITS—COLLATERAL SALES

[This instruction should only be given in the event that patent holder is seeking lost profits from collateral sales.]

In this case, [patent holder] is seeking lost profits from sales of [ ], which [patent holder] contends it would have sold along with the product it sells that competes with the infringing products [ ]. These products sold along with the competitive product are called collateral products.

To recover lost profits on sales of such collateral products, [patent holder] must establish two things. First, [patent holder] must establish it is more likely than not that [patent holder] would have sold the collateral products but for the infringement. Second, a collateral product and the competitive product together must be analogous to components of a single assembly or parts of a complete machine, or, in other words, they must constitute a single functional unit.

Recovery for lost profits on sales of collateral products must not include items that essentially have no functional relationship to the competitive product and that have been sold with the competitive product only as a matter of convenience or business advantage.

Committee Comments and Authorities

The relationship required to recover lost profits on collateral sales is outlined in *Rite-Hite Corp. v. Kelley Co.*, 56 F.3d 1538, 1550 (Fed. Cir. 1995) (en banc) (denying recovery for lost profits on collateral sales where nonpatented product lacked a functional relationship to the patented product); *see also State Indus., Inc. v. Mar-Flo Indus., Inc.*, 883 F.2d 1573, 1580 (Fed. Cir. 1989); *Panduit Corp. v. Stahlin Bros. Fibre Works, Inc.*, 575 F.2d 1152, 1157-58 (6th Cir. 1978).

B.6 Patent Damages

6.4 LOST PROFITS—PRICE EROSION

[This instruction should only be given in the event that patent holder contends it should be compensated for price erosion.]

[Patent holder] can recover additional damages if it can establish that it is more likely than not that, if there had been no infringement, [patent holder] would have been able to charge higher prices for some of its products. If this fact is established, you may award as additional damages the difference between:

(A) the amount of profits [patent holder] would have made by selling its product at the higher price, and

(B) the amount of profits [patent holder] actually made by selling its product at the lower price [patent holder] actually charged for its product.

This type of damage is referred to as price-erosion damage.

If you find that [patent holder] suffered price erosion, you may also use the higher price in determining [patent holder]'s lost profits from sales that were lost because of the infringement. In calculating [patent holder]'s total losses from price erosion, you must take into account any drop in sales that would have resulted from charging a higher price.

You may also award as damages the amount of any increase in [patent holder]'s costs, such as additional marketing costs, caused by competition from the infringing product.

<u>Authorities</u>

Compare Crystal Semiconductor Corp. v. Tritech Microelectronics Int'l, Inc., 246 F.3d 1336, 1357-58 (Fed. Cir. 2001) (upholding denial of price-erosion damages where patentee failed to show how higher prices would have affected demand for the patented product), *with Ericsson, Inc. v. Harris Corp.*, 352 F.3d 1369, 1377-79 (Fed. Cir. 2003) (upholding award of price-erosion damages where patentee offered sufficient proof of an inelastic market that would support price increases without a drop in sales of the patented product); *see also Vulcan Eng'g Co. v. FATA Aluminum, Inc.*, 278 F.3d 1366, 1377 (Fed. Cir. 2002); *Minco, Inc. v. Combustion Eng'g, Inc.*, 95 F.3d 1109, 1120 (Fed. Cir. 1996); *BIC Leisure Prods., Inc. v. Windsurfing Int'l, Inc.*, 1 F.3d 1214, 1220 (Fed. Cir. 1993); *Kalman v. Berlyn Corp.*, 914 F.2d 1473, 1485 (Fed. Cir. 1990).

B.6 Patent Damages

6.5 REASONABLE ROYALTY—ENTITLEMENT

If you find that [patent holder] has established infringement, [patent holder] is entitled to at least a reasonable royalty to compensate it for that infringement. If you find that [patent holder] has not proved its claim for lost profits, or has proved its claim for lost profits for only a portion of the infringing sales, then you must award [patent holder] a reasonable royalty for all infringing sales for which it has not been awarded lost profits damages.

Authorities

35 U.S.C. § 284; *Lucent Techs., Inc. v. Gateway, Inc.*, 580 F.3d 1301, 1340 (Fed. Cir. 2009) (vacating and remanding jury award as excessive); *Crystal Semiconductor Corp. v. Tritech Microelectronics Int'l, Inc.*, 246 F.3d 1336 (Fed. Cir. 2001); *Fromson v. W. Litho Plate & Supply Co.*, 853 F.2d 1568, 1574 (Fed. Cir. 1998); *Minco, Inc. v. Combustion Eng'g, Inc.*, 95 F.3d 1109, 1119-20 (Fed. Cir. 1996); *Mahurkar v. C.R. Bard, Inc.*, 79 F.3d 1572, 1579 (Fed. Cir. 1996); *Rite-Hite Corp. v. Kelley Co.*, 56 F.3d 1538, 1554 (Fed. Cir. 1995) (en banc).

B.6 Patent Damages

6.6 REASONABLE ROYALTY—DEFINITION

A royalty is a payment made to a patent holder in exchange for the right to make, use, or sell the claimed invention. A reasonable royalty is the amount of royalty payment that a patent holder and the alleged infringer would have agreed to in a hypothetical negotiation taking place at a time prior to when the infringement first began. In considering this hypothetical negotiation, you should focus on what the expectations of the patent holder and the alleged infringer would have been had they entered into an agreement at that time, and had they acted reasonably in their negotiations. In determining this, you must assume that both parties believed the patent was valid and infringed and that both parties were willing to enter into an agreement. The reasonable royalty you determine must be a royalty that would have resulted from the hypothetical negotiation, and not simply a royalty either party would have preferred. Evidence of things that happened after the infringement first began can be considered in evaluating the reasonable royalty only to the extent that the evidence aids in assessing what royalty would have resulted from a hypothetical negotiation. Although evidence of the actual profits an alleged infringer made may be used to determine the anticipated profits at the time of the hypothetical negotiation, the royalty may not be limited or increased based on the actual profits the alleged infringer made.

Authorities

Uniloc USA, Inc. v. Microsoft Corp., 632 F.3d 1292 (Fed. Cir. 2011) (25% "rule of thumb" inadmissible); *ResQNet.com, Inc. v. Lansa, Inc.*, 594 F.3d 860 (Fed. Cir. 2010) (per curiam) (licenses must be related to patent at issue to be relevant to a reasonable royalty); *Lucent Techs., Inc. v. Gateway, Inc.*, 580 F.3d 1301, 1340 (Fed. Cir. 2009) *cert. denied*, 130 S. Ct. 3324 (2010) (vacating and rewarding jury award as excessive); *Golight, Inc. v. Wal-Mart Stores, Inc.*, 355 F.3d 1327, 1338 (Fed. Cir. 2004); *Maxwell v. J. Baker, Inc.*, 86 F.3d 1098, 1108-10 (Fed. Cir. 1996); *Mahurkar v. C.R. Bard, Inc.*, 79 F.3d 1572, 1579-81 (Fed. Cir. 1996); *Rite-Hite Corp. v. Kelley Co.*, 56 F.3d 1538, 1554 (Fed. Cir. 1995) (en banc); *Georgia-Pacific Corp. v. U.S. Plywood Corp.*, 318 F. Supp. 1116, 1120 (S.D.N.Y. 1970); *Interactive Pictures Corp. v. Infinite Pictures, Inc.*, 274 F.3d 1371 (Fed. Cir. 2001); *Trans-World Mfg. Corp. v. Al Nyman & Sons, Inc.*, 750 F.2d 1552 (Fed. Cir. 1984).

B.6 Patent Damages

6.7 REASONABLE ROYALTY—RELEVANT FACTORS

In determining the reasonable royalty, you should consider all the facts known and available to the parties at the time the infringement began. Some of the kinds of factors that you may consider in making your determination are:

(1) The value that the claimed invention contributes to the accused product.

(2) The value that factors other than the claimed invention contribute to [the accused product].

(3) Comparable license agreements, such as those covering the use of the claimed invention or similar technology.

[Add if a Standard Essential Patent or a patent otherwise subject to a RAND obligation is involved] You have heard evidence that the asserted patent is a standard essential patent, that is, the [industry standard] cannot be practiced without infringing the patent. If you agree that the patent is essential to the [standard], you must ensure that your damages award reflects only the value of the patented invention and not the additional value that resulted from the patent's inclusion in the [standard]. In other words, you may not consider the success of the standard itself in determining a reasonable royalty for the patent(s)-in-suit.]

No one factor is dispositive and you can and should consider the evidence that has been presented to you in this case on each of these factors. You may also consider any other factors which in your mind would have increased or decreased the royalty the alleged infringer would have been willing to pay and the patent holder would have been willing to accept, acting as normally prudent business people.

<u>Committee Comments and Authorities</u>

The so-called "*Georgia-Pacific*" factors, which can be considered in appropriate cases to inform the hypothetical negotiations, include the following:

(1) The royalties received by the patentee for the licensing of the patent-in-suit, proving or tending to prove an established royalty

(2) The rates paid by the licensee for the use of other patents comparable to the patent-in-suit.

(3) The nature and scope of the license, as exclusive or nonexclusive, or as restricted or nonrestricted in terms of territory or with respect to whom the manufactured product may be sold.

(4) The licensor's established policy and marketing program to maintain his or her patent monopoly by not licensing others to use the invention or by granting licenses under special conditions designed to preserve that monopoly.

(5) The commercial relationship between the licensor and licensee, such as whether they are competitors in the same territory in the same line of business, or whether they are inventor and promoter.

(6) The effect of selling the patented specialty in promoting sales of other products of the licensee, the existing value of the invention to the licensor as a generator of sales of his nonpatented items, and the extent of such derivative or convoyed sales.

(7) The duration of the patent and the term of the license.

(8) The established profitability of the product made under the patents, its commercial success, and its current popularity.

(9) The utility and advantages of the patented property over the old modes or devices, if any, that had been used for working out similar results.

(10) The nature of the patented invention, the character of the commercial embodiment of it as owned and produced by the licensor, and the benefits to those who have used the invention.

(11) The extent to which the infringer has made use of the invention and any evidence probative of the value of that use.

(12) The portion of the profit or of the selling price that may be customary in the particular business or in comparable business to allow for the use of the invention or analogous inventions.

(13) The portion of the realizable profits that should be credited to the invention as distinguished from nonpatented elements, the manufacturing process, business risks, or significant features or improvements added by the infringer.

(14) The opinion and testimony of qualified experts.

(15) The amount that a licensor (such as the patentee) and a licensee (such as the infringer) would have agreed upon (at the time the infringement began) if both had been reasonably and voluntarily trying to reach an agreement; that is, the amount which a prudent licensee—who desired, as a business proposition, to obtain a license to manufacture and sell a particular article embodying the patented invention—would have been willing to pay as a royalty and yet be able to make a reasonable profit and which amount would have been acceptable by a prudent patentee who was willing to grant a license.

The Federal Circuit has made it clear that the *Georgia Pacific* factors are not mandatory. *See, e.g., Energy Transp. Group, Inc. v. William Demant Holding A/S/*, 697 F.3d 1342, 1357 (Fed. Cir. 2012) ("[T]his court does not endorse *Georgia-Pacific* as setting forth a test for royalty calculations, but only as a list of admissible factors informing a reliable economic analysis."). But if they are used, the jury should be instructed only on the factors that are relevant to the evidence before the jury. *Ericsson, Inc. v. D-Link Sys.*, 773 F.3d 1201, 1231 (Fed. Cir. 2014) (stating that "the district court erred by instructing the jury on multiple *Georgia-Pacific* factors that are not relevant, or are misleading, on the record before it"); *Uniloc USA, Inc. v. Microsoft Corp.*, 632 F.3d 1292 (Fed. Cir. 2011) (25% "rule of thumb" inadmissible); *ResQNet.com, Inc. v. Lansa, Inc.*, 594 F.3d 860 (Fed. Cir. 2010) (per curiam) (licenses must be related to patent at issue to be relevant to a reasonable royalty); *Lucent Techs., Inc. v. Gateway, Inc.*, 580 F.3d 1301, 1340 (Fed. Cir. 2009), cert. denied, 130 S. Ct. 3324 (2010) (vacating and rewarding jury award as excessive); *Golight, Inc. v. Wal-Mart Stores, Inc.*, 355 F.3d 1327, 1338 (Fed. Cir. 2004); *Maxwell v. J. Baker, Inc.*, 86 F.3d 1098, 1108-10 (Fed. Cir. 1996); *Mahurkar v. C.R. Bard, Inc.*, 79 F.3d 1572, 1579-81 (Fed. Cir. 1996); *Rite-Hite Corp. v. Kelley Co.*, 56 F.3d 1538, 1554 (Fed. Cir. 1995) (en banc); *Georgia-Pacific Corp. v. U.S. Plywood Corp.*, 318 F. Supp. 1116, 1120 (S.D.N.Y. 1970).

If a Standard Essential Patent is involved, the jury must be instructed to separate out the value of the patented invention from any value that arises from the fact that the patent is essential to a standard:

> Because SEP holders should only be compensated for the added benefit of their inventions, the jury must be told to differentiate the added benefit from any value the innovation gains because it has become standard essential. Although the jury, as the fact finder, should determine the appropriate value for that added benefit and may do so with some level of imprecision, we conclude that they must be told to consider the difference between the added value of the technological invention and the added value of that invention's standardization.

Ericsson, Inc. v. D-Link Sys., 773 F.3d at 1233.

B.6 Patent Damages

6.8 DATE OF COMMENCEMENT OF DAMAGES—PRODUCTS

In determining the amount of damages, you must determine when the damages began. Damages commence on the date that [alleged infringer] has both infringed and been notified of the alleged infringement of the [ ] patent [choose those that apply]:

Alternative A:
[Patent holder] and [alleged infringer] agree that date was [insert date].

Alternative B:
If you find that [patent holder] sells a product that includes the claimed invention, you must determine whether [patent holder] has "marked" that product with the patent number. "Marking" is placing either the word "patent" or the abbreviation "pat." with the patent's number on substantially all of the products that include the patented invention. [Patent holder] has the burden of establishing that it substantially complied with the marking requirement. This means [patent holder] must show that it marked substantially all of the products it made, offered for sale, or sold under the [ ] patent, [and that [patent holder] made reasonable efforts to ensure that its licensees who made, offered for sale, or sold products under the [ ] patent marked the products].

[If [patent holder] has not marked that product with the patent number, you must determine the date that [alleged infringer] received actual notice of the [ ] patent and the specific product alleged to infringe.] [Actual notice means that [patent holder] communicated to [alleged infringer] a specific charge of infringement of the [ ] patent by a specific accused product or device. The filing of the complaint in this case qualified as actual notice, so the damages period begins no later than the date the complaint was filed.] [However, [patent holder] claims to have provided actual notice prior to filing of the complaint, on [date], when it [sent a letter to [alleged infringer]]. [Patent holder] has the burden of establishing that it is more probable than not [alleged infringer] received notice of infringement on [date].]

[If you find that [patent holder] *[choise A]* does not sell a product covered by the [ ] patent *[or choise B]* sells such a product but marks the product with the patent number, damages begin without the requirement for actual notice. If you find that the [ ] patent was granted before the infringing activity began, damages should be calculated as of the date you determine that the infringement began. If you find that the [ ] patent was granted after the infringing activity began, damages should be calculated as of [date patent issued].]

<u>Committee Comments and Authorities</u>

35 U.S.C. § 287; *Crystal Semiconductor Corp. v. Tritech Microelectronics Int'l, Inc.*, 246 F.3d 1336 (Fed. Cir. 2001); *Nike Inc. v. Wal-Mart Stores*, 138 F.3d 1437, 1443-44 (Fed. Cir. 1998); *Maxwell v. J. Baker, Inc.*, 86 F.3d 1098, 1108-09 (Fed. Cir. 1996); *Am. Med. Sys. v. Med. Eng'g Corp.*, 6 F.3d 1523, 1534 (Fed. Cir. 1993); *Devices for Med., Inc. v. Boehl*, 822 F.2d 1062, 1066 (Fed. Cir. 1987).
Notice through marking is constructive notice. *See Maxwell*, 86 F.3d at 1111-12 (holding that when 95% of patented product offered for sale was marked by licensee retailer with "patent

pending," even after the patent had been granted and remaining 5% of product remained unmarked, constructive notice had been made under 35 U.S.C. § 287(a) where patentee demonstrated efforts to correct licensee's mistakes).

In determining when damages begin with regard to method claims, there is no notice requirement. 35 U.S.C. § 287(c)(2)(F); *see Am. Med. Sys.*, 6 F.3d at 1538 ("The law is clear that the notice provisions of section 287 do not apply where the patent is directed to a process or method."). Accordingly, the calculation of damages for infringement of method claims should begin as of the date the patent issued or the date the infringement began, whichever was first. *Crystal Semiconductor*, 246 F.3d at 1353.

C. Appendix

GLOSSARY

Some of the terms in this glossary will be defined in more detail in the legal instructions you are given. The definitions in the instructions must be followed and must control your deliberations.

[Add any technical terms from the art involved that may be used during trial and have agreed upon definitions. Delete any of the following terms which may not be applicable in a particular case.]

Abstract: A brief summary of the technical disclosure in a patent to enable the U.S. Patent and Trademark Office and the public to determine quickly the nature and gist of the technical disclosure in the patent.

Amendment: A patent applicant's change to one or more claims or to the specification either in response to an office action taken by an Examiner or independently by the patent applicant during the patent application examination process.

Anticipation: A situation in which a claimed invention describes an earlier invention and, therefore, is not considered new and is not entitled to be patented.

Assignment: A transfer of patent rights to another called an "assignee" who, upon transfer, becomes the owner of the rights assigned.

Claim: Each claim of a patent is a concise, formal definition of an invention and appears at the end of the specification in a separately numbered paragraph. In concept, a patent claim marks the boundaries of the patent in the same way that a legal description in a deed specifies the boundaries of land, i.e., similar to a landowner who can prevent others from trespassing on the bounded property, the inventor can prevent others from using what is claimed. Claims may be independent or dependent. An independent claim stands alone. A dependent claim does not stand alone and refers to one or more other claims. A dependent claim incorporates whatever the other referenced claim or claims say.

Conception: The complete mental part of the inventive act which must be capable of proof, as by drawings, disclosure to another, etc.

Drawings: The drawings are visual representations of the claimed invention contained in a patent application and issued patent, and usually include several figures illustrating various aspects of the claimed invention.

Elements: The required parts of a device or the required steps of a method. A device or method infringes a patent if it contains each and every requirement of a patent claim.

Embodiment: A product or method that contains the claimed invention.

Enablement: A description of the invention that is sufficient to enable persons skilled in the field of the invention to make and use the invention. The specification of the patent must contain such an enabling description.

Examination: Procedure before the U.S. Patent and Trademark Office whereby an Examiner reviews the filed patent application to determine if the claimed invention is patentable.

Filing Date: Date a patent application, with all the required sections, has been submitted to the U.S. Patent and Trademark Office.

Infringement: Violation of a patent occurring when someone makes, uses, or sells a patented invention, without permission of the patent holder, within the United States during the term of the patent. Infringement may be direct, by inducement, or contributory. Direct infringement is making, using, or selling the patented invention without permission. Inducing infringement is intentionally causing another to directly infringe a patent. Contributory infringement is offering to sell or selling an item that is a significant part of the invention, so that the buyer directly infringes the patent. To be a contributory infringer, one must know that the part being offered or sold is designed specifically for infringing the patented invention and is not a common object suitable for noninfringing uses.

Limitation: A required part of an invention set forth in a patent claim. A limitation is a requirement of the invention. The word "limitation" is often used interchangeably with the word "requirement."

Nonobviousness: One of the requirements for securing a patent. To be valid, the subject matter of the invention must not have been obvious to a person of ordinary skill in the field at the time of the earlier of the filing date of the patent application or the date of invention.

Office Action: A written communication from the Examiner to the patent applicant in the course of the application examination process.

Patent: A patent is an exclusive right granted by the U.S. Patent and Trademark Office to an inventor to prevent others from making, using, or selling an invention for a term of 20 years from the date the patent application was filed (or 17 years from the date the patent issued). When the patent expires, the right to make, use, or sell the invention is dedicated to the public. The patent has three parts, which are a specification, drawings and claims. The patent is granted after examination by the U.S. Patent and Trademark Office of a patent application filed by the inventor which has these parts, and this examination is called the prosecution history.

Patent and Trademark Office (PTO): An administrative branch of the U.S. Department of Commerce that is charged with overseeing and implementing the federal laws of patents and trademarks. It is responsible for examining all patent applications and issuing all patents in the United States.

Prior Art: Previously known subject matter in the field of a claimed invention for which a patent is being sought. It includes issued patents, publications, and knowledge deemed to be publicly available, such as trade skills, trade practices, and the like.

Prosecution History: The prosecution history is the complete written record of the proceedings in the PTO from the initial application to the issued patent. The prosecution history includes the office actions taken by the PTO and the amendments to the patent application filed by the applicant during the examination process.

Reads On: A patent claim "reads on" a device or method when each required part (requirement) of the claim is found in the device or method.

Reduction to Practice: The invention is "reduced to practice" when it is sufficiently developed to show that it would work for its intended purpose.

Requirement: A required part or step of an invention set forth in a patent claim. The word "requirement" is often used interchangeably with the word "limitation."

Royalty: A royalty is a payment made to the owner of a patent by a nonowner in exchange for rights to make, use, or sell the claimed invention.

Specification: The specification is a required part of a patent application and an issued patent. It is a written description of the invention and of the manner and process of making and using the claimed invention.

Model Patent Jury Instructions
for the Northern District of California

June 17, 2014

Working Committee

Professor Mark Lemley
Kathi Lutton David McIntyre Matthew Powers
Honorable Ronald Whyte
James Yoon

I. Introduction

These Model Patent Jury Instructions have been adopted by the Northern District of California and have been revised to account for changes in the law as of June 1, 2014. However, several patent cases are pending before the Supreme Court and further modifications may be required.

Additionally, Congress has amended the patent laws in the America Invents Act ("AIA"), signed by the President on September 16, 2011. Most notably, the First Inventor to File Provision of the AIA redefines Prior Art for those patent applications filed under the First Inventor to File system. The prior art jury instructions provided in this model set of instructions are therefore inapplicable to any claimed invention having an effective filing date on or after March 16, 2013.

The court is indebted to the Working Committee which spent many hours drafting the original model instructions and subsequent revisions. The court specially recognizes the contributions of Martin Fleisler who acted as chair of the Committee prior to his recent passing.

The instructions have been prepared to assist judges in communicating effectively and in plain English with jurors in patent cases. The instructions are models and are not intended to be used without tailoring. They are not substitutes for the individual research and drafting that may be required in a particular case.

These instructions include only instructions on patent law. They will need to be supplemented with standard instructions on, among other things, the duties of the judge and jury, the consideration of evidence, the duty to deliberate, and the return of a verdict. The Ninth Circuit's Manual of Model Civil Jury Instructions (download from Civil_Jury_Instructions_2014.pdf or Civil_Jury_Instructions_2014.wpd) is a good reference for standard instructions for civil cases.

The instructions use the terms "patent holder" and "alleged infringer" in brackets. The names of the parties should be substituted for these terms as appropriate. Other language is bracketed as it may not be appropriate for a particular case. Empty brackets signify additional case specific information to be added, such as patent or claim numbers.

Suggested revisions to these instructions may be sent to the Honorable Ronald M. Whyte at the e-mail address: Ronald_Whyte@cand.uscourts.gov or at his U.S. mail address: U.S. Court Building, 280 S. First Street, San Jose, California 95113.

June 17, 2014

II. Table of Contents

A.1. Preliminary Instructions

WHAT A PATENT IS AND HOW ONE IS OBTAINED

This case involves a dispute relating to a United States patent. Before summarizing the positions of the parties and the legal issues involved in the dispute, let me take a moment to explain what a patent is and how one is obtained.

Patents are granted by the United States Patent and Trademark Office (sometimes called "the PTO"). The process of obtaining a patent is called patent prosecution. A valid United States patent gives the patent owner the right to prevent others from making, using, offering to sell, or selling the patented invention within the United States, or from importing it into the United States, during the term of the patent without the patent holder's permission. A violation of the patent owner's rights is called infringement. The patent owner may try to enforce a patent against persons believed to be infringers by a lawsuit filed in federal court.

To obtain a patent one must file an application with the PTO. The PTO is an agency of the federal government and employs trained examiners who review applications for patents. The application includes what is called a "specification," which must contain a written description of the claimed invention telling what the invention is, how it works, how to make it and how to use it so others skilled in the field will know how to make or use it. The specification concludes with one or more numbered sentences. These are the patent "claims." When the patent is eventually granted by the PTO, the claims define the boundaries of its protection and give notice to the public of those boundaries.

After the applicant files the application, a PTO patent examiner reviews the patent application to determine whether the claims are patentable and whether the specification adequately describes the invention claimed. In examining a patent application, the patent examiner reviews records available to the PTO for what is referred to as "prior art." The examiner also will review prior art if it is submitted to the PTO by the applicant. Prior art is defined by law, and I will give you at a later time specific instructions as to what constitutes prior art. [However, in general, prior art includes things that existed before the claimed invention, that were publicly known, or used in a publicly accessible way in this country, or that were patented or described in a publication in any country. The examiner considers, among other things, whether each claim defines an invention that is new, useful, and not obvious in view of the prior art.]* A patent lists the prior art that the examiner considered; this list is called the "cited references."

---

* The preceding two sentences are inapplicable to any post-AIA claims, i.e., to any claimed invention having an effective filing date on or after March 16, 2013.

After the prior art search and examination of the application, the patent examiner then informs the applicant in writing what the examiner has found and whether any claim is patentable, and thus will be "allowed." This writing from the patent examiner is called an "office action." If the examiner rejects the claims, the applicant then responds and sometimes changes the claims or submits new claims. This process, which takes place only between the examiner and the patent applicant, may go back and forth for some time until the examiner is satisfied that the application and claims meet the requirements for a patent. The papers generated during this time of communicating back and forth between the patent examiner and the applicant make up what is called the "prosecution history." All of this material becomes available to the public no later than the date when the patent issues.

The fact that the PTO grants a patent does not necessarily mean that any invention claimed in the patent, in fact, deserves the protection of a patent. For example, the PTO may not have had available to it all the information that will be presented to you. A person accused of infringement has the right to argue here in federal court that a claimed invention in the patent is invalid because it does not meet the requirements for a patent.

A.2. Preliminary Instructions

PATENT AT ISSUE

[The court should show the jury the patent at issue and point out the parts including the specification, drawings and claims including the claims at issue.]

A.3. Preliminary Instructions

SUMMARY OF CONTENTIONS

To help you follow the evidence, I will now give you a summary of the positions of the parties.

The parties in this case are [patent holder] and [alleged infringer]. The case involves a United States patent obtained by [inventor], and transferred by [inventor] to [patent holder]. The patent involved in this case is United States Patent Number [patent number] which lists [inventor] as the inventor. For convenience, the parties and I will often refer to this patent as the [last three numbers of the patent] patent, [last three numbers of patent] being the last three numbers of its patent number.

[Patent holder] filed suit in this court seeking money damages from [alleged infringer] for allegedly infringing the [ ] patent by [making], [importing], [using], [selling], and [offering for sale] [products] [methods] that [patent holder] argues are covered by claims [ ] of the patent. [[Patent holder] also argues that [alleged infringer] has [actively induced infringement of these claims of the [ ] patent by others] [and] [contributed to the infringement of these claims of the [ ] patent by others].] The [products] [methods] that are alleged to infringe are [list of accused products or methods].

[Alleged infringer] denies that it has infringed claims [ ] of the [ ] patent and argues that, in addition, the claims are invalid. [Add other defenses, if applicable]. Invalidity is a defense to infringement.

Your job will be to decide whether claims [ ] of the [ ] patent have been infringed and whether those claims are invalid. If you decide that any claim of the [ ] patent has been infringed and is not invalid, you will then need to decide any money damages to be awarded to [patent holder] to compensate it for the infringement. [You will also need to make a finding as to whether the infringement was willful. If you decide that any infringement was willful, that decision should not affect any damage award you give. I will take willfulness into account later.]

You may hear evidence that [alleged infringer] has its own patent(s) or that [alleged infringer] improved on the [ ] patent. While this evidence is relevant to some issues you will be asked to decide, a party can still infringe even if it has its own patents in the same area. You will be instructed after trial as to what, if any, relevance these facts have to the particular issues in this case. Meanwhile, please keep an open mind.

Before you decide whether [alleged infringer] has infringed the claim[s] of the patent or whether the claim[s] [is][are] invalid, you will need to understand the patent claims. As I mentioned, the patent claims are numbered sentences at the end of the patent that describe the boundaries of the patent's protection. It is my job as judge to explain to you the meaning of any language in the claim[s] that needs interpretation.

[The Court may wish to hand out its claim constructions (if the claims have been construed at this point) and the glossary at this time. If the claim constructions are handed out, the following instruction should be read:

I have already determined the meaning of certain terms of the claims of the [ ] patent. You have been given a document reflecting those meanings. You are to apply my definitions of these terms throughout this case. However, my interpretation of the language of the claims should not be taken as an indication that I have a view regarding issues such as infringement and invalidity. Those issues are yours to decide. I will provide you with more detailed instructions on the meaning of the claims before you retire to deliberate your verdict.]

A.4. Preliminary Instructions

OVERVIEW OF APPLICABLE LAW

[The court may want to consider giving preliminary instructions on the patent law applicable to the specific issues in the case. This could help focus the jury on the facts relevant to the issues it will have to decide. If this is done, the instructions intended to be given after the close of evidence could be adapted and given as preliminary instructions. This, of course, would not negate the need to give complete instructions at the close of evidence.]

A.5. Preliminary Instructions

OUTLINE OF TRIAL

The trial will now begin. First, each side may make an opening statement. An opening statement is not evidence. It is simply an outline to help you understand what that party expects the evidence will show.

The presentation of evidence will then begin. Witnesses will take the witness stand and the documents will be offered and admitted into evidence. There are two standards of proof that you will apply to the evidence, depending on the issue you are deciding. On some issues, you must decide whether something is more likely true than not. On other issues you must use a higher standard and decide whether it is highly probable that something is true.

[Patent holder] will present its evidence on its contention that [some] [the] claims of the [ ] patent have been [and continue to be] infringed by [alleged infringer] [and that the infringement has been [and continues to be] willful.] These witnesses will be questioned by [Patent holder]'s counsel in what is called direct examination. After the direct examination of a witness is completed, the opposing side has an opportunity to cross-examine the witness. To prove infringement of any claim, [patent holder] must persuade you that it is more likely than not that [alleged infringer] has infringed that claim. [To persuade you that any infringement was willful, [patent holder] must prove that it is highly probable that the infringement was willful.]

After [Patent holder] has presented its witnesses, [alleged infringer] will call its witnesses, who will also be examined and cross-examined. [Alleged infringer] will present its evidence that the claims of the [ ] patent are invalid. To prove invalidity of any claim, [alleged infringer] must persuade you that it is highly probable that the claim is invalid. In addition to presenting its evidence of invalidity, [alleged infringer] will put on evidence responding to [patent holder]'s infringement [and willfulness] contention[s].

[Patent holder] will then return and will put on evidence responding to [alleged infringer]'s contention that the claims of the [ ] patent are invalid. [Patent holder] will also have the option to put on what is referred to as "rebuttal" evidence to any evidence offered by [alleged infringer] of non-infringement [or lack of willfulness].

Finally, [alleged infringer] will have the option to put on "rebuttal" evidence to any evidence offered by [patent holder] on the validity of [some] [the] claims of the [ ] patent.

[During the presentation of the evidence, the attorneys will be allowed brief opportunities to explain what they believe the evidence has shown or what they believe upcoming evidence will show. Such comments are not evidence and are being allowed solely for the purpose of helping you understand the evidence.]

Because the evidence is introduced piecemeal, you need to keep an open mind as the evidence comes in and wait for all the evidence before you make any decisions. In other words, you should keep an open mind throughout the entire trial.

[The parties may present the testimony of a witness by reading from his or her deposition transcript or playing a videotape of the witness's deposition testimony. A deposition is the sworn testimony of a witness taken before trial and is entitled to the same consideration as if the witness had testified at trial.]

After the evidence has been presented, [the attorneys will make closing arguments and I will give you final instructions on the law that applies to the case] [I will give you final instructions on the law that applies to the case and the attorneys will make closing arguments]. Closing arguments are not evidence. After the [closing arguments and instructions] [instructions and closing arguments], you will then decide the case.

B.1. Summary of Contentions

SUMMARY OF CONTENTIONS

I will first give you a summary of each side's contentions in this case. I will then tell you what each side must prove to win on each of its contentions. As I previously told you, [patent holder] seeks money damages from [alleged infringer] for allegedly infringing the [ ] patent by [making,] [importing,] [using,] [selling] and [offering for sale] [products] [methods] that [patent holder] argues are covered by claims [ ] of the patent. These are the asserted claims of the [ ] patent. [Patent holder] also argues that [alleged infringer] has [actively induced infringement of these claims of the [ ] patent by others] [contributed to the infringement of these claims of the [ ] patent by others]. The [products] [methods] that are alleged to infringe are [list of accused products or methods].

[Alleged infringer] denies that it has infringed the asserted claims of the patent and argues that, in addition, claims [ ] are invalid. [Add other defenses if applicable.]

Your job is to decide whether the asserted claims of the [ ] patent have been infringed and whether any of the asserted claims of the [ ] patent are invalid. If you decide that any claim of the patent has been infringed and is not invalid, you will then need to decide any money damages to be awarded to [patent holder] to compensate it for the infringement. [You will also need to make a finding as to whether the infringement was willful. If you decide that any infringement was willful, that decision should not affect any damage award you make. I will take willfulness into account later.]

B.2. Claim Construction

2.1 INTERPRETATION OF CLAIMS

Before you decide whether [alleged infringer] has infringed the claim[s] of the patent or whether the claim[s] [is][are] invalid, you will need to understand the patent claims. As I mentioned, the patent claims are numbered sentences at the end of the patent that describes the boundaries of the patent's protection. It is my job as judge to explain to you the meaning of any language in the claim[s] that needs interpretation.

I have interpreted the meaning of some of the language in the patent claims involved in this case. You must accept those interpretations as correct. My interpretation of the language should not be taken as an indication that I have a view regarding the issues of infringement and invalidity. The decisions regarding infringement and invalidity are yours to make.

[Court gives its claim interpretation. This instruction must be coordinated with instruction 3.5 "Means-Plus-Function Claims—Literal Infringement" if the claims at issue include means-plus- function limitations.]

Authorities

Markman v. Westview Instruments, Inc., 517 U.S. 370, 384–91 (1996); *Phillips v. AWH Corp.*, 415 F.3d 1303, 1324 (Fed. Cir. 2005); *Pitney Bowes, Inc. v. Hewlett-Packard Co.*, 182 F.3d 1298, 1304–13 (Fed. Cir. 1999); *Cybor Corp. v. FAS Techs.*, 138 F.3d 1448 (Fed. Cir. 1998) (en banc); *Markman v. Westview Instruments, Inc.*, 52 F.3d 967, 977 (Fed. Cir. 1995) (en banc).

B.3. Infringement

3.1 INFRINGEMENT – BURDEN OF PROOF

I will now instruct you on the rules you must follow in deciding whether [patent holder] has proven that [alleged infringer] has infringed one or more of the asserted claims of the [ ] patent. To prove infringement of any claim, [patent holder] must persuade you that it is more likely than not that [alleged infringer] has infringed that claim.

Authorities

Warner-Lambert Co. v. Teva Pharm. USA, Inc., 418 F.3d 1326, 1341 n.15 (Fed. Cir. 2005); *Seal- Flex, Inc. v. Athletic Track and Court Constr.*, 172 F.3d 836, 842 (Fed. Cir. 1999); *Morton Int'l, Inc. v. Cardinal Chem. Co.*, 5 F.3d 1464, 1468–69 (Fed. Cir. 1993).

B.3. Infringement

3.2 DIRECT INFRINGEMENT

A patent's claims define what is covered by the patent. A [product] [method] directly infringes a patent if it is covered by at least one claim of the patent.

Deciding whether a claim has been directly infringed is a two-step process. The first step is to decide the meaning of the patent claim. I have already made this decision, [and I will instruct you later as to the meaning of the asserted patent claims] [and I have already instructed you as to the meaning of the asserted patent claims]. The second step is to decide whether [alleged direct infringer] has [made,] [used,] [sold,] [offered for sale] or [imported] within the United States a [product] [method] covered by a claim of the [ ] patent.[1] If it has, it infringes. You, the jury, make this decision.

[With one exception,] you must consider each of the asserted claims of the patent individually, and decide whether [alleged direct infringer]'s [product] [method] infringes that claim. [The one exception to considering claims individually concerns dependent claims. A dependent claim includes all of the requirements of a particular independent claim, plus additional requirements of its own. As a result, if you find that an independent claim is not infringed, you must also find that its dependent claims are not infringed. On the other hand, if you find that an independent claim has been infringed, you must still separately decide whether the additional requirements of its dependent claims have also been infringed.]

[You have heard evidence about both [patent holder]'s commercial [[product] [method]] and [alleged infringer]'s accused [[product] [method]]. However, in deciding the issue of infringement you may not compare [alleged infringer]'s accused [[product] [method]] to [patent holder]'s commercial [[product] [method]]. Rather, you must compare the [alleged infringer]'s accused [[product] [method]] to the claims of the [ ] patent when making your decision regarding infringement.][2]

Whether or not [alleged infringer] knew its [product][method] infringed or even knew of the patent does not matter in determining direct infringement.

---

1. Consistent with the policy of these instructions not to propose instructions on issues that arise only rarely, we have not proposed instructions on international infringement under sections 35 U.S.C. 271(f) and (g). If those issues arise, the reference in this instruction to infringement "within the United States" should be modified accordingly. *See Microsoft Corp. v. AT&T Corp.*, 550 U.S. 437 (2007); *Bayer AG v. Housey Pharms. Inc.*, 340 F.3d 1367 (Fed. Cir. 2003).

2. This instruction is appropriate in cases where the plaintiff sells a commercial product and contends that such product practices at least one of the asserted patent claims.

There are two ways in which a patent claim may be directly infringed. A claim may be "literally" infringed, or it may be infringed under the "doctrine of equivalents." The following instructions will provide more detail on these two types of direct infringement. [You should note, however, that what are called "means-plus-function" requirements in a claim are subject to different rules for deciding direct infringement. These separate rules apply to claims [ ]. I will describe these separate rules shortly.]

Authorities

35 U.S.C. § 271; *Warner-Jenkinson Co., Inc. v. Hilton Davis Chem. Co.*, 520 U.S. 17 (1997); *Cross Med. Prods., Inc. v. Medtronic Sofamor Danek, Inc.*, 424 F.3d 1293, 1310-11 (Fed. Cir. 2005); *DeMarini Sports, Inc. v. Worth, Inc.*, 239 F.3d 1314, 1330-34 (Fed. Cir. 2001); *Seal-Flex, Inc. v. Athletic Track and Court Constr.*, 172 F.3d 836, 842 (Fed. Cir. 1999); *Carroll Touch, Inc. v. Electro Mech. Sys., Inc.*, 15 F.3d 1573, 1576 (Fed. Cir. 1993).

B.3. Infringement

3.3 LITERAL INFRINGEMENT

To decide whether [alleged infringer]'s [product] [method] literally infringes a claim of the [ ] patent, you must compare that [product] [method] with the patent claim and determine whether every requirement of the claim is included in that [product] [method]. If so, [alleged infringer]'s [product] [method] literally infringes that claim. If, however, [alleged infringer]'s [product] [method] does not have every requirement in the patent claim, [alleged infringer]'s [product] [method] does not literally infringe that claim. You must decide literal infringement for each asserted claim separately.

[If the patent claim uses the term "comprising," that patent claim is to be understood as an open claim. An open claim is infringed as long as every requirement in the claim is present in [alleged infringer]'s [product] [method]. The fact that [alleged infringer]'s [product] [method] also includes other [parts] [steps] will not avoid infringement, as long as it has every requirement in the patent claim.]

[If the patent claim uses the term "consisting of," that patent claim is to be understood as a closed claim. To infringe a closed claim, [alleged infringer]'s [product] [method] must have every requirement in the claim and no other [parts] [steps].]

[If the patent claim uses the term "consisting essentially of," that patent claim is to be understood as a partially closed claim. A partially closed claim is infringed as long as every requirement in the claim is present in [alleged infringer]'s [product] [method]. The fact that [alleged infringer]'s [product] [method] also includes other [parts] [steps] will not avoid infringement so long as those [parts] [steps] do not materially affect the basic and novel properties of the invention. If [accused infringer]'s [product] [method] includes other [parts] [steps] that do change those basic and novel properties, it does not infringe.[3]]

[If [alleged infringer's] [product] [method] does not itself include every requirement in the patent claim, [alleged infringer] cannot be liable for infringement merely because other parties supplied the missing elements, unless [accused infringer] directed or controlled the acts by those parties.] [Alleged infringer] does not direct or control someone else's action merely because [alleged infringer] entered into a business relationship with that person. Instead, [alleged infringer] must specifically instruct or cause that other person to perform each step in an in-

---

3. Generally, only one of the three preceding paragraphs will be appropriate, depending on the transition used in the claim; the others should be omitted. In cases in which more than one claim is at issue, and the claims use different transitions, more than one paragraph will be used.

fringing manner, so that every step is attributable to [alleged infringer] as controlling party.

[If one party controls and makes use of a system that contains all the requirements of the claim, that party may be an infringer even though the parts of the system do not all operate in the same place or at the same time.][4]

Authorities

MicroStrategy Inc. v. Bus. Objects, S.A., 429 F.3d 1344, 1352-53 (Fed. Cir. 2005); *Netword, LLC v. Centraal Corp.*, 242 F.3d 1347, 1353 (Fed. Cir. 2001); *Cole v. Kimberly-Clark Corp.*, 102 F.3d 524, 532 (Fed. Cir. 1996); *Ecolab, Inc. v. FMC Corp.*, 535 F.3d 1369 (Fed. Cir. 2009); *Cross Med. Prods. v. Medtronic Sofamor Danek*, 424 F.3d 1293 (Fed. Cir. 2005); *BMC Res., Inc. v. Paymentech, L.P.*, 498 F.3d 1373 (Fed. Cir. 2007).

4. The final sentence of this instruction is appropriate in cases involving system claims, but not method claims. *Centillion Data Sys., LLC v. Qwest Comm'ns Int'l*, 631 F.3d 1279 (Fed. Cir. 2011).

B.3. Infringement

3.4 INFRINGEMENT UNDER THE DOCTRINE OF EQUIVALENTS

If you decide that [alleged infringer]'s [product] [method] does not literally infringe an asserted patent claim, you must then decide whether that [product] [method] infringes the asserted claim under what is called the "doctrine of equivalents."

Under the doctrine of equivalents, the [product] [method] can infringe an asserted patent claim if it includes [parts] [steps] that are identical or equivalent to the requirements of the claim. If the [product] [method] is missing an identical or equivalent [part] [step] to even one requirement of the asserted patent claim, the [product] [method] cannot infringe the claim under the doctrine of equivalents. Thus, in making your decision under the doctrine of equivalents, you must look at each individual requirement of the asserted patent claim and decide whether the [product] [method] has either an identical or equivalent [part] [step] to that individual claim requirement.

A [part] [step] of a [product] [method] is equivalent to a requirement of an asserted claim if a person of ordinary skill in the field would think that the differences between the [part] [step] and the requirement were not substantial as of the time of the alleged infringement.

Changes in technique or improvements made possible by technology developed after the patent application is filed may still be equivalent for the purposes of the doctrine of equivalents if it still meets the other requirements of the doctrine of equivalents set forth in this instruction.

[One way to decide whether any difference between a requirement of an asserted claim and a [part] [step] of the [product] [method] is not substantial is to consider whether, as of the time of the alleged infringement, the [part] [step] of the [product] [method] performed substantially the same function, in substantially the same way, to achieve substantially the same result as the requirement in the patent claim.]

[In deciding whether any difference between a claim requirement and the [product] [method] is not substantial, you may consider whether, at the time of the alleged infringement, persons of ordinary skill in the field would have known of the interchangeability of the [part] [step] with the claimed requirement. The known interchangeability between the claim requirement and the [part] [step] of the [product] [method] is not necessary to find infringement under the doctrine of equivalents. However, known interchangeability may support a conclusion that the difference between the [part] [step] in the [product] [method] and the claim requirement is not substantial. The fact that a [part] [step] of the [product] [method] performs the same function as the claim requirement is not, by itself, sufficient to show known interchangeability.]

[You may not use the doctrine of equivalents to find infringement if you find that [alleged infringer]'s [product] [method] is the same as what was in the prior art before the application for the [ ] patent or what would have been obvious to persons of ordinary skill in the field in light of what was in the prior art. A patent holder may not obtain, under the doctrine of equivalents, protection that it could not have lawfully obtained from the Patent and Trademark Office.][5]

[You may not use the doctrine of equivalents to find infringement if you find that the subject matter alleged to be equivalent to a requirement of the patent claim was described in the [ ] patent but not covered by any of its claims. The subject matter described but not claimed must be specific enough that one of ordinary skill in the art would understand that it was present in the patent.]

Authorities

Festo Corp. v. Shoketsu Kinzoku Kogyo Kabushiki Co., 535 U.S. 722 (2002); *Warner-Jenkinson Co., Inc. v. Hilton Davis Chem. Co.,* 520 U.S. 17 (1997); *Graver Tank & Mfg. Co. v. Linde Air Prods. Co.,* 339 U.S. 605, 609 (1950); *Abraxis Bioscience, Inc. v. Mayne Pharma (USA) Inc.*, 467 F.3d 1370, 1379-82 (Fed. Cir. 2006); *Pfizer, Inc. v. Teva Pharms., USA, Inc.*, 429 F.3d 1364, 1378 (Fed. Cir. 2005); *Johnston & Johnston Assoc. v. R.E. Service Co.,* 285 F.3d 1046 (Fed. Cir. 2002) (en banc); *Multiform Desiccants, Inc. v. Medzam, Ltd.*, 133 F.3d 1473, 1480 (Fed. Cir. 1998); *Dolly, Inc. v. Spalding & Evenflo Cos.*, 16 F.3d 394, 397 (Fed. Cir. 1994).
B.3. Infringement

---

5. If this instruction is applicable in a given case, then the court should instruct the jury that if [alleged infringer] has offered evidence sufficient to show that the accused [product] [method] is in the prior art, the burden shifts to the [patent holder] to prove that what it attempts to cover under the doctrine of equivalents is not in the prior art or would not have been obvious from the prior art. *See Fiskares, Inc. v. Hunt Mfg. Co.*, 221 F.3d 1318, 1323 (Fed. Cir. 2000); *Ultra-Tex Surfaces, Inc. v. Hill Bros. Chem. Co.*, 204 F.3d 1360, 1364-66 (Fed. Cir. 2000); *Streamfeeder, LLC v. Sure-Feed Sys., Inc.*, 175 F.3d 974, 981-84 (Fed. Cir. 1999).

3.5 MEANS-PLUS-FUNCTION CLAIMS – LITERAL INFRINGEMENT[6]

I will now describe the separate rules that apply to "means-plus-function" requirements that are used in some claims. Claims [ ] in the [ ] patent contain "means-plus-function" requirements. A means-plus-function requirement only covers the specific [structure] disclosed in a patent specification for performing the claimed function and the equivalents of those specific [structure] that perform the claimed function. A means-plus-function requirement does not cover all possible structures that could be used to perform the claimed function.

As an example, the term "means for processing data" might be understood to encompass a variety of different ways of making a calculation, including not only a computer or calculator but a pencil and paper or even the human brain. But because the phrase is a means-plus-function requirement, we interpret that phrase not to cover every possible means for processing data, but instead to cover the actual means disclosed in the patent for processing data and other means that are equivalent to it.

For purposes of this trial, I have interpreted each means-plus-function requirement for you and identified the structure in the patent specification that corresponds to these means-plus-function requirements. Specifically, I have determined that:

> [X. [ ] is the structure that perform[s] the [ ] function identified in the means- plus-function requirement of claim [ ].]

> [X. [ ] is the structure that perform[s] the [ ] function identified in the means- plus-function requirement of claim [ ].]

In deciding if [patent holder] has proven that [alleged infringer]'s [product] includes structure covered by a means-plus-function requirement, you must first decide whether the [product] has any structure that performs the function I just described to you. If not, the claim containing that means-plus-function requirement is not infringed.

If you find that the [alleged infringer]'s [accused product] does have structure that performs the claimed function, you must then determine whether that structure is the same as or equivalent to the structure I have identified in the specification. If they are the same or equivalent, the means- plus-function requirement is satisfied by that structure of the [accused product]. If all the other requirements of the claim are satisfied, the [accused product] infringes the claim.

---

6. If a claim at issue is a method claim with a limitation written in "step-plus-function" format, this instruction should be modified accordingly, for example, substituting "acts" for "structure."

In order to prove that [a structure] in the [accused product] is equivalent to the structure in the [ ] patent, the [patent holder] must show that a person of ordinary skill in the field would have considered that the differences between the structure described in the [ ] patent and the structure in the [accused product] are not substantial. The [patent holder] must also show that the structure was available on the date the [ ] patent was granted.[7]

Authorities

35 U.S.C. § 112(6); *Frank's Casing Crew & Rental Tools, Inc. v. Weatherford Int'l, Inc.*, 389 F.3d 1370, 1378 (Fed. Cir. 2004); *Odetics, Inc. v. Storage Tech. Corp.*, 185 F.3d 1259, 1266 (Fed. Cir. 1999); *Chiuminatta Concrete Concepts, Inc. v. Cardinal Indus., Inc.*, 145 F.3d 1303, 1307 (Fed. Cir. 1998); *Micro Chem., Inc. v. Great Plains Chem. Co., Inc.*, 103 F.3d 1538, 1547 (Fed. Cir. 1997); *Valmont Indus., Inc. v. Reinke Mfg. Co., Inc.*, 983 F.2d 1039, 1042 (Fed. Cir. 1993).

---

7. There is an important difference between what can be an equivalent under § 112(6) and what can be an equivalent under the doctrine of equivalents. An equivalent structure or act under § 112(6) cannot embrace technology developed after the issuance of the patent because the literal meaning of a claim is fixed upon its issuance. *Chiuminatta Concrete Concepts, Inc. v. Cardinal Indus., Inc.*, 145 F.3d 1303, 1310 (Fed. Cir. 1998); *Al-Site Corp. v. VSI Int'l, Inc.*, 174 F.3d 1308, 1320 (Fed. Cir. 1999). Although new matter cannot be added to a patent application after it has been filed, current Federal Circuit law nevertheless uses the patent issuance date, as opposed to the effective filing date, to distinguish what constitutes an "after arising equivalent." An after arising equivalent infringes, if at all, under the doctrine of equivalents and could infringe under the doctrine of equivalents and could infringe under the doctrine of equivalents without infringing literally under § 112(6). Furthermore, under § 112(6) the accused device must perform the identical function as recited in the claim element while the doctrine of equivalents may be satisfied when the function performed by the accused device is only substantially the same. *Al-Site*, 174 F3d. at 1320-21

B.3. Infringement

3.6 MEANS-PLUS-FUNCTION CLAIMS – INFRINGEMENT UNDER THE DOCTRINE OF EQUIVALENTS

[No model instruction is provided since an instruction on this subject is necessarily case specific. However, a means-plus-function requirement can be met under the doctrine of equivalents if the function is not the same but is equivalent (*see, e.g.*, *WMS Gaming Inc. v. Int'l Game Tech.*, 184 F.3d 1339, 1353 (Fed. Cir. 1999) or the corresponding structure in the accused product is later developed technology. *See Chiuminatta Concrete Concepts, Inc. v. Cardinal Indus., Inc.*, 145 F.3d 1303, 1310 (Fed. Cir. 1998); *Al-Site Corp. v. VSI Int'l, Inc.*, 174 F.3d 1308, 1320 (Fed. Cir. 1999).]

B.3. Infringement

3.7 LIMITATIONS ON THE DOCTRINE OF EQUIVALENTS

Because [patent holder] made certain claim changes or statements during the patent application process for the [   ] patent, the doctrine of equivalents analysis cannot be applied to the following requirements of the asserted claims:

[List requirements on a claim-by-claim basis]

Unless each of these requirements is literally present within the [alleged infringer]'s [product] [method], there can be no infringement of the claim.

Authorities

Honeywell Int'l Inc. v. Hamilton Sundstrand Corp., 370 F.3d 1131 (Fed. Cir. 2004) (en banc); *Festo Corp. v. Shoketsu Kinzoku Kogyo Kabushiki Co., Ltd.*, 344 F.3d (Fed. Cir. 2003) (en banc).

B.3. Infringement

3.8 CONTRIBUTORY INFRINGEMENT

[Patent holder] [also] argues that [alleged infringer] has contributed to infringement by another. Contributory infringement may arise when someone supplies something that is used to infringe one or more of the patent claims.

In order for there to be contributory infringement by [alleged infringer], someone other than [alleged infringer] must directly infringe a claim of the [ ] patent; if there is no direct infringement by anyone, there can be no contributory infringement.

If you find someone has directly infringed the [ ] patent, then contributory infringement exists if:

(1) [Alleged infringer] supplied an important component of the infringing part of the [product] or [method];

(2) The component is not a common component suitable for non-infringing use; and

(3) [Alleged infringer] supplied the component with the knowledge of the [ ] patent and knowledge that the component was especially made or adapted for use in an infringing manner.

A "common component suitable for non-infringing use" is a component that has uses [other than as a component of the patented product][other than in the patented method], and those other uses are not occasional, farfetched, impractical, experimental, or hypothetical.

Authorities

35 U.S.C. § 271(c); *PharmaStem Therapeutics, Inc. v. ViaCell, Inc. et. al.*, 491 F.3d 1342, 1356-58 (Fed. Cir. 2007); *Aro Mfg. Co. v. Convertible Top Replacement Co.*, 377 U.S. 476 (1964); *DSU Med. Corp. v. JMS Co.*, 471 F.3d 1293, 1303 (Fed. Cir. 2006); *Mentor H/S, Inc. v. Med. Device All., Inc.*, 244 F.3d 1365 (Fed. Cir. 2001); *Hewlett-Packard Co. v. Bausch & Lomb, Inc.*, 909 F.2d 1464, 1469 (Fed. Cir. 1990); *Preemption Devices, Inc. v. Minn. Mining & Mfr. Co.*, 803 F.2d 1170, 1174 (Fed. Cir. 1986).

B.3. Infringement

3.9 INDUCING PATENT INFRINGEMENT

[Patent holder] argues that [alleged infringer] has actively induced another to infringe the [ ] patent. In order for the [alleged infringer] to induce infringement, [alleged infringer] must have induced another to directly infringe a claim of the [ ] patent; if there is no direct infringement by anyone, there can be no induced infringement. In order to be liable for inducement of infringement, [alleged infringer][8] must:

1. have intentionally taken action that actually induced direct infringement;
2. have been aware of the [ ] patent;
3. have known that the acts it was causing would infringe the patent; and
4. not have had a good faith belief the patent was invalid.

If the four requirements just stated are not met, [alleged infringer] cannot be liable for inducement unless it actually believed that it was highly probable its actions would encourage infringement of a patent it believed to be valid and that it deliberately chose to avoid learning the truth. To prove inducement, it is not enough that [accused infringer] was merely indifferent to the possibility that its actions might encourage infringement of a valid patent. Nor is it enough that [accused infringer] took a risk that was substantial and unjustified.

In deciding whether the [alleged infringer] induced infringement, you may consider whether [accused infringer] actually believed that the acts it encouraged did not infringe the patent[, and whether [accused infringer] had a good-faith belief that the patent would be held invalid][, and whether [alleged infringer] relied on advice given by its lawyers].

<u>Authorities</u>

35 U.S.C. § 271(b): *Global-Tech Appliances, Inc. et al. v. SEB S.A.*, 131 S.Ct. 2060, ___ (2011); *DSU Med. Corp. v. JMS Co.*, 471 F.3d 1293, 1304-06 (Fed. Cir. 2006) (en banc) (quoting *Metro-Goldwyn-Mayer Studios Inc. v. Grokster, Ltd.*, 545 U.S. 913, 936 (2005)); *Broadcom Corp. v. Qualcomm, Inc.*, 543 F.3d 683 (Fed. Cir. 2008); *Limelight Networks, Inc. v. Akamai Techs.*, 134 S.Ct. 2111, 572 U.S. ___ (2014); *Commil USA v. Cisco Sys.*, 720 F.3d 1361 (Fed. Cir. 2013).

---

8. [Alleged Infringer] in this instance refers to the alleged inducer infringer, not the alleged direct infringer.

B.3. Infringement

3.10 WILLFUL INFRINGEMENT

In this case, [patent holder] argues that [alleged infringer] willfully infringed the [patent holder]'s patent.

To prove willful infringement, [patent holder] must first persuade you that the [alleged infringer] infringed a valid [and enforceable] claim of the [patent holder]'s patent. The requirements for proving such infringement were discussed in my prior instructions.

In addition, to prove willful infringement, the [patent holder] must persuade you that it is highly probable that [alleged infringer] acted with reckless disregard of the claims of the [patent holder]'s [patent].

To demonstrate such "reckless disregard," [patent holder] must persuade you that [alleged infringer] actually knew, or it was so obvious that [alleged infringer] should have known, that its actions constituted infringement of a valid [and enforceable] patent.

In deciding whether [alleged infringer] acted with reckless disregard for [patent holder]'s patent, you should consider all of the facts surrounding the alleged infringement including, but not limited to, the following factors.

Factors that may be considered as evidence that [alleged infringer] was not willful include:

(1) Whether [alleged infringer] acted in a manner consistent with the standards of commerce for its industry; [and]

(2) Although there is no obligation to obtain an opinion of counsel whether [alleged infringer] relied on a legal opinion that was well-supported and believable and that advised [alleged infringer] (1) that the [product] [method] did not infringe [patent holder]'s patent or (2) that the patent was invalid [or unenforceable].[9]

Factors that may be considered as evidence that [alleged infringer] was willful include:

---

9. This bracketed language should only be included if the alleged infringer relies on advice of counsel. There is no affirmative obligation to obtain opinion of counsel. *In re Seagate Tech., LLC*, 497 F.3d 1360 (Fed. Cir. 2007) (en banc).

(1) Whether [alleged infringer] intentionally copied a product of [patent holder] covered by the patent.

Authorities

35 U.S.C. § 284; *In re Seagate Tech., LLC*, 497 F.3d 1360 (Fed. Cir. 2007); *Knorr-Bremse Systeme Fuer Nutzfahrzeuge GmbH v. Dana Corp.*, 383 F.3d 1337, 1345 (Fed. Cir. 2004) (en banc); *Crystal Semiconductor Corp. v. Tritech Microelectronics Int'l, Inc.*, 246 F.3d 1336, 1346 (Fed. Cir. 2001); *WMS Gaming Inc. v. Int'l Game Tech.*, 184 F.3d 1339, 1354 (Fed. Cir. 1999); *Read Corp. v. Portec, Inc.*, 970 F.2d 816 (Fed. Cir. 1992); *Gustafson, Inc. v. Intersystems Indus. Prods., Inc.*, 897 F.2d 508, 510 (Fed. Cir. 1990).

[Note to judges: the Federal Circuit has held that "the judge may when the defense is a question of fact or a mixed question of law and fact allow the jury to determine the underlying facts relevant to the defense in the first instance, for example, the questions of anticipation or obviousness. But, consistent with this court's holding today, the ultimate legal question of whether a reasonable person would have considered there to be a high likelihood of infringement of a valid patent should always be decided as a matter of law by the judge." *Bard Peripheral Vascular v. W.L. Gore & Assocs.*, 682 F.3d 1003 (Fed. Cir. 2012). So the jury's finding on the subjective prong *does not mean* that infringement was willful; it is the obligation of the judge to independently evaluate the objective basis for the underlying defense.]

B.4.1 Validity

4.1 INVALIDITY – BURDEN OF PROOF

I will now instruct you on the rules you must follow in deciding whether [alleged infringer] has proven that claims [ ] of the [ ] patent are invalid. Before discussing the specific rules, I want to remind you about the standard of proof that applies to this defense. To prove invalidity of any patent claim, [alleged infringer] must persuade you that it is highly probable that the claim is invalid.

[During this case, the [alleged infringer] has submitted prior art that was not considered by the United States Patent and Trademark Office (PTO) during the prosecution of the [ ] patent. The [alleged infringer] contends that such prior art invalidates certain claims of the [ ] patent. In deciding the issue of invalidity, you may take into account the fact that the prior art was not considered by the PTO when it issued the [ ] patent. Prior art that differs from the prior art considered by the PTO may carry more weight than the prior art that was considered and may make the [alleged infringer's] burden of showing that it is highly probable that a patent claim is invalid easier to sustain.

<u>Authorities</u>

Microsoft Corp. v. i4i Ltd. P'ship, 131 S.Ct. 2238, 2242, 2251, ___ U.S.____ (2011); *Buildex. Inc. v. Kason Indus., Inc.*, 849 F.2d 1461, 1463 (Fed. Cir. 1988); *Hybritech, Inc. v. Monoclonal Antibodies, Inc.*, 802 F.2d 1367, 1375 (Fed. Cir. 1986).

B.4.2 Validity—Adequacy of Patent Specification

4.2a WRITTEN DESCRIPTION REQUIREMENT

A patent claim is invalid if the patent does not contain an adequate written description of the claimed invention. The purpose of this written description requirement is to demonstrate that the inventor was in possession of the invention at the time the application for the patent was filed, even though the claims may have been changed or new claims added since that time. The written description requirement is satisfied if a person of ordinary skill in the field reading the original patent application at the time it was filed would have recognized that the patent application described the invention as claimed, even though the description may not use the exact words found in the claim. A requirement in a claim need not be specifically disclosed in the patent application as originally filed if a person of ordinary skill would understand that the missing requirement is necessarily implied in the patent application as originally filed.

Authorities

35 U.S.C. § 112(1) and (2); *In Re Skvorecz,* 580 F.3d 1262, 1269 (Fed. Cir. 2009); *Kao Corp. v. Unilever U.S., Inc.*, 441 F.3d 963, 968 (Fed. Cir. 2006); *Chiron Corp. v. Genentech, Inc.*, 363 F.3d 1247 (Fed. Cir. 2004); *Purdue Pharma L.P. v. Faulding, Inc.*, 230 F.3d 1320, 1323 (Fed. Cir. 2000); *Lampi Corp. v. Am. Power Prods., Inc.*, 228 F.3d 1365, 1377-78 (Fed. Cir. 2000); *Gentry Gallery, Inc. v. Berkline Corp.*, 134 F.3d 1473, 1478-80 (Fed. Cir. 1998); *In re Alton*, 76 F.3d 1168, 1172 (Fed. Cir. 1996); *Univ. of Rochester v. G.D. Searle & Co.,* 358 F.3d 916, 926-928 (Fed. Cir. 2004).

B.4.2 Validity—Adequacy of Patent Specification

4.2b ENABLEMENT

A patent claim is invalid if the patent at the time it was originally filed did not contain a description of the claimed invention that is sufficiently full and clear to enable a person of ordinary skill in the field at the time to make and use the full scope of the invention. This is known as the "enablement" requirement.

The patent may be enabling even though it does not expressly state some information if a person of ordinary skill in the field could make and use the invention without having to do excessive experimentation. In determining whether excessive experimentation is required, you may consider the following factors:

the scope of the claimed invention;

the amount of guidance presented in the patent;

the amount of experimentation necessary;

the time and cost of any necessary experimentation;

how routine any necessary experimentation is in the field of [identify field]; whether the patent discloses specific working examples of the claimed invention; the nature and predictability of the field; and

the level of ordinary skill in the field of [identity field].

The question of whether a patent is enabling is judged as of the date the original application for the patent was first filed.[10]

Authorities

35 U.S.C. § 112(1); *Sitrick v. Dreamworks, LLC,* 516 F.3d 993, 999 (Fed. Cir. 2008); *Auto. Techs. Int'l, Inc. v. BMW of N. Am., Inc.,* 501 F.3d 1274, 1285 (Fed. Cir. 2007); *AK Steel Corp. v. Sollac & Ugine,* 344 F.3d 1234, 1244 (Fed. Cir. 2003); *Union Pac. Res. Co. v. Chesapeake Energy Corp.*, 236 F.3d 684, 690–92 (Fed. Cir. 2001); *Ajinomoto Co. v. Archer-Daniels-Midland Co.*, 228 F.3d 1338, 1345–46 (Fed. Cir. 2000); *In re Wands,* 858 F.2d 731, 737 (Fed. Cir. 1988).

---

10. Where a claim is the result of a continuation-in-part application and the priority date is disputed, this language will need to be revised to reflect the concept of effective filing date.

B.4.2 Validity—Adequacy of Patent Specification

4.2c BEST MODE[11]

A patent claim is invalid if the patent does not disclose what [the inventor] [any of the inventors] believed was the best way to carry out the claimed invention at the time the patent application was filed. This is known as the "best mode" requirement. It ensures that the public obtains a full disclosure of the best way to carry out the claimed invention known to [the inventor] [any of the inventors] at the time the [original] patent application was first filed. The disclosure of the best mode must be detailed enough to enable the persons of ordinary skill in the field of [identity] field to carry out that best mode without excessive experimentation.

The best mode requirement focuses on what [the inventor] [any of the inventors] believed at the time the [original] patent application was first filed. It does not matter whether the best mode contemplated by [the inventor] [any of the inventors] was, in fact, the best way to carry out the invention. The question is whether the patent includes what [the inventor] [any of the inventors] believed was the best mode at the time the [original] patent application was filed. If [the inventor did not believe] [none of the inventors believed] there was a best way to carry out the invention at the time that application was filed, there is no requirement that the patent describe a best mode. Although a patent specification must disclose the best mode, it may disclose other modes as well and need not state which of the modes disclosed is best. If [the inventor] [any of the inventors] believed there was a better way to carry out the invention and the patent does not disclose it, the patent is invalid.

<u>Authorities</u>

35 U.S.C. § 112(1); *Pfizer, Inc. v. Teva Pharms. USA, Inc.*, 518 F.3d 1353, 1364–64 (Fed. Cir. 2008); *Cardiac Pacemaker, Inc. v. St. Jude Medical, Inc.*, 381 F.3d 1371, 1378–79 (Fed. Cir. 2004); *Glaxo Inc. v. Novopharm Ltd.*, 52 F.3d 1043, 1049–52 (Fed. Cir. 1995); *Transco Prods. v. Performance Contracting*, 38 F.3d 551 (Fed. Cir. 1994); *Wahl Instruments v. Acvious*, 950 F.2d 1575 (Fed. Cir. 1991); *Chemcast Corp. v. Arco Indus. Corp.*, 913 F.2d 923, 926–28 (Fed. Cir. 1990); *Spectra-Physics Inc. v. Coherent, Inc.*, 827 F.2d 1524 (Fed. Cir. 1987).

---

11. Applies only to civil actions commenced prior to September 16, 2011, the enactment date of the AIA. For civil actions commenced on or after September 16, 2011, Section 15 of the AIA (amended 35 U.S.C. § 282) provides"that the failure to disclose the best mode shall not be a basis on which any claim of a patent may be ... held invalid."

B.4.3 Validity—The Claims

4.3a1 ANTICIPATION[12]

A patent claim is invalid if the claimed invention is not new. For the claim to be invalid because it is not new, all of its requirements must have existed in a single device or method that predates the claimed invention, or must have been described in a single previous publication or patent that predates the claimed invention. In patent law, these previous devices, methods, publications or patents are called "prior art references." If a patent claim is not new we say it is "anticipated" by a prior art reference.

The description in the written reference does not have to be in the same words as the claim, but all of the requirements of the claim must be there, either stated or necessarily implied, so that someone of ordinary skill in the field of [identify field] looking at that one reference would be able to make and use the claimed invention.

Here is a list of the ways that [alleged infringer] can show that a patent claim was not new [use those that apply to this case]:

> [– if the claimed invention was already publicly known or publicly used by others in the United States before [insert date of conception unless at issue];]
>
> [– if the claimed invention was already patented or described in a printed publication anywhere in the world before [insert date of conception unless at issue]. [A reference is a "printed publication" if it is accessible to those interested in the field, even if it is difficult to find.];]
>
> [– if the claimed invention was already made by someone else in the United States before [insert date of conception unless in issue], if that other person had not abandoned the invention or kept it secret;]
>
> [– if the claimed invention was already described in another issued U.S. patent or published U.S. patent application that was based on a patent application filed before [insert date of the patent holder's application filing date] [or] [insert date of conception unless at issue];]
>
> [– if [named inventor] did not invent the claimed invention but instead learned of the claimed invention from someone else;]

---

12. This Section 4.3a1 is inapplicable to any post-AIA claims, i.e., to any claimed invention having an effective filing date on or after March 16, 2013.

[– if the [patent holder] and [alleged infringer] dispute who is a first inventor, the person who first conceived of the claimed invention and first reduced it to practice is the first inventor. If one person conceived of the claimed invention first, but reduced to practice second, that person is the first inventor only if that person (a) began to reduce the claimed invention to practice before the other party conceived of it and (b) continued to work diligently to reduce it to practice. [A claimed invention is "reduced to practice" when it has been tested sufficiently to show that it will work for its intended purpose or when it is fully described in a patent application filed with the PTO].]

[Since it is in dispute, you must determine a date of conception for the [claimed invention] [and/or] [prior invention]. Conception is the mental part of an inventive act and is proven when the invention is shown in its complete form by drawings, disclosure to another or other forms of evidence presented at trial.]

Authorities

35 U.S.C. § 102(a), (c), (e), (f) and (g); *Flex-Rest, LLC v. Steelcase, Inc.*, 455 F.3d 1351, 1358–60 (Fed. Cir. 2006); *Invitrogen Corp. v. Biocrest Mfg., L.P.*, 424 F.3d 1374, 1379–82 (Fed. Cir. 2005); *Apotex U.S.A., Inc. v. Merck & Co.*, 254 F.3d 1031, 1035 (Fed. Cir. 2001); *Mycogen Plant Sci., Inc. v. Monsanto Co.*, 243 F.3d 1316, 1330 (Fed. Cir. 2001); *Ecolochem, Inc. v. S. Cal. Edison Co.*, 227 F.3d 1361, 1367–70 (Fed. Cir. 2000); *Singh v. Brake*, 222 F.3d 1362, 1366–70 (Fed. Cir. 2000); *Pannu v. Iolab Corp.*, 155 F.3d 1344, 1349 (Fed. Cir. 1998); *Gambro Lundia AB v. Baxter Healthcare Corp.*, 110 F.3d 1573, 1576–78 (Fed. Cir. 1997); *Lamb-Weston, Inc. v. McCain Foods, Ltd.*, 78 F.3d 540, 545 (Fed. Cir. 1996); *In re Bartfeld*, 925 F.2d 1450 (Fed. Cir. 1985); *Ralston Purina Co. v. Far-Mar-Co, Inc.*, 772 F.2d 1570, 1574 (Fed. Cir. 1985); *Am. Stock Exch., LLC v. Mopies*, 250 F. Supp. 2d 323 (S.D.N.Y. 2003); *In re Wyer*, 655 F.2d 221, 226 (C.C.P.A. 1981).

B.4.3 Validity—The Claims

4.3a2 STATUTORY BARS[13]

A patent claim is invalid if the patent application was not filed within the time required by law. This is called a "statutory bar." For a patent claim to be invalid by a statutory bar, all of its requirements must have been present in one prior art reference dated more than one year before the patent application was filed. Here is a list of ways [alleged infringer] can show that the patent application was not timely filed: [choose those that apply]

[– if the claimed invention was already patented or described in a printed publication anywhere in the world before [insert date that is one year before effective filing date of patent application]. [A reference is a "printed publication" if it is accessible to those interested in the field, even if it is difficult to find.];]

[– if the claimed invention was already being openly used in the United States before [insert date that is one year before application filing date] and that use was not primarily an experimental use (a) controlled by the inventor, and (b) to test whether the invention worked for its intended purpose;]

[– if a device or method using the claimed invention was sold or offered for sale in the United States, and that claimed invention was ready for patenting, before [insert date that is one year before application filing date]. [The claimed invention is not being [sold] [or] [offered for sale] if the [patent holder] shows that the [sale] [or] [offer for sale] was primarily experimental.] [The claimed invention is ready for patenting if it was actually built, or if the inventor had prepared drawings or other descriptions of the claimed invention that were sufficiently detailed to enable a person of ordinary skill in the field to make and use the invention based on them.];]

[– if the [patent holder] had already obtained a patent on the claimed invention in a foreign country before filing the original U.S. application, and the foreign application was filed at least one year before the U.S. application.]

For a claim to be invalid because of a statutory bar, all of the claimed requirements must have been either (1) disclosed in a single prior art reference, (2) implicitly disclosed in a reference to one skilled in the field, or (3) must have been present in

---

13. This Section 4.3a2 is inapplicable to any post-AIA claims, i.e., to any claimed invention having an effective filing date on or after March 16, 2013.

the reference, whether or not that was understood at the time. The disclosure in a reference does not have to be in the same words as the claim, but all the requirements must be there, either described in enough detail or necessarily implied, to enable someone of ordinary skill in the field of [identify field] looking at the reference to make and use the claimed invention.

Authorities

35 U.S.C. § 102(b) and (d); *Pfaff v. Wells Elec. Inc.*, 525 U.S. 55 (1998); *Schering Corp. v. Geneva Pharms.*, 339 F.2d 1273 (Fed Cir. 2003); *Helifix Ltd. v. Blok-Lok, Ltd.*, 208 F.3d 1339, 1346 (Fed. Cir. 2000); *Abbot Labs. v. Geneva Pharms., Inc.*, 182 F.3d 1315, 1318 (Fed. Cir. 1999); *Finnigan Corp. v. Int'l Trade Comm'n*, 180 F.3d 1354 (Fed. Cir. 1999); *J.A. LaPorte, Inc. v. Norfolk Dredging Co.*, 787 F.2d 1577, 1581 (Fed. Cir. 1986); *In re Hall*, 781 F.2d 897, 898–99 (Fed. Cir. 1986); *D.L. Auld Co. v. Chroma Graphics Corp.*, 714 F.2d 1144, 1150 (Fed. Cir. 1983).

B.4.3 Validity—The Claims

4.3b OBVIOUSNESS[14] – (Alternative 1)

Not all innovations are patentable. A patent claim is invalid if the claimed invention would have been obvious to a person of ordinary skill in the field [at the time the application was filed][as of [insert date]]. The court, however, is charged with the responsibility of making the determination as to whether a patent claim was obvious based upon your determination of several factual questions.

First, you must decide the level of ordinary skill in the field that someone would have had [at the time the claimed invention was made] [as of the effective filing date of the claimed invention][16][15]. In deciding the level of ordinary skill, you should consider all the evidence introduced at trial, including:

(1) the levels of education and experience of persons working in the field;
(2) the types of problems encountered in the field; and
(3) the sophistication of the technology.

[Patent holder] contends that the level of ordinary skill in the field was [ ]. [Alleged infringer] contends that the level of ordinary skill in the field was [ ].

Second, you must decide the scope and content of the prior art. [Patent holder] and [alleged infringer] disagree as to whether [identify prior art reference(s)] should be included in the prior art you use to decide the validity of claims [ ] of the [ ] patent. In order to be considered as prior art to the [ ] patent, these references must be reasonably related to the claimed invention of that patent. A

---

14. This instruction provides the jury with an instruction on the underlying factual questions it must answer to enable the court to make the ultimate legal determination of the obviousness question. The court, not the jury, should make the legal conclusion on the obviousness question based on underlying factual determinations made by the jury. *KSR Int'l Co. v. Teleflex, Inc.*, 550 U.S. 398, 427 (2007)("The ultimate judgment of obviousness is a legal determination."); *see Dippin' Dots, Inc. v. Mosey*, 476 F.3d 1337, 1343 (Fed. Cir. 2007). It is anticipated that these factual issues will be presented to the jury as specifically as possible. For example, if the only dispute between the parties is whether a particular reference is with the "scope and content" of the prior art, that is the only *Graham* factor that should be presented to the jury. As another example, if the only factual dispute between the parties on the "difference between the prior art and the claimed invention" is whether a prior art reference discloses a particular claim limitation, that is the only issue that should be presented to the jury on that *Graham* factor. The introductory comment to the sample verdict form discusses further the functions of the judge and jury in determining obviousness.

15. The "effective filing date of the claimed invention" option is applicable to any post-AIA claims, i.e., to any claimed invention having an effective filing date on or after March 16, 2013.

reference is reasonably related if it is in the same field as the claimed invention or is from another field to which a person of ordinary skill in the field would look to solve a known problem.

Third, you must decide what difference, if any, existed between the claimed invention and the prior art.

Finally, you must determine which, if any, of the following factors have been established by the evidence:

[(1) commercial success of a product due to the merits of the claimed invention];]
[(2) a long felt need for the solution provided by the claimed invention];]
[(3) unsuccessful attempts by others to find the solution provided by the claimed invention[;]
[(4) copying of the claimed invention by others];]
[(5) unexpected and superior results from the claimed invention]]
[(6) acceptance by others of the claimed invention as shown by praise from others in the field or from the licensing of the claimed invention];]
[(7) other evidence tending to show nonobviousness];]
[(8) independent invention of the claimed invention by others before or at about the same time as the named inventor thought of it]; and]
[(9) other evidence tending to show obviousness].]

Authorities

35 U.S.C. § 103; *Graham v. John Deere Co.*, 383 U.S. 1 (1966); *KSR Int'l Co. v. Teleflex, Inc.*, 550 U.S. 398, 407 (2007); *Ruiz v. A.B. Chance Co.*, 234 F.3d 654 (Fed. Cir. 2000); *Arkie Lures, Inc. v. Gene Larew Tackle, Inc.*, 119 F.3d 953, 957 (Fed. Cir. 1997); *Specialty Composites v. Cabot Corp.*, 845 F.2d 981, 991 (Fed. Cir. 1988); *Windsurfing Int'l, Inc. v. AMF, Inc.*, 782 F.2d 995, 1000 (Fed. Cir. 1986); *Pentec. Inc. v. Graphic Controls Corp.*, 776 F.2d 309, 313 (Fed. Cir. 1985). *See Novo Nordisk A/S v. Becton Dickinson & Co.*, 304 F.3d 1216, 1219–20 (Fed. Cir. 2002); *Wang Labs. v. Toshiba Corp.*, 993 F.2d 858, 864 (Fed. Cir. 1993); *Daiichi Sankyo Co. v. Apotex, Inc.*, 501 F.3d. 1254, 1256 (Fed. Cir. 2007); *Brown & Williamson Tobacco Corp. v. Philip Morris Inc.*, 229 F.3d 1120, 1125 (Fed. Cir. 2000); *SIBIA Neurosciences, Inc. v. Cadus Pharm. Corp.*, 225 F.3d 1349, 1355 (Fed. Cir. 2000); *Ryko Mfg. Co. v. Nu-Star, Inc.*, 950 F.2d 714, 718–19 (Fed. Cir. 1991).

4.3b OBVIOUSNESS[16] – (Alternative 2)

Not all innovations are patentable. A patent claim is invalid if the claimed invention would have been obvious to a person of ordinary skill in the field [at the time the claimed invention was made] [as of the effective filing date of the claimed invention][17] [as of [insert date]]. This means that even if all of the requirements of the claim cannot be found in a single prior art reference that would anticipate the claim or constitute a statutory bar to that claim, a person of ordinary skill in the field of [identify field] who knew about all this prior art would have come up with the claimed invention.

The ultimate conclusion of whether a claim is obvious should be based upon your determination of several factual decisions.

First, you must decide the level of ordinary skill in the field that someone would have had [at the time the claimed invention was made] [as of the effective filing date of the claimed invention]. In deciding the level of ordinary skill, you should consider all the evidence introduced at trial, including:

(1) the levels of education and experience of persons working in the field;
(2) the types of problems encountered in the field; and
(3) the sophistication of the technology.

[Patent holder] contends that the level of ordinary skill in the field was [ ]. [Alleged infringer] contends that the level of ordinary skill in the field was [ ].

Second, you must decide the scope and content of the prior art. [Patent holder] and [alleged infringer] disagree as to whether [identify prior art reference(s)] should be included in the prior art you use to decide the validity of claims [ ] of the [ ] patent. In order to be considered as prior art to the [ ] patent, these references must be reasonably related to the claimed invention of that patent. A ref-

---

16. This instruction provides the jury with an instruction on how to analyze the obviousness question and reach a conclusion on it in the event that the Court decides to allow the jury to render an advisory verdict on the ultimate question of obviousness. However, the court, not the jury, should make the legal conclusion on the obviousness question based on underlying factual determinations made by the jury. *KSR Int'l Co. v. Teleflex, Inc.*, 550 U.S. 398, 427(2007) ("The ultimate judgment of obviousness is a legal determination."); *see Dippin' Dots, Inc. v. Mosey*, 476 F.3d 1337, 1343 (Fed. Cir. 2007). The introductory comment to the sample verdict form discusses further the functions of the judge and jury in determining obviousness.

17. The "effective filing date of the claimed invention" option is applicable to any post-AIA claims, i.e., to any claimed invention having an effective filing date on or after March 16, 2013.

erence is reasonably related if it is in the same field as the claimed invention or is from another field to which a person of ordinary skill in the field would look to solve a known problem.

Third, you must decide what difference, if any, existed between the claimed invention and the prior art.

Finally, you should consider any of the following factors that you find have been shown by the evidence:

[(1) commercial success of a product due to the merits of the claimed invention];]
[(2) a long felt need for the solution provided by the claimed invention];]
[(3) unsuccessful attempts by others to find the solution provided by the claimed invention];]
[(4) copying of the claimed invention by others];]
[(5) unexpected and superior results from the claimed invention];]
[(6) acceptance by others of the claimed invention as shown by praise from others in the field or from the licensing of the claimed invention];]
[(7) other evidence tending to show nonobviousness];]
[(8) independent invention of the claimed invention by others before or at about the same time as the named inventor thought of it] [; and]
[(9) other evidence tending to show obviousness].]

[The presence of any of the [list factors 1–7 as appropriate] may be considered by you as an indication that the claimed invention would not have been obvious [at the time the claimed invention was made] [as of the effective filing date of the claimed invention], and the presence of the [list factors 8–9 as appropriate] may be considered by you as an indication that the claimed invention would have been obvious at such time. Although you should consider any evidence of these factors, the relevance and importance of any of them to your decision on whether the claimed invention would have been obvious is up to you.]

A patent claim composed of several elements is not proved obvious merely by demonstrating that each of its elements was independently known in the prior art. In evaluating whether such a claim would have been obvious, you may consider whether [the alleged infringer] has identified a reason that would have prompted a person of ordinary skill in the field to combine the elements or concepts from the prior art in the same way as in the claimed invention. There is no single way to define the line between true inventiveness on the one hand (which is patentable) and the application of common sense and ordinary skill to solve a problem on the other hand (which is not patentable). For example, market forces or other design incentives may be what produced a change, rather than true inventiveness. You may consider whether the change was merely the predictable result of using prior art elements according to their known functions, or whether it was the result of true inventiveness. You may also consider whether there is some teaching or suggestion in the prior art to make the modification or combination of elements claimed in the patent. Also, you may consider whether the innovation applies a known technique that had been used to improve a similar device or method in a similar way. You may also consider whether the claimed invention would have been obvious to try, meaning that the claimed innovation was one of a relatively small number of possible approaches to the problem with a reasonable expectation of success by those skilled in the art. However, you must be careful not to determine obviousness using the benefit of hindsight; many true inventions might seem obvious after the fact. You should put yourself in the position of a person of ordinary skill in the field [at the time the claimed invention was made] [as of the effective filing date of the claimed invention] and you should not consider what is known today or what is learned from the teaching of the patent.

Authorities

35 U.S.C. § 103; *Graham v. John Deere Co.*, 383 U.S. 1 (1966); *KSR Int'l Co. v. Teleflex, Inc.*, 550 U.S. 398, 407 (2007); *Ruiz v. A.B. Chance Co.*, 234 F.3d 654 (Fed. Cir. 2000); *Arkie Lures, Inc. v. Gene Larew Tackle, Inc.*, 119 F.3d 953, 957 (Fed. Cir. 1997); *Specialty Composites v. Cabot Corp.*, 845 F.2d 981, 991 (Fed. Cir. 1988); *Windsurfing Int'l, Inc. v. AMF, Inc.*, 782 F.2d 995, 1000 (Fed. Cir. 1986); *Pentec. Inc. v. Graphic Controls Corp.*, 776 F.2d 309, 313 (Fed. Cir. 1985). *See Novo Nordisk A/S v. Becton Dickinson & Co.*, 304 F.3d 1216, 1219–20 (Fed. Cir. 2002); *Wang Labs. v. Toshiba Corp.*, 993 F.2d 858, 864 (Fed. Cir. 1993); *Daiichi Sankyo Co. v. Apotex, Inc.*, 501 F.3d. 1254, 1256 (Fed. Cir. 2007); *Brown & Williamson Tobacco Corp. v. Philip Morris Inc.*, 229 F.3d 1120, 1125 (Fed. Cir. 2000); *SIBIA Neurosciences, Inc. v. Cadus Pharm. Corp.*, 225 F.3d 1349, 1355 (Fed. Cir. 2000); *Ryko Mfg. Co. v. Nu-Star, Inc.*, 950 F.2d 714, 718–19 (Fed. Cir. 1991).

B.4.3 Validity—The Claims

4.3c INVENTORSHIP

[[Alleged infringer] can meet its burden of proving that a patent is invalid by showing that it fails to name all actual inventors and only the actual inventors. This is known as the "inventorship" requirement.]

or

[To obtain correction of the inventors listed on the patent, or to prove a claim for [type of state law claim that requires proof of patent law inventorship], [plaintiff] must show that it is highly probable that [s]he is an actual inventor of the patent.][18]

To be an inventor, one must make a significant contribution to the conception of one or more claims of the patent.[19] Persons may be inventors even though they do not physically work together or make the same type or amount of contribution, or contribute to the subject matter of each claim of the patent. However, merely helping with experimentation by carrying out the actual inventor's instructions or explaining the actual inventor's well-known concepts or the current state of the art does not make someone an inventor.

Authorities

35 U.S.C. § 102(f) and 35 U.S.C. § 256; *Pannu v. Iolab Corp.*, 155 F.3d 1344, 1349–50 (Fed. Cir. 1998); *Hess v. Advanced Cardiovascular Sys.*, 106 F.3d 976, 980 (Fed. Cir. 1997); *Burroughs Wellcome Co. v. Barr Lab.*, 40 F.3d 1223, 1227–28 (Fed. Cir.

---

18. The former paragraph is appropriate where the defendant in an infringement suit claims that the patent is invalid for failure to name the correct inventors. The latter paragraph is appropriate when a plaintiff brings state-law claims that depend on the plaintiff proving his or her status as an inventor. *Shum v. Intel Corp.*, 499 F.3d 1272 (Fed. Cir. 2007). Those claims must apply the federal patent law standard. *Univ. of Colo. Found. v. Am. Cyanamid*, 196 F.3d 1366 (Fed. Cir. 1999). Fraud and unjust enrichment claims are examples, if the basis of the claim is that the plaintiff in fact invented the subject matter of the patent. Correction of inventorship is not an issue for the jury, and may be ordered in one set of circumstances if the omission of an inventor is without deceptive intention, but not in another set of circumstances. *Stark v. Advanced Magnetics, Inc., et al.*, 119 F.3d 1551 (Fed Cir. 1997).

19. Alleged infringer, in order to meet its burden of proof, must present corroborating evidence of a contemporaneous disclosure that would enable one skilled in the field to make the claimed invention. Corroborating evidence may take many forms and is evaluated under a rule of reason analysis. The court should tailor instructions to the specific facts of the case. *See Linear Tech. Corp. v. Impala Linear Corp.*, 379 F.3d 1311 (Fed. Cir. 2004); *Univ. of Colo. Found., Inc. v. Am. Cyanimid Co.*, 342 F.3d 1298 (Fed. Cir. 2003).

1994); *Shatterproof Glass Corp. v. Libbey-Owens Ford Co.*, 758 F.2d 613, 624 (Fed. Cir. 1985).

B.5. Patent Damages

5.1 DAMAGES – BURDEN OF PROOF

I will instruct you about the measure of damages. By instructing you on damages, I am not suggesting which party should win on any issue. If you find that [alleged infringer] infringed any valid claim of the [ ] patent, you must then determine the amount of money damages to be awarded to [patent holder] to compensate it for the infringement.

The amount of those damages must be adequate to compensate [patent holder] for the infringement. A damages award should put the patent holder in approximately the financial position it would have been in had the infringement not occurred, but in no event may the damages award be less than a reasonable royalty. You should keep in mind that the damages you award are meant to compensate the patent holder and not to punish an infringer.

[Patent holder] has the burden to persuade you of the amount of its damages. You should award only those damages that [patent holder] more likely than not suffered. While [patent holder] is not required to prove its damages with mathematical precision, it must prove them with reasonable certainty. [Patent holder] is not entitled to damages that are remote or speculative.

Authorities

35 U.S.C. § 284; *Dow Chem. Co. v. Mee Indus., Inc.*, 341 F.3d 1370, 1381–82 (Fed. Cir. 2003); *Grain Processing Corp. v. Am. Maize-Prod. Co.*, 185 F.3d 1341, 1349 (Fed. Cir. 1999); *Maxwell v. J. Baker, Inc.*, 86 F.3d 1098, 1108–09 (Fed. Cir. 1996); *Rite-Hite Corp. v. Kelley Co.*, 56 F.3d 1538, 1544–45 (Fed. Cir. 1995) (en banc).

B.5. Patent Damages

5.2 LOST PROFITS - GENERALLY

In this case, [patent holder] seeks to recover lost profits for some of [alleged infringer]'s sales of [infringing product], and a reasonable royalty on the rest of [alleged infringer]'s sales.

To recover lost profits for infringing sales, [patent holder] must show that but for the infringement there is a reasonable probability that it would have made sales that [alleged infringer] made of the infringing product. [Patent holder] must show the share of [alleged infringer]'s sales that it would have made if the infringing product had not been on the market.

Authorities

Aro Mfg. Co. v. Convertible Top Co., 377 U.S. 476, 502–07 (1964); *Beauregard v. Mega Sys., LLC*, 350 F.3d 1327, 1345–46 (Fed. Cir. 2003); *Central Soya Co. v. George A. Hormel & Co.*, 723 F.2d 1573, 1579 (Fed. Cir. 1983); *Lam, Inc. v. Johns-Manville Corp.*, 718 F.2d 1056, 1065 (Fed. Cir. 1983); *Versata Software, Inc. v. SAP Am., Inc.*, 717 F.3d 1255, 1265 (Fed. Cir. 2013); *Presidio Components, Inc. v. Am. Tech. Ceramics Corp.*, 702 F.3d 1351, 1360 (Fed. Cir. 2012).

B.5. Patent Damages

5.3 LOST PROFITS – FACTORS TO CONSIDER

[Patent holder] is entitled to lost profits if it proves all of the following:

(1) that there was a demand for the patented [product] [method] [product produced by the method];

(2) that there were no acceptable non-infringing substitutes for the [product] [method] for which [patent holder] seeks lost profits, or, if there were, the number of sales made by [alleged infringer] that [patent holder] would have made despite the availability of any acceptable non-infringing substitutes. An acceptable non- infringing substitute may involve modifying the [alleged infringer's] product to avoid infringement by adding an available alternative or by removing the patented feature from the product altogether.

An alternative may be considered available as a potential substitute even if it was not actually on sale during the infringement period. Factors suggesting that the alternative was available include whether the material, experience, and know-how for the alleged substitute were readily available and potential customers would have believed that the alternative was an acceptable substitute. Factors suggesting that the alternative was not available include whether the material was of such high cost as to render the alternative unavailable, whether potential customers would have believed that the alternative was an acceptable substitute and whether [alleged infringer] had to design or invent around the patented technology to develop an alleged substitute;

(3) that [patent holder] had the manufacturing and marketing capacity to make any infringing sales actually made by the infringer and for which [patent holder] seeks an award of lost profits; and

(4) the amount of profit that [patent holder] would have made if [alleged infringer] had not infringed.

Authorities

Versata Software, Inc. v. SAP Am., Inc., 717 F.3d 1255, 1264 (Fed. Cir. 2013); *Presidio Components, Inc. v. Am. Tech. Ceramics Corp.*, 702 F.3d 1351, 1360–61 (Fed. Cir. 2012).

B.5. Patent Damages

5.3a LOST PROFITS – MARKET SHARE

One way [patent holder] may prove the number of sales it would have made if the infringement had not happened is to prove its share of the relevant market excluding infringing products. You may award [patent holder] a share of profits equal to that market share.

In deciding [patent holder]'s market share, you must decide which products are in [patent holder]'s market. Products are in the same market if they are sufficiently similar to compete against each other. Two products are sufficiently similar if one does not have a significantly higher price than or possess characteristics significantly different than the other.

Authorities

Micro Chem., Inc. v. Lextron, Inc., 318 F.3d 1119, 1124 (Fed. Cir. 2003); *Crystal Semiconductor Corp. v. Tritech Microelectronics Int'l, Inc.*, 246 F.3d 1336, 1354–55 (Fed. Cir. 2001); *State Indus., Inc. v. Mor-Flo Indus., Inc.*, 883 F.2d 1573, 1580 (Fed. Cir. 1989).

B.5. Patent Damages

5.4 LOST PROFITS - COLLATERAL SALES

In this case, [patent holder] is seeking profits from sales of [x], which it contends it would have sold along with [y]. These products are called collateral products.

To recover lost profits on sales of such collateral products [patent holder] must prove two things. First, that it is more likely than not that [patent holder] would have sold the collateral products but for the infringement. Second, a collateral product and the patented product together must be analogous to components of a single assembly or parts of a complete machine, or they must constitute a functional unit.

Authorities

Rite-Hite Corp. v. Kelley Co., 56 F.3d 1538, 1550 (Fed. Cir. 1995) (en banc); *State Indus., Inc. v. Mor-Flo Indus., Inc.*, 883 F.2d 1573, 1580 (Fed. Cir. 1989); *Panduit Corp. v. Stahlin Bros. Fibre Works, Inc.*, 575 F.2d 1152, 1157–58 (6th Cir. 1978).

B.5. Patent Damages

5.5 LOST PROFITS – PRICE EROSION

[Patent holder] can recover additional damages if it can show to a reasonable probability that, if there had been no infringement, [patent holder] would have been able to charge higher prices for some of its products. In that case, you may also award as additional damages the amount represented by the difference between the amount of profits that [patent holder] would have made by selling its product at the higher price and the amount of profits [patent holder] actually made by selling its product at the lower price that [patent holder] charged for its product. This type of damage is referred to as price erosion damage.

If you find that [patent holder] suffered price erosion, you may also use the higher price in determining [patent holder]'s lost profits from sales lost because of the infringement. In calculating a patentee's total losses from price erosion, you must take into account any drop in sales that would have resulted from a higher price.

You may also award as damages the amount of any increase in costs of [patent holder], such as additional marketing costs, caused by competition from the infringing product.

Authorities

Ericsson, Inc. v. Harris Corp., 352 F.3d 1369, 1377–79 (Fed. Cir. 2003); *Vulcan Eng'g Co. v. FATA Aluminum, Inc.*, 278 F.3d 1366, 1377 (Fed. Cir. 2002); *Crystal Semiconductor Corp. v. Tritech Microelectronics Int'l, Inc.*, 246 F.3d 1336, 1357–58 (Fed. Cir. 2001); *Minco, Inc. v. Combustion Eng'g, Inc.*, 95 F.3d 1109, 1120 (Fed. Cir. 1996); *BIC Leisure Prods., Inc. v. Windsurfing Int'l, Inc.*, 1 F.3d 1214, 1220 (Fed. Cir. 1993); *Kalman v. Berlyn Corp.*, 914 F.2d 1473, 1485 (Fed. Cir. 1990); *Wechsler v. Macke Int. Trade, Inc.,* 486 F. 3d 1286, 1293–94 (Fed. Cir. 2007).

B.5. Patent Damages

5.6 REASONABLE ROYALTY – ENTITLEMENT

If [patent holder] has not proved its claim for lost profits, or has proved its claim for lost profits for only a portion of the infringing sales, then [patent holder] should be awarded a reasonable royalty for all infringing sales for which it has not been awarded lost profits damages.

Authorities

35 U.S.C. § 284; *Crystal Semiconductor Corp. v. Tritech Microelectronics Int'l, Inc.*, 246 F.3d 1336 (Fed. Cir. 2001); *Fromson v. Western Litho Plate & Supply Co.*, 853 F.2d 1568, 1574 (Fed. Cir. 1998) (overruled on other grounds); *Minco, Inc. v. Combustion Eng'g, Inc.*, 95 F.3d 1109, 1119–20 (Fed. Cir. 1996); *Mahurkar v. C.R. Bard, Inc.*, 79 F.3d 1572, 1579 (Fed. Cir. 1996); *Rite-Hite Corp. v. Kelley Co.*, 56 F.3d 1538, 1554 (Fed. Cir. 1995) (en banc).

B.5. Patent Damages

5.7 REASONABLE ROYALTY – DEFINITION

A royalty is a payment made to a patent holder in exchange for the right to make, use or sell the claimed invention. This right is called a "license." A reasonable royalty is the payment for the license that would have resulted from a hypothetical negotiation between the patent holder and the infringer taking place at the time when the infringing activity first began. In considering the nature of this negotiation, you must assume that the patent holder and the infringer would have acted reasonably and would have entered into a license agreement. You must also assume that both parties believed the patent was valid and infringed. Your role is to determine what the result of that negotiation would have been. The test for damages is what royalty would have resulted from the hypothetical negotiation and not simply what either party would have preferred.

A royalty can be calculated in several different ways and it is for you to determine which way is the most appropriate based on the evidence you have heard. One way to calculate a royalty is to determine what is called an "ongoing royalty." To calculate an ongoing royalty, you must first determine the "base," that is, the product on which the infringer is to pay. You then need to multiply the revenue the defendant obtained from that base by the "rate" or percentage that you find would have resulted from the hypothetical negotiation. For example, if the patent covers a nail, and the nail sells for $1, and the licensee sold 200 nails, the base revenue would be $200. If the rate you find would have resulted from the hypothetical negotiation is 1%, then the royalty would be $2, or the rate of 0.01 times the base revenue of $200. By contrast, if you find the rate to be 5%, the royalty would be $10, or the rate of 0.05 times the base revenue of $200. These numbers are only examples, and are not intended to suggest the appropriate royalty rate.

Instead of a percentage royalty, you may decide that the appropriate royalty that would have resulted from a hypothetical negotiation is a fixed number of dollars per unit sold. If you do, the royalty would be that fixed number of dollars times the number of units sold.

If the patent covers only part of the product that the infringer sells, then the base would normally be only that feature or component. For example, if you find that for a $100 car, the patented feature is the tires which sell for $5, the base revenue would be $5. However, in a circumstance in which the patented feature is the reason customers buy the whole product, the base revenue could be the value of the whole product. Even if the patented feature is not the reason for customer demand, the value of the whole product could be used if, for example, the value of the patented feature could not be separated out from the value of the whole product. In such a case, however, the rate resulting from the hypothetical negotiation would be a lower rate because it is being applied to the value of the whole product and the patented feature is not the reason for the customer's purchase of the whole product.

Another way to calculate a royalty is to determine a one-time lump sum payment that the infringer would have paid at the time of the hypothetical negotiation for a license covering all sales of the licensed product both past and future. This differs from payment of an ongoing royalty because, with an ongoing royalty, the licensee pays based on the revenue of actual licensed products it sells. When a one-time lump sum is paid, the infringer pays a single price for a license covering both past and future infringing sales.

It is up to you, based on the evidence, to decide what type of royalty is appropriate in this case. Authorities

Golight, Inc., v. Wal-Mart Stores, Inc., 355 F.3d 1327, 1338 (Fed. Cir. 2004); *Maxwell v. Baker, Inc.*, 86 F.3d 1098, 1108–10 (Fed. Cir. 1996); *Mahurkar v. C.R. Bard, Inc.*, 79 F.3d 1572, 1579–81 (Fed. Cir. 1996); *Rite-Hite Corp. v. Kelley Co.*, 56 F.3d 1538, 1554 (Fed. Cir. 1995)(en banc); *Georgia-Pacific Corp. v. United States Plywood Corp.*, 318 F. Supp. 1116, 1120 (S.D.N.Y. 1970).

B.5. Patent Damages

5.8 DATE OF COMMENCEMENT - PRODUCTS[2120]

Damages that [patent holder] may be awarded by you commence on the date that [alleged infringer] has both infringed and been notified of the [ ] patent: [use those that apply to this case]

> [[Patent holder] and [alleged infringer] agree that date was [insert date];]
>
> [Since [patent holder] sells a product that includes the claimed invention but has not marked that product with the patent number, you must determine the date that [alleged infringer] received actual written notice of the [ ] patent and the specific product alleged to infringe;]
>
> [Since [patent holder] [marks the product] or [does not sell a product covered by the patent], then damages begin without the requirement for actual notice under the following circumstances:
>
>> If the [ ] patent was granted before the infringing activity began, damages should be calculated as of the date you determine that the infringement began; or
>>
>> If the [ ] patent was granted after the infringing activity began as determined by you, damages should be calculated as of [date patent issued].]

<u>Authorities</u>

35 U.S.C. § 287; *Crystal Semiconductor Corp. v. Tritech Microelectronics Int'l, Inc.*, 246 F.3d 1336 (Fed. Cir. 2001); *Nike Inc. v. Wal-Mart Stores*, 138 F.3d 1437, 1443–44 (Fed. Cir. 1998); *Maxwell v. Baker, Inc.*, 86 F.3d 1098, 1111–12 (Fed. Cir. 1996); *Am. Med. Sys. v. Med. Eng'g Corp.*, 6 F.3d 1523, 1534 (Fed. Cir. 1993); *Devices for Med., Inc. v. Boehl*, 822 F.2d 1062, 1066 (Fed. Cir. 1987).

---

20. This instruction may be used when the claim is an apparatus or product claim and [alleged infringer] is a direct infringer. Different rules may apply if the claim is a method claim or [alleged infringer] is an inducer or contributory infringer

B.5. Patent Damages

5.9 CALCULATING DAMAGES IN CASES OF INDUCEMENT OR CONTRIBUTORY INFRINGEMENT

In order to recover damages for induced infringement, [patent holder] must either prove that the [accused product] necessarily infringes the [patent in suit] or prove acts of direct infringement by others that were induced by [accused infringer]. Because the amount of damages for induced infringement is limited by the number of instances of direct infringement, [patent holder] must further prove the number of direct acts of infringement of the [patent in suit], for example, by showing individual acts of direct infringement or by showing that a particular class of [products] [uses] directly infringes.

In order to recover damages for contributory infringement, [patent holder] must either prove that the [accused product] necessarily infringes the [patent in suit] or prove acts of direct infringement by others to which [accused infringer] made a substantial contribution. Because the amount of damages for contributory infringement is limited by the number of instances of direct infringement, [patent holder] must further prove the number of direct acts of infringement of the [patent in suit], for example, either by showing individual acts of direct infringement or by showing that a particular class of [products] [uses] directly infringes.

Authorities

Dynacore Holdings Corp. v. U.S. Philips Corp., 363 F.3d 1263 (Fed. Cir. 2004); *Cardiac Pacemakers, Inc. v. St. Jude Med., Inc.*, 576 F.3d 1348 (Fed. Cir. 2009).

C.1 Appendix

GLOSSARY

Some of the terms in this glossary will be defined in more detail in the instructions you are given. The definitions in the instructions must be followed and must control your deliberations.

[Add any technical terms from the art involved that may be used during trial and have agreed- upon definitions and delete any of the following terms which may not be applicable in a particular case.]

Abstract: A brief summary of the technical disclosure in a patent to enable the U.S. Patent and Trademark Office and the public to determine quickly the nature and gist of the technical disclosure in the patent.

Amendment: A patent applicant's change to one or more claims or to the specification either in response to an office action taken by a Patent Examiner or independently by the patent applicant during the patent application examination process.

Anticipation: A situation in which a claimed invention describes an earlier invention and, therefore, is not considered new and is not entitled to be patented.

Assignment: A transfer of patent rights to another called an "assignee" who upon transfer becomes the owner of the rights assigned.

Best Mode: The best way the inventor actually knew to make or use the invention at the time of the patent application. If the applicant had a best mode as of the time the application was first filed, it must be set forth in the patent specification.

Claim: Each claim of a patent is a concise, formal definition of an invention and appears at the end of the specification in a separately numbered paragraph. In concept, a patent claim marks the boundaries of the patent in the same way that a legal description in a deed specifies the boundaries of land, i.e. similar to a land owner who can prevent others from trespassing on the bounded property, the inventor can prevent others from using what is claimed. Claims may be independent or dependent. An independent claim stands alone. A dependent claim does not stand alone and refers to one or more other claims. A dependent claim incorporates whatever the other referenced claim or claims say.

Conception: The complete mental part of the inventive act which must be capable of proof, as by drawings, disclosure to another, etc.

Continuation Application: A patent application filed during the examination process of an earlier application which has the same disclosure as the original application and does not include anything which would constitute new matter if inserted in the original application.

Continuation-In-Part (C-I-P) Application: A patent application filed during the application process of an earlier application which repeats some or all of the earlier application and adds matter not disclosed in the earlier application to support the addition of new patent claims.

Drawings: The drawings are visual representations of the claimed invention contained in a patent application and issued patent, and usually include several figures illustrating various aspects of the claimed invention.

Elements: The required parts of a device or the required steps of a method. A device or method infringes a patent if it contains each and every requirement of a patent claim.

Embodiment: A product or method that contains the claimed invention.

Enablement: A description of the invention that is sufficient to enable persons skilled in the field of the invention to make and use the invention. The specification of the patent must contain such an enabling description.

Examination: Procedure before the U.S. Patent and Trademark Office whereby a Patent Examiner reviews the filed patent application to determine if the claimed invention is patentable.

Filing Date: Date a patent application, with all the required sections, has been submitted to the U.S. Patent and Trademark Office.

Infringement: Violation of a patent occurring when someone makes, uses or sells a patented invention, without permission of the patent holder, within the United States during the term of the patent. Infringement may be direct, by inducement, or contributory. Direct infringement is making, using or selling the patented invention without permission. Inducing infringement is intentionally causing another to directly infringe a patent. Contributory infringement is offering to sell or selling an item that is an important component of the invention, so that the buyer directly infringes the patent. To be a contributory infringer one must know that the part being offered or sold is designed specifically for infringing the patented invention and is not a common component suitable for non-infringing uses.

Limitation: A required part of an invention set forth in a patent claim. A limitation is a requirement of the invention. The word "limitation" is often used interchangeably with the word "requirement."

Nonobviousness: One of the requirements for securing a patent. To be valid, the subject matter of the invention must not have been obvious to a person of ordinary skill in the field of the invention at the time of the earlier of the filing date of the patent application or the date of invention.

Office Action: A written communication from the Patent Examiner to the patent applicant in the course of the application examination process.

Patent: A patent is an exclusive right granted by the U.S. Patent and Trademark Office to an inventor to prevent others from making, using, offering to sell, or selling an invention within the United States, or from importing it into the United States, during the term of the patent. When the patent expires, the right to make, use or sell the invention is dedicated to the public. The patent has three parts, which are a specification, drawings and claims. The patent is granted after examination by the U.S. Patent and Trademark Office of a patent application filed by the inventor which has these parts, and this examination is called the prosecution history.

Patent and Trademark Office (PTO): An administrative branch of the U.S. Department of Commerce that is charged with overseeing and implementing the federal laws of patents and trademarks. It is responsible for examining all patent applications and issuing all patents in the United States.

Prior Art: Previously known subject matter in the field of a claimed invention for which a patent is being sought. It includes issued patents, publications, and knowledge deemed to be publicly available such as trade skills, trade practices and the like.

Prosecution History: The prosecution history is the complete written record of the proceedings in the PTO from the initial application to the issued patent. The prosecution history includes the office actions taken by the PTO and the amendments to the patent application filed by the applicant during the examination process.

Reads On: A patent claim "reads on" a device or method when each required part (requirement) of the claim is found in the device or method.

Reduction to Practice: The invention is "reduced to practice" when it is sufficiently developed to show that it would work for its intended purpose.

Reexamination: A process in which a patent is reexamined by the PTO to determine whether one or more of the claims are patentable with respect to submitted prior art which may consist only of prior patents or printed publications. An "ex parte" reexamination is initiated by the patent holder or a third party, but does not include the further participation of any third party. An "inter partes" reexamination is initiated by a third party who continues to participate in the proceedings.

Requirement: A required part or step of an invention set forth in a patent claim. The word "requirement" is often used interchangeably with the word "limitation."

Royalty: A royalty is a payment made to the owner of a patent by a non-owner in exchange for rights to make, use or sell the claimed invention.

Specification: The specification is a required part of a patent application and an issued patent. It is a written description of the invention and of the manner and process of making and using the claimed invention.

C.2. Appendix

COMMENTS REGARDING USE OF SAMPLE VERDICT FORM

The following sample verdict form is provided for guidance in preparing an appropriate special verdict form tailored for your specific case. The sample is for a hypothetical case in which the patent holder alleges direct and indirect infringement of a single claim of one patent and seeks a combination of lost profits and a reasonable royalty for the allegedly infringing sales. The alleged infringer raises a number of invalidity defenses. No issue is raised, however, as to the conception date of the claimed invention. The issue of willfulness has not been bifurcated.

The form requires the jury to make specific findings on the bases for the affirmative defenses of "anticipation" and "statutory bars."

The form also requires the jury to make factual determinations underlying a conclusion of "obviousness" or "nonobviousness." It is expected that these issues will be presented to the jury as specifically as possible. For example, if the only dispute between the parties is whether a particular reference is within the "scope and content" of the prior art, that is the only question on that *Graham* factor that should be presented to the jury. As another example, if the only factual dispute between the parties on the "differences between the prior art and the claimed invention" is whether a prior art reference discloses a particular claim limitation, that is the only issue that should be presented to the jury on that *Graham* factor.

This form also provides two alternative section 11's on obviousness. One asks the jury to only answer the underlying factual questions. The other permits the jury to give an advisory verdict on the ultimate question of obviousness. It must be remembered, however, that the ultimate question of obviousness is a question of law for the court. *KSR Int'l Co. v. Teleflex, Inc.*, 550 U.S. 398, 427 (2007) ("The ultimate judgment of obviousness is a legal determination."); *see Dippin' Dots, Inc. v. Mosey*, 476 F.3d 1337, 1343 (Fed. Cir. 2007). Both alternatives are designed to focus the parties and the court on the factual disputes on the obviousness question. For example, the form requires that each party specify exactly what it contends constitutes the scope and content of the prior art. Although trial courts have often permitted the jury to reach the final conclusion of obviousness without specifying its underlying factual determinations, such an approach is not recommended. The verdict form should require the jury's finding on each factual issue so that the trial judge may make the final determination on the obviousness question. As Judge Michel pointed out in his dissent in *McGinley v. Franklin Sports, Inc.*, 262 F.3d 1339 (Fed. Cir. 2001):

> The issue presented in this appeal derives from the common, if unfortunate, practice of allowing the jury to render a general verdict on the ultimate legal conclusion of obviousness without re-

> quiring express findings on the underlying factual issues through a special verdict or special interrogatories under Fed. R. Civ. P. 49. Nevertheless, since the inception of our court, we have recognized that a court may submit this legal question to a jury and that doing so by general verdict rather than by Rule 49 is not ordinarily an abuse of discretion. We have emphasized, however, that there is no question that the judge must remain the ultimate arbiter on the question of obviousness.

Id. at 1358 (internal citations and quotation marks omitted). The fact that the verdict form allows the jury to give an advisory conclusion on obviousness should not be construed as suggesting that the court defer to the jury's ultimate determination on obviousness. The law is clear that the ultimate question is a legal one for the court.

C.3. Appendix

SAMPLE VERDICT FORM

When answering the following questions and filling out this Verdict Form, please follow the directions provided throughout the form. Your answer to each question must be unanimous. Some of the questions contain legal terms that are defined and explained in detail in the Jury Instructions. Please refer to the Jury Instructions if you are unsure about the meaning or usage of any legal term that appears in the questions below.

We, the jury, unanimously agree to the answers to the following questions and return them under the instructions of this court as our verdict in this case.

FINDINGS ON INFRINGEMENT CLAIMS

(The questions regarding infringement should be answered regardless of your findings with respect to the validity or invalidity of the patent.)

A. Direct Infringement

1. Has Patent Holder proven that it is more likely than not that every requirement of claim 1 of its patent is included in Alleged Infringer's accused product?

Yes ______ No ______

If your answer to question 1 is "yes," go to question 3. If your answer to question 1 is "no," go to question 2.

B. Infringement Under the Doctrine of Equivalents

2. Has Patent Holder proven that it is more likely than not that the accused product includes parts that are identical or equivalent to every requirement of claim 1 of Patent Holder's patent? In other words, for any requirement that is not literally found in the Alleged Infringer's accused product, does the accused product have an equivalent part to that requirement?

Yes ______ No ______

C. Contributory Infringement

3. Has Patent Holder proven that it is more likely than not: (i) that Direct Infringer infringed claim 1 of Patent Holder's patent; (ii) that Alleged Infringer supplied an

important component of the infringing part of the product; (iii) that the component was not a common component suitable for non-infringing use; and (iv) that Alleged Infringer supplied the component with knowledge of the patent and knowledge that the component was especially made or adapted for use in an infringing manner?

Yes ______ No ______

D. Inducing Infringement

4. Has Patent Holder proven that it is more likely than not: (i) that Direct Infringer infringed claim 1 of Patent Holder's patent; (ii) that Alleged Infringer took action that actually induced that infringement by Direct Infringer; and (iii) that Alleged Infringer was aware of the patent and believed that its actions would encourage infringement of a valid patent, or alternatively that it was willfully blind as to whether its actions would encourage infringement of the patent?

Yes ______ No ______

E. Willful Infringement

5a. Has the Patent Holder proven that it is highly probable that from an objective point of view the defenses put forth by Alleged Infringer failed to raise any substantial question with regard to infringement, validity or enforceability of the patent claim?

Yes ______ No ______

[If the answer to question 5a is "yes," answer question 5b. If your answer to question 5a is "no," go to question 6.]

5b. Has the Patent Holder proven that it is highly probable that the Alleged Infringer actually knew, or it was so obvious that Alleged Infringer should have known, that its actions constituted infringement of a valid and enforceable patent?

FINDINGS ON INVALIDITY DEFENSES

(The questions regarding invalidity should be answered regardless of your findings with respect to infringement.)

A. Written Description Requirement

6. Has Alleged Infringer proven that it is highly probable that the specification of the Patent Holder's patent does not contain an adequate written description of the claimed invention?

Yes ______ No ______

B. Enablement

7. Has Alleged Infringer proven that it is highly probable that the specification of the Patent Holder's patent does not contain a description of the claimed invention that is sufficiently full and clear to enable persons of ordinary skill in the field to make and use the invention?

Yes ______ No ______

C. Best Mode

8. Has Alleged Infringer proven that it is highly probable that the patent does not disclose what the inventor believed was the best way to carry out the claimed invention at the time the patent application was filed?

Yes ______ No ______

D. Anticipation

9. Has Alleged Infringer proven that it is highly probable that claim 1 of Patent Holder's patent was "anticipated," or, in other words, not new?

Yes ______ No ______

[If the answer is "yes," check any reason below that is applicable:

_____ The claimed invention was already publicly known or publicly used by others in the United States before the date of conception of the claimed invention.

_____ The claimed invention was already patented or described in a printed publication anywhere in the world before the date of conception.

_____ The claimed invention was already made by someone else in the United States before the date of conception and that other person had not abandoned the invention or kept it secret.

_____ The claimed invention was already described in another issued U.S. patent or published U.S. patent application that was based on a patent application filed before the date of conception.

_____ The named inventor did not invent the claimed invention but instead learned of the claimed invention from someone else.

_______ The named inventor was not the first inventor of the claimed invention.]

E. Statutory Bar

10. Has Alleged Infringer proven that it is highly probable that claim 1 of Patent Holder's patent was not filed within the time required by law?

Yes ______ No ______

If the answer is "yes," check any reason below that is applicable:

_____ The claimed invention was already patented or described in a printed publication anywhere in the world at least one year before the filing date of the patent application.

_____ The claimed invention was already being openly used in the United States at least one year before the filing date of the patent application and that use was not primarily an experimental use to test whether the invention worked for its intended purpose which was controlled by the inventor.

_____ A device or method using the claimed invention was sold or offered for sale in the United States and the claimed invention was ready for patenting at least one year before the filing date of the patent application and that offer or sale was not primarily for experimental purposes to test whether the invention worked for its intended purpose and which was controlled by the inventor.

_____ Patent Holder had already obtained a patent on the claimed invention in a foreign country before the original U.S. application, and the foreign application was filed at least one year before the U.S. application.

F. Obviousness

[Alternative 1 – Jury decides underlying factual issues only]

11. The ultimate legal conclusion on the obviousness question will be made by the court. However, in order for the court to do so, you must answer the following preliminary factual questions:

a. What was the level of ordinary skill in the field that someone would have had at the time the claimed invention was made? (check the applicable answer)

_______ set forth Alleged Infringer's contention, e.g., an individual with at least 3 years of experience in both furniture design and manufacture]

_______ [set forth Patent Holder's contention, e.g., anyone who has worked in the field of furniture design or manufacture for at least two years]

_______ [other, specify _______________________________]

b. What was the scope and content of the prior art at the time of the claimed invention? (check the applicable answer)

_______ [set forth what the Alleged Infringer has offered as the invalidating prior art, e.g., '123 patent on fixed sitting device with four legs, general knowledge in field of industrial design that a horizontal surface may be held parallel to the ground using three legs and common knowledge that a person can easily move an object weighing under 25 pounds]

_______ [set forth what the Patent Holder asserts was within the scope and content of the prior art, e.g., '123 patent on fixed sitting device with four legs]

_______ [other, specify _______________________________]

c. What difference, if any, existed between the claimed invention and the prior art at the time of the claimed invention?

_______ [set forth the Alleged Infringer's contention as to the difference, e.g., no difference between scope of invention and what is known in prior art]

_______ [set forth the Patent Holder's contention as to the difference, e.g., only 3 legs on a sitting device and portability]

_______ [other, specify ______________________________]

d. Which of the following factors has been established by the evidence with respect to the claimed invention: (check those that apply)[verdict form should list only those factors for which a *prima facie* showing has been made]:

_______ commercial success of a product due to the merits of the claimed invention

_______ a long felt need for the solution that is provided by the claimed invention

_______ unsuccessful attempts by others to find the solution that is provided by the claimed invention

_______ copying of the claimed invention by others

_______ unexpected and superior results from the claimed invention

_______ acceptance by others of the claimed invention as shown by praise from others in the field or from the licensing of the claimed invention

_______ independent invention of the claimed invention by others before or at about the same time as the named inventor thought of it

[_______ other factor(s) indicating obviousness or nonobviousness—describe the factor(s)______________________]

[Alternative 2 - Jury decides underlying factual issues and renders advisory verdict on obviousness]

11. The ultimate conclusion that must be reached on the obviousness question is whether Alleged Infringer has proven that it is highly probable that the claimed invention would have been obvious to a person of ordinary skill in the field at the time the patent application was filed. In order to properly reach a conclusion the following preliminary questions must be answered:

a. What was the level of ordinary skill in the field that someone would have had at the time the claimed invention was made? (check the applicable answer)

_________ [set forth Alleged Infringer's contention, e.g., an individual with at least 3 years of experience in both furniture design and manufacture]

_________ [set forth Patent Holder's contention, e.g., anyone who has worked in the field of furniture design or manufacture for at least two years]

_________ [other, specify ______________________________________]

b. Was [disputed reference] within the scope and content of the prior art at the time of the claimed invention? (check only if reference was within the scope and content of the prior art)

_____ [set forth the prior art reference [alleged infringer] has offered as prior art that the [patent holder] disputes as being in the scope and content of the prior art. If there is more than one reference in dispute, each disputed reference should be listed separately.]

c. What difference, if any, existed between the claimed invention and the prior art at the time of the claimed invention?

_____ [set forth the Alleged Infringer's contention as to the difference, e.g., no difference between scope of invention and what is known in prior art]

______ [set forth the Patent Holder's contention as to the difference, e.g., only 3 legs on a sitting device and portability]

______ [other, specify ______________________________]

d. Which of the following factors has been established by the evidence with respect to the claimed invention: (check those that apply)[verdict form should list only those factors for which a *prima facie* showing has been made]

_________ commercial success of a product due to the merits of the claimed invention

_________ a long felt need for the solution that is provided by the claimed invention

_________ unsuccessful attempts by others to find the solution that is provided by the claimed invention

_________ copying of the claimed invention by others

_________ unexpected and superior results from the claimed invention

_________ acceptance by others of the claimed invention as shown by praise from others in the field or from the licensing of the claimed invention

_________ independent invention of the claimed invention by others before or at about the same time as the named inventor thought of it

[_________ other factor(s) indicating obviousness or nonobviousness—describe the factor(s)_________________________]

After consideration of the answers to the preliminary questions above, do you find that the Alleged Infringer has proven that it is highly probable that the claim of Patent Holder's patent would have been obvious to a person of ordinary skill in the field at the time the patent application was filed?

Yes ______ No ______

G. Inventorship

12. Has Alleged Infringer proven that it is highly probable that Patent Holder's patent fails to meet the requirement to name all actual inventors and only the actual inventors?

Yes ______ No ______

FINDINGS ON DAMAGES (IF APPLICABLE)

If you answered question 1, 2, 3 or 4 "yes" and questions 6, 7, 8, 9, 10, 11 and 12 "no," proceed to answer the remaining questions. If you did not so answer, do not answer the remaining questions and proceed to check and sign the verdict form.

13. What lost profits, if any, did Patent Holder show it more likely than not suffered as a result of sales that it would with reasonable probability have made but for Alleged Infringer's infringement?

$________________________

14. For those infringing sales for which Patent Holder has not proved its entitlement to lost profits, what has it proved it is entitled to as a reasonable royalty:

a) on-going royalty payment of (1) $_____ [per unit sold] or ____ % of $_____ in total sales; or

b) one-time payment of $______________ for the life of the patent.

You have now reached the end of the verdict form and should review it to ensure it accurately reflects your unanimous determinations. The Presiding Juror should then sign and date the verdict form in the spaces below and notify the Security Guard that you have reached a verdict. The Presiding Juror should retain possession of the verdict form and bring it when the jury is brought back into the courtroom.

DATED: ___________, 20 By: _________________________________

Presiding Juror

AIPLA's Model Patent Jury Instructions

Disclaimer

The Model Jury Instructions are provided as general assistance for the litigation of patent issues. While efforts have been and will be made to ensure that the Model Jury Instructions accurately reflect existing law, this work is not intended to replace the independent research necessary for formulating jury instructions that are best suited to particular facts and legal issues. AIPLA does not represent that the information contained in the Model Jury Instructions is accurate, complete, or current. The work could contain typographical errors or technical inaccuracies, and AIPLA reserves the right to add, change, or delete its contents or any part thereof without notice.

Table of Contents

I. Introduction

The 2015 Version

In the Winter of 2013, the Patent Litigation Committee of the American Intellectual Property Law Association once again undertook the task of updating the AIPLA Model Patent Jury Instructions ("Instructions") to take into account changes to the law since the previous version of the Instructions were published. The Instructions were originally created in 1997 and were updated previously in 2005, 2008, and 2012. A Subcommittee was formed to review recent case law and make any necessary changes to the Instructions to conform to the significant changes in patent law over the last several years. The Subcommittee also continued its effort to simplify the Instructions and to improve the formatting so that the electronic version of the Instructions is easier to navigate. The current revision includes case law through December 31, 2014.

One of the fundamental goals of the Instructions is to provide a model set of jury instructions that would not be biased in favor of either the patent owner or the accused infringer. These Model Instructions are not intended to address every conceivable issue that might arise in patent litigation. Instead, Instructions are provided on those issues that typically arise in patent litigation and that have clear precedential support. It is incumbent upon the litigants to tailor these instructions to the specific issues in their particular case and to simplify the tasks for the Court and the jury by not providing superfluous or confusing instructions. It is also intended that these Instructions will be used in conjunction with other instructions dealing with non-patent issues such as credibility and that the trial court will further the jury's understanding of these Instructions by relating the legal principles in the Instructions to the particular factual contentions of the parties.

To further these goals and to enhance the litigants' ability to customize the Instructions to a particular case, these revised Instructions continue the use of bracketed terminology for certain consistent terms. This enables the litigants to use the find-and-replace feature of a word processing program to insert case specific facts. Examples of the terms are:

[subject matter]
[the patentee]
[the Plaintiff]
[the Defendant]
[full patent number]
[abbreviated patent number]
[claims in dispute]
[allegedly infringing product]
[invention date]
[U.S. filing date]
[critical date]
[effective filing date]

[anticipating patent]
[alleged analogous art]
[alleged prior publication]
[alleged device on sale]
[infringement notice date]
[lawsuit filing date]
[beginning infringement date]
[collateral products]
[the Plaintiff's product]

In addition to these "find-and-replace" terms, brackets were also used to indicate where various terminology could be used to customize these Instructions to a particular case. For example, to take into account the differences between product and method patents, there will be instructions that include "[[product] [method]]" and the like. Other examples include "[[product] [system]]," "[importing] [selling] [offering to sell] [using]" and "[method] [process]]."

The Subcommittee substantially completed these revisions in the fourth quarter of 2014. The AIPLA Board of Directors approved these Instructions for publication in June 2015. These Instructions, however, do not take into account case law or statutory changes that occurred in 2015.

December 2014
Felicia J. Boyd
Chair, Model Patent Jury Instructions Subcommittee
Patent Litigation Committee
American Intellectual Property Law Association

II. Preliminary Jury Instructions

Members of the jury:

Now that you have been sworn, I have the following preliminary instructions for your guidance on the nature of the case and on your role as jurors.

A. The Nature of the Action and the Parties

This is a patent case. The patents involved in this case relate to [subject matter] technology. [BRIEFLY DESCRIBE TECHNOLOGY INVOLVED].

During the trial, the parties will offer testimony to familiarize you with this technology. For your convenience, the parties have also prepared a Glossary of some of the technical terms to which they may refer during the trial, which will be distributed to you.

[The Plaintiff] is the owner of a patent, which is identified by the Patent Office number: [full patent number] (which may be called "the [abbreviated patent number] patent"); [IDENTIFY ADDITIONAL PATENTS]. This patent may also be referred to as "[the Plaintiff]'s patent." [The Defendant] is the other party here.

i. United States Patents

Patents are granted by the United States Patent and Trademark Office (sometimes called the "PTO" or "USPTO"). A patent gives the owner the right to exclude others from making, using, offering to sell, or selling [[the patented invention] [a product made by the patented process]] within the United States or importing it into the United States. During the trial, the parties may offer testimony to familiarize you with how one obtains a patent from the PTO, but I will give you a general background here.

To obtain a patent, an application for a patent must be filed with the PTO. The application includes a specification, which should have a written description of the invention, and telling how it works and how to make and use it so as to enable others skilled in the art to do so. [The specification should also describe what the inventor believed at the time of filing to be the best way of making his or her invention.][21] The specification concludes with one or more numbered sentences or paragraphs. These are called the "claims" of the patent. The purpose of the claims is to particularly point out what the applicant regards as the invention and to define the scope of the patent owner's exclusive rights.

After an application for a patent is filed with the PTO, the application is reviewed by a trained PTO Patent Examiner. The Patent Examiner reviews (or examines) the patent application to determine whether the claims are patentable and whether the specification adequately describes the invention claimed. In examining a patent application, the patent examiner searches records available to the PTO for

21. The bracketed sentence should only be read if a defense of failure to comply with best mode is raised against an asserted patent having a pre-AIA priority date.

what is referred to as "prior art," and he or she also reviews prior art submitted by the applicant.

When the parties are done presenting evidence, I will give you more specific instructions as to what constitutes prior art in this case. Generally, prior art is previously existing technical information and knowledge against which the Patent Examiners determine whether or not the claims in the application are patentable.[22] The Patent Examiner considers, among other things, whether each claim defines an invention that is new, useful, and not obvious in view of this prior art.

Following the prior art search and examination of the application, the Patent Examiner advises the applicant in writing what the patent examiner has found and whether any claim is patentable (in other words, "allowed"). This writing from the Patent Examiner is called an "office action." More often than not, the initial Office Action by the Patent Examiner rejects the claims. The Applicant then responds to the Office Action and sometimes changes the claims or submits new claims. This process may go back and forth between the Patent Examiner and the Applicant for several months or even years until the Patent Examiner is satisfied that the Application and claims are patentable. At that time, the PTO "issues" or "grants" a patent with the allowed claims.

The collection of papers generated by the patent examiner and the applicant during this time of corresponding back and forth is called the "prosecution history." You may also hear the "prosecution history" referred to as the "file history" or the "file wrapper."

In this case, it is ultimately for you to decide, based on my instructions to you, whether the accused infringer has shown that the patent claims are invalid.

ii. Patent Litigation

Someone is said to be infringing a claim of a patent when they, without permission from the patent owner, import, make, use, offer to sell, or sell [[the patented invention] [a product made by the patented process]], as defined by the claims, within the United States before the term of the patent expires. A patent owner who believes someone is infringing the exclusive rights of a patent may bring a lawsuit, like this one, to attempt to address the alleged infringing acts and to recover damages, which generally means money paid by the infringer to the patent owner to compensate for the harm caused by the infringement. The patent owner must prove infringement of the claims of the patent. The patent owner must also prove the amount of damages he or she is entitled to.

A patent is presumed to be valid. In other words, it is presumed to have been properly granted. But that presumption of validity can be overcome if clear and convincing evidence is presented that proves the patent is invalid. One example

---

22. If the litigation involves a patent governed by the AIA, prior art is art that was effectively filed or published before the filing of the application or patent.

of a way in which the presumption may be overcome is if the PTO has not considered, for whatever reason, invalidating prior art that is presented to you. Someone accused of infringing a patent may deny that they infringe and/or prove that the asserted claims of the patent are invalid. If the opposing party challenges the validity of the patent, you must decide based on the instructions I will give you, whether the challenger has overcome the presumption of validity with proof that the asserted claims of the patent are invalid. The party challenging validity must prove invalidity by clear and convincing evidence. I will discuss more of this topic later.

I will now briefly explain the parties' basic contentions in more detail.

B. Contentions of the Parties

[The Plaintiff] contends that [the Defendant] makes, uses, offers to sell, or sells a [[product] [method]] that infringes [claim(s) in dispute] of the [abbreviated patent number] patent. [The Plaintiff] must prove that [the Defendant] infringes the [abbreviated patent number] patent by a preponderance of the evidence. That means that [the Plaintiff] must show that it is more likely that [the Defendant]'s [allegedly infringing product] infringes than it does not infringe.

There are two ways in which a patent claim can be directly infringed.[23] First, a claim can be literally infringed. Second, a claim can be infringed under what is called the "doctrine of equivalents." To determine infringement, you must compare the accused [[product] [method]] with each claim from the [abbreviated patent number] that [the Plaintiff] asserts is infringed. It will be my job to tell you what the language of the patent claims mean. You must follow my instructions as to the meaning of the patent claims. You are not to define the patent claims yourselves.

A patent claim is literally infringed only if [the Defendant]'s [[product] [method]] includes each and every [[element] [method step]] in that patent claim. If [the Defendant]'s [[product] [method]] does not contain one or more [[elements] [method steps]] in that claim, [the Defendant] does not literally infringe that claim. You must determine literal infringement with respect to each patent claim individually.

> **Practice Note:** To avoid jury confusion, it is important to distinguish those claims that are allegedly infringed literally from those that are allegedly infringed under the doctrine of equivalents. Rather than submit both to the jury, the Court should narrow the infringement contentions before the jury is charged in order to provide the jury clear guidance and avoid instructions that may be confusing.

A patent claim is infringed under the doctrine of equivalents only if there is an equivalent [[component] [part] [method step]] in [the Defendant]'s [[product] [method]] for each [[element] [method step]] of the patent claim that is not literally

23. This section and below should be modified in accordance with the patent owner's infringement contentions, *e.g.*, where the doctrine of equivalents is not at issue,.

present in [the Defendant]'s [[product] [method]]. In other words, [the Plaintiff] must prove that it is more likely than not that [the Defendant]'s [[product] [method]] contains the equivalent of each element of the claimed invention that is not literally present in the [allegedly infringing product]. An equivalent of an element is a [[component]] [[action]] that is insubstantially different from the claimed element. One way of showing that an element is insubstantially different is to show that it performs substantially the same function, in substantially the same way, to achieve substantially the same result as would be achieved by the element that is not literally present in the accused [[product]] [[method]].

[The Defendant] denies that it is infringing the [abbreviated patent number] patent and contends that the [abbreviated patent number] patent is invalid [and/or unenforceable].[24] [INSERT BRIEF DESCRIPTION OF THE PARTICULAR INVALIDITY AND UNENFORCEABILITY DEFENSES BEING ASSERTED].

Invalidity of the asserted patent claim(s) is a defense to infringement. Therefore, even though the PTO examiner has allowed the claims of the [abbreviated patent number] patent, you, the jury, must decide whether each claim of the [abbreviated patent number] patent that is challenged by [Defendant] is invalid. [The Defendant] must prove invalidity of each challenged claim by clear and convincing evidence in order to overcome the presumption of validity. Clear and convincing evidence means that it is highly probable that the fact is true. This standard is different than the standard that applies to other issues in this case. I have instructed you that other issues, such as infringement, may be found under a lower standard, name ly, by a preponderance of the evidence. You may think of this "preponderance of the evidence" as slightly greater than 50%. This is different that the criminal law standard of "beyond a reasonable doubt." You may think of this "beyond a reasonable doubt" standard as approaching certainty, without reasonable doubt. The "clear and convincing" standard is between the two.

C. Trial Procedure

We are about to commence the opening statements in the case. Before we do that, I want to explain the procedures that we will be following during the trial and the format of the trial. This trial, like all jury trials, comes in six phases. We have completed the first phase, which was to select you as jurors.

We are now about to begin the second phase, the Opening Statements. The opening statements of the lawyers are statements about what each side expects the evidence to show. The Opening Statements are not evidence for you to consider in your deliberations. You must make your decision based on the evidence and not the lawyers' statements and arguments.

In the third phase, the evidence will be presented to you. Witnesses will take the witness stand and documents will be offered and admitted into evidence. [Plain-

---

24. This section and below should be modified in accordance with the Defendant's defenses, e.g., where the Defendant has opted to not allege non-infringement or invalidity.

tiff] goes first in calling witnesses to the witness stand. These witnesses will be questioned by [the Plaintiff]'s counsel in what is called direct examination. After the direct examination of a witness is completed, the opposing side has an opportunity to cross-examine the witness. After [the Plaintiff] has presented its witnesses, [the Defendant] will call its witnesses, who will also be examined and cross-examined. The parties may present the testimony of a witness by having the individual testify live for you, by reading from their deposition transcript, or by playing a videotape of the witness's deposition testimony. All three are acceptable forms of testimony. A deposition is the sworn testimony of a witness taken before trial and is entitled to the same consideration as if the witness had testified at trial.

The evidence often is introduced piecemeal, meaning that all of the evidence relating to an issue may not be presented all at one time but, rather, may be presented at different times during the trial. You need to keep an open mind as the evidence comes in. You are to wait until all the evidence comes in before you make any decisions. In other words, keep an open mind throughout the entire trial.

In the fourth phase, the lawyers will again have an opportunity to talk to you in what is called "Closing Argument." As with the Opening Statements, what the lawyers say in the Closing Arguments is not evidence for you to consider in your deliberations.

In the fifth phase, I will read you the final jury instructions. I will instruct you on the law that you must apply in this case. I have already explained to you a little bit about the law. In the fifth phase, I will explain the law to you in more detail.

Finally, the sixth phase is the time for you to deliberate and reach a verdict. You will evaluate the evidence, discuss the evidence among yourselves, and make a decision in this case. We both have a job to do. You will decide the facts, and I will apply the law. I will explain the rules of law that apply to this case, and I will also explain the meaning of the patent claim language. You must follow my explanation of the law and the patent claim language, even if you do not agree with me. Nothing I say or do during the course of the trial is intended to indicate what your verdict should be on those facts that you must decide.

III. Glossary of Patent Terms

Application – The initial papers filed by the applicant in the United States Patent and Trademark Office (also called the Patent Office or PTO).

Claims – The numbered sentences or paragraphs appearing at the end of the patent that define the invention. The words of the claims define the scope of the patent owner's exclusive rights during the life of the patent.

File wrapper – See "prosecution history" below.

License – Permission to use the patented invention(s), which may be granted by a patent owner (or a prior licensee) in exchange for a fee called a "royalty" or other compensation.

Office action – Communication from the patent examiner regarding the specification (see definition below) and/or the claims in the patent application.

Ordinary skill in the art – The level of experience, education, and/or training generally possessed by those individuals who work in the area of the invention at the time of the invention.

Patent Examiners – Personnel employed by the PTO in a specific technical area who review (examine) the patent application to determine (1) whether the claims of a patent application are patentable over the prior art considered by the examiner, and (2) whether the specification/application describes the invention with the required specificity.

Prior art (pre-AIA) – Knowledge that is available to the public either prior to the invention by the applicant or more than one year prior to the filing date of the application.

Prior Art (Post-AIA) – Knowledge that is publicly available before the effective filing date of the patent application.

Prosecution history – The written record of proceedings between the applicant and the PTO, including the original patent application and later communications between the PTO and applicant. The prosecution history may also be referred to as the "file history" or "file wrapper" of the patent during the course of this trial.

References – Any item of prior art used to determine patentability.

Specification – The information that appears in the patent and concludes with one or more claims. The specification includes the written text, the claims, and the drawings. In the specification, the inventor describes the invention, how it works, and how to make and use it.

[Others to be agreed upon between the parties]

IV. Glossary of Technical Terms

[To be agreed upon between the parties]

V. Post-Trial Instructions[25]

1. Summary of Patent Issues

I will now summarize the issues that you must decide and for which I will provide instructions to guide your deliberations. You must decide the following [three] main issues:

1. Whether [the Plaintiff] has proved that [the Defendant] infringed Claim[s] [claims in dispute] of the [abbreviated patent number] patent.

2. Whether [the Defendant] has proved that Claim[s] [claims in dispute] of the [abbreviated patent number] patent are invalid.

3. What amount of damages, if any, [the Plaintiff] has proved.

[LIST ANY OTHER PATENT ISSUES]

2. Claim Construction

2.0 Claim Construction – Generally

Before you decide whether [the Defendant] has infringed the claims of [the Plaintiff]'s patent or whether [the Plaintiff]'s patent is invalid, you will have to understand the patent claims. The patent claims are numbered sentences at the end of the patent. The patent claims involved here are [claims in dispute], beginning at column ___, line ___ of the patent, which is exhibit ___ in evidence. The claims are intended to define, in words, the boundaries of the inventor's rights. Only the claims of the patent can be infringed. Neither the written description, nor the drawings of a patent can be infringed. Each of the claims must be considered individually. You must use the same claim meaning for both your decision on infringement and your decision on invalidity.

35 U.S.C. § 112; *Source Search Techs., LLC v. LendingTree, LLC*, 588 F.3d 1063, 1075 (Fed. Cir. 2009); *Computer Docking Station Corp. v. Dell, Inc.*, 519 F.3d 1366, 1373 (Fed. Cir. 2008); *Phillips v. AWH Corp.*, 415 F.3d 1303 (Fed. Cir. 2005) (*en banc*); *Catalina Lighting, Inc. v. Lamps Plus, Inc.*, 295 F.3d 1277, 1286 (Fed. Cir. 2002); *Amazon. com, Inc. v. Barnesandnoble.com, Inc.*, 239 F.3d 1343, 1351 (Fed. Cir. 2001); *Markman v. Westview Instruments, Inc.*, 52 F.3d 967 (Fed. Cir. 1995) (*en banc*), *aff'd*, 517 U.S. 370 (1996); *SmithKline Diagnostics, Inc. v. Helena Labs. Corp.*, 859 F.2d 878, 882 (Fed. Cir. 1988).

---

25. AIPLA drafted these Model Jury Instructions assuming the litigated issues included in the instructions will be submitted to the jury. AIPLA is not suggesting that the parties have a right to a jury trial on all issues included in the instructions. The instructions used in your case should be tailored to the specific issues being litigated.

2.1 Claim Construction for the Case

It is my job as judge to provide to you the meaning of any claim language that must be interpreted. You must accept the meanings I give you and use them when you decide whether any claim has been infringed and whether any claim is invalid. I will now tell you the meanings of the following words and groups of words from the patent claims.

[READ STIPULATIONS AND COURT'S CLAIM CONSTRUCTIONS]

Phillips v. AWH Corp., 415 F.3d 1303 (Fed. Cir. 2005) (en banc); *Markman v. Westview Instruments, Inc.,* 52 F.3d 967 (Fed. Cir. 1995) (*en banc*) *aff'd,* 517 U.S. 370 (1996).

2.2 Construction of Means-Plus-Function Claims for the Case[26]

The patentee may express an element for a claim in the form of a "means" or step for performing a function.

The asserted claims of the [abbreviated patent number] patent include the following clause: "____". I have determined, as a matter of law, that this is a means-plus-function element, as described in the section of the statute I read to you. This clause requires special interpretation. This element does not cover all [[means] [steps]] that perform the recited function of "____." Rather, I have determined that the recited function is "________________________________." I have determined that [[structure] [step]] described in the patent specification and drawings that perform this recited function is "____," or an equivalent this [[structure] or [step]]. You must use this interpretation of the means-plus-function [[element] [step]] in your deliberations regarding infringement and validity, as further discussed below.

35 U.S.C. § 112; *Chicago Bd. Of Options Exchange, Inc. v. Int'l Secs. Exchange, LLC*, 677 F,3d 1361, 1366-69 (Fed. Cir. 2012); *Mettler-Toledo, Inc. v. B-Tek Scales, LLC*, 671 F.3d 1291, 1295-96 (Fed. Cir. 2012); *JVW Enters., Inc. v. Interact Accessories, Inc.*, 424 F.3d 1324, 1330-32 (Fed. Cir. 2005); *Utah Med. Prods., Inc. v. Graphic Controls Corp.*, 350 F.3d 1376, 1381 (Fed. Cir. 2003); *Carroll Touch, Inc.*

26. Give Instruction 2.2 only if the case involves means-plus-function claims. In Instruction 2.1, the court provides its construction of any terms for which a construction is needed. This should include its construction of any limitations governed by 35 U.S.C. § 112 ¶ 6, or § 112(f). Where the limitation uses the phrase "means for" or "step for," a jury may nonetheless incorrectly conclude that the limitation includes any component or any step that accomplishes the specified function. To avoid confusing the jury, we recommend use of Instruction 2.2. Where the limitation is governed by 35 U.S.C. § 112 ¶ 6, or § 112(f), but does not use the phrase "means for" or "step for," consideration should be given to whether Instruction 2.2 is unnecessary.

v. Electro Mech. Sys., Inc., 15 F.3d 1573, 1578 (Fed. Cir. 1993); *Valmont Indus., Inc. v. Reinke Mfg. Co., Inc.*, 983 F.2d 1039, 1042 (Fed. Cir. 1993).]

3. Infringement

3.0 Infringement – Generally

Questions _____ through _____ of the Verdict Form read as follows: [READ TEXT OF INFRINGEMENT VERDICT QUESTIONS].

I will now instruct you as to the rules you must follow when deciding whether [the Plaintiff] has proven that [the Defendant] infringed any of the claims of the [abbreviated patent number] patent.

Patent law gives the owner of a valid patent the right to exclude others from importing, making, using, offering to sell, or selling [[the patented invention] [a product made by a patented method]] within the United States during the term of the patent. Any person or business entity that has engaged in any of those acts without the patent owner's permission infringes the patent. Here, [the Plaintiff] alleges that [the Defendant]'s [allegedly infringing product] infringes claim[s] [claims in dispute] of [the Plaintiff]'s [abbreviated patent number] patent.

You have heard evidence about both [the Plaintiff]'s commercial [[product] [method]] and [the Defendant]'s accused [[product] [method]]. However, in deciding the issue of infringement you may not compare [the Defendant]'s accused [[product] [method]] to [the Plaintiff]'s commercial [[product] [method]]. Rather, you must compare the [Defendant]'s accused [[product] [method]] to the claims of the [abbreviated patent number] patent when making your decision regarding infringement.

> **Practice Note:** To avoid jury confusion, it is important to distinguish those claims that are allegedly infringed directly from those that are allegedly infringed indirectly. In addition, it is important to distinguish those claims that are allegedly infringed literally from those allegedly infringed under the doctrine of equivalents. Finally, for indirect infringement, induced infringement should be distinguished from contributory infringement. In order to provide the jury with clear guidance and avoid confusion, the Court should only charge the jury on the specific infringement issues that are actually at issue. For example, if only literal infringement is asserted, there is no need to instruct the jury on the doctrine of equivalents.

A patent may be infringed directly or indirectly. As explained further in the following instructions, direct infringement results if the accused [[product] [method]] is covered by at least one claim of the patent. Indirect infringement results if the defendant induces another to infringe a patent or contributes to the infringement of a patent by another.

35 U.S.C. § 271; *Limelight Networks, Inc. v. Akamai Techs., Inc.*, 572 U.S. ___, 134 S. Ct. 2111, 189 L.Ed.2d 52 (2014); *Merial Ltd. v. CIPLA Ltd.*, 681 F.3d 1283, 1302-03 (Fed. Cir. 2012); *WiAV Solutions LLC v. Motorola, Inc.*, 631 F.3d 1257, 1264 (Fed. Cir. 2010); *WordTech Sys., Inc. v. Integrated Network Solutions, Inc.*, 609 F.3d 1308, 1313-18 (Fed. Cir. 2010).

3.1 Direct Infringement – Knowledge of the Patent and Intent to Infringe are Immaterial

In this case, [the Plaintiff] asserts that [the Defendant] has directly infringed the patent. [the Defendant] is liable for directly infringing [the Plaintiff]'s patent if you find that [the Plaintiff] has proven that it is more likely than not that [the Defendant] made, used, imported, offered to sell, or sold the invention defined in at least one claim of [the Plaintiff]'s patent.

Someone can directly infringe a patent without knowing of the patent or without knowing that what they are doing is an infringement of the patent. They also may directly infringe a patent even though they believe in good faith that what they are doing does not infringe a patent or if they believe in good faith that the patent is invalid.

35 U.S.C. § 271(a); *Medtronic, Inc. v. Mirowski Family Ventures, LLC*, 571 U.S. ___, 124 S. Ct. 843 (2014); *Global-Tech Appliances, Inc., v. SEB, S.A.*, 563 U.S. ___ , n.2, 131 S. Ct. 2060, 2065 n.2 (2011); *Warner-Jenkinson Co. v. Hilton Davis Chem. Co.*, 520 U.S. 17, 35 (1997); *DeMarini Sports, Inc. v. Worth, Inc.*, 239 F.3d 1314, 1330 (Fed. Cir. 2001); *Seal-Flex, Inc. v. Athletic Track & Court Constr.*, 172 F.3d 836, 842 (Fed. Cir. 1999); *SmithKline Diagnostics, Inc. v. Helena Labs. Corp.*, 859 F.2d 878, 889 (Fed. Cir. 1988).

3.2 Direct Infringement – Literal Infringement

To determine literal infringement, you must compare the accused [[product] [method]] with each claim that [the Plaintiff] asserts is infringed, using my instructions as to the meaning of the patent claims.

A patent claim is literally infringed only if [the Defendant]'s [[product] [method]] includes each and every [[element] [method step]] in that patent claim. If [the Defendant]'s [[product] [method]] does not contain one or more [[elements] [method steps]] recited in a claim, [the Defendant] does not literally infringe that claim.

You must determine literal infringement with respect to each patent claim individually.

The accused [[product] [method]] should be compared to the invention described in each patent claim it is alleged to infringe. The same [[element] [method step]] of the accused [product] [method] may satisfy more than one element of a claim.

Intellectual Sci. & Tech. v. Sony Elect., 589 F.3d 1179, 1183 (Fed. Cir. 2009); *Hutchins v. Zoll Med. Corp.*, 492 F.3d 1377, 1380 (Fed. Cir. 2007); *BMC Resources v. Paymentech, L.P.*, 498 F.3d 1373, 1381-82 (Fed. Cir. 2007); *DeMarini Sports, Inc. v. Worth, Inc.*, 239 F.3d 1314, 1330-31 (Fed. Cir. 2001); *Gen. Mills, Inc. v. Hunt-Wesson, Inc.*, 103 F.3d 978, 981 (Fed. Cir. 1997); *Martin v. Barber*, 755 F.2d 1564, 1567 (Fed. Cir. 1985); *Amstar Corp. v. Envirotech Corp.*, 730 F.2d 1476, 1481-82 (Fed. Cir. 1984).

3.2.1 Direct Infringement – Joint Infringement[27]

In this case, [the Defendant] is accused of direct infringement. [the Defendant] asserts that it has not directly infringed the [abbreviated patent number] patent because it did not perform each step of a claimed method or did not perform all the steps necessary to make, sell, offer for sale, or import [allegedly infringing product] because [another party] performed one of more of the acts necessary to infringe. If you find that one or more of the steps cannot be attributed to [the Defendant], then you must find that there is no joint infringement. For example, if you find that several parties have collectively committed the acts necessary to infringe but no single party has committed all of the required acts, then you must find that there is no joint infringement.

However, if you find that [the Defendant] performed all of the acts necessary to infringe, either personally or that the steps performed by the other person are attributable to [the Defendant], [the Defendant] directly infringes. In determining whether the steps are attributable to [the Defendant], you should consider whether [the Defendant] exercised direction or control over [the other party] when it performed these acts.

If you find that [the Defendant] and [the other party] have a contract that requires [the other party] to perform a step [[steps]] of the claimed method on [the Defendant]'s behalf, then you should find that [the Defendant] has granted [the other party] authority to act on [the Defendant]'s behalf and that [the other party] has agreed to so act.

Muniauction, Inc. v. Thomson Corp., 532 F.3d 1318 (Fed. Cir. 2008); *BMC Resources v. Paymentech, L.P.*, 498 F.3d 1373, 1381-82 (Fed. Cir. 2007). *Limelight Networks, Inc. v. Akami Techs., Inc.*, 572 U.S. ___, 134 S. Ct. 2111, 189 L.Ed.2d 52 (2014).

> **Practice Note:** The concepts of direct infringement based on joint infringement and indirect infringement based on inducement to infringe (Instruction 3.10) are closely-related and may be confusing to the jury. Care should be taken to be clear regarding the instructions on each issue and what findings the jury is being

27. Give instructions on Joint Infringement and Active Inducement to Infringe only if these issues are raised and are adequately supported by the evidence.

asked to make. Only if these theories of infringement are alleged and have been adequately supported by sufficient evidence should these instructions be given. If both instructions are being given, consideration should be given to instructing on joint infringement and inducement to infringe (Instruction 3.10) back-to-back and in a manner that readily allows the jury to appreciate the difference between the two theories, the evidence required to support each, and the specific findings they are being asked to make on each.

3.3 Literal Infringement of Means-Plus-Function or Step-Plus Function Claims[28]

The Court has instructed you that claims _____ through _____of the [abbreviated patent number] patent contain [[means-plus-function] [step-plus-function]] clauses. To establish infringement, [the Plaintiff] must prove that it is more likely than not that the [[part of the Defendant's product] [step in the Defendant's method]]: (1) performs the recited function of "_______________________________"; and (2) is identical or equivalent to the [[structure] [step]] described in the patent specification and drawings for performing this recited function, namely, "_______________________________."

In deciding whether [the Plaintiff] has proven that [the Defendant]'s [[product] [method]] includes structure covered by a [[means-plus-function] [step-plus-function]] requirement, you must first decide whether the [[product] [method]] has any [[structure] [step]] that performs the specific function [step] that I just described to you. If not, the claim containing that means-plus-function [or step-plus-function] requirement is not infringed.

Even if you find that [the Defendant]'s [product] [method] includes some [structure] [step] that performs this specific function, you must next decide whether the [structure] [step] in [the Defendant]'s [[product] [method] is the same as, or equivalent to, the structure recited in the specification for performing this specific function.

Whether the [[structure] [act]] of the accused product is equivalent to a [[structure] [act]] described in the patent specification is decided from the perspective of a person of ordinary skill in the art. If a person of ordinary skill in the art would consider the differences between the [[structure] [act]] found in [the Defendant]'s product and a [[structure] [act]] described in the patent specification to be insubstantial, the [[structures] [acts]] are equivalent. One way of showing that an element is insubstantially different is to show that it performs substantially the same

28. This Instruction should be given only if infringement of a means-plus-function claim is asserted and there is sufficient evidence to support this assertion.

function, in substantially the same way, to achieve substantially the same result as would be achieved by the element that is not literally present in the accused [[structure]][[act]].

Only if you find both that [the Defendant]'s [product] [method] has the same or equivalent [structure] [step] for performing the specific function can you find that the claim containing the [means-plus-function] or [step-plus-function] limitation is infringed. If you find that either the recited [structure] [step] is not performed or that the [structure] [step] in [the Defendant]'s product that performs this specific function is not the same or equivalent, you must find that the claim containing the means-plus-function limitation is not infringed.

35 U.S.C. § 112; *Cybor Corp. v. FAS Techs., Inc.*, 138 F.3d 1448, 1457 (Fed. Cir. 1998) (*en banc*); *In re Donaldson Co., Inc.*, 16 F.3d 1189, 1193 & 1195 (Fed. Cir. 1994) (*en banc*); *Chicago Bd. Options Exchange, Inc. v. Int'l. Secs. Exchange, LLC*, 677 F.3d 1361, 1366-69 (Fed. Cir. 2012); *Uniloc USA, Inc. v. Microsoft Corp.*, 632 F.3d 1292, 1304-05 (Fed. Cir. 2011); *General Protecht Gp., Inc. v. Int'l Trade Comm'n.*, 619 F.3d 1303, 1312-13 (Fed. Cir. 2010); *Baran v. Med. Device Tech., Inc.*, 616 F.3d 1309, 1316-17, (Fed. Cir. 2010); *Intellectual Sci. and Tech., Inc. v. Sony Elecs., Inc.*, 589 F.3d 1179, 1183 (Fed. Cir. 2009); *Applied Med. Resources Corp. v. U.S. Surgical Corp.*, 448 F.3d 1324, 1333-34 (Fed. Cir. 2006); *Chiuminatta Concrete Concepts, Inc. v. Cardinal Indus., Inc.*, 145 F.3d 1303, 1307-09 (Fed. Cir. 1998); *Kraft Foods Inc. v. Int'l Trade Comm.*, 203 F.3d 1362, 1371-73 (Fed. Cir. 2000).

3.4 Infringement of Dependent Claims

There are two different types of claims in the patent. One type is called an independent claim. The other is called a dependent claim.

An independent claim does not refer to any other claim of the patent. For example, [Independent Claim] is an independent claim. An independent claim must be read separately from the other claims to determine the scope of the claim.

A dependent claim refers to at least one other claim in the patent. For example, [Dependent Claim] is a dependent claim that refers to claim [Independent Claim]. A dependent claim includes all of the elements recited in the dependent claim, as well as all of the elements of [Independent Claim] the claim to which it refers.

To establish literal infringement of [Dependent Claim], [the Plaintiff] must show that it is more likely than not that the [Defendant]'s [[product] [method]] includes each and every element of [Independent Claim] and [Dependent Claim].

If you find that [Independent Claim] from which [Dependent Claim] depends is not literally infringed, then you must find that [Dependent Claim] is also not literally infringed.

Wolverine World Wide v. Nike Inc., 38 F.3d 1192, 1196-99 (Fed. Cir. 1994) (citing Johnston v. IVAC Corp., 885 F.2d 1574, 1577-89 (Fed. Cir. 1989)); *Wilson Sporting Goods v. David Geoffrey & Assocs.*, 904 F.2d 677, 685-86 (Fed. Cir. 1990); *Wahpeton Canvas Co., Inc. v. Frontier, Inc.*, 870 F.2d 1546, 1552-53 nn.9&10 (Fed. Cir. 1989); *Shatterproof Glass Corp. v. Libbey-Owens Ford Co.*, 758 F.2d 613, 626 (Fed. Cir. 1985).

3.5 Infringement of Open Ended or "Comprising" Claims

(Alternative 1: "comprising") The preamble to claim _____ uses the phrase [RECITE THE PREAMBLE "_________ comprising"]. The word "comprising" means "including the following but not excluding others."

If you find that [the Defendant]'s [[product] [method]] includes all of the elements in claim _____, and that [the Defendant]'s [[product] [method]] it may include additional [[components] [method steps]], you must find that [the Defendant]'s [product] [method] literally infringes claim _____.

(Alternative 2: "consisting of") The preamble to claim _____ uses the phrase [RECITE THE PREAMBLE "_________ consisting of"]. The word "consisting of" means "including the following and excluding others."

If you find that [the Defendant]'s [[product] [method]] includes all of the elements in claim _____, and that [the Defendant]'s [[product] [method]] includes additional [[components] [method steps]], you must find that [the Defendant]'s product does not literally infringe claim _____.

(Alternative 3: "consisting essentially of") The preamble to claim _____ uses the phrase [RECITE THE PREAMBLE "_________ consisting essentially of"]. The words "consisting essentially of" mean "including the following and possibly including unlisted [components][method steps] that do not materially affect the invention."

CIAS Inc. v. Alliance Gaming Corp., 504 F.3d 1356 (Fed. Cir. 2007); *Norian Corp. v. Stryker Corp.*, 363 F.3d 1321, 1331(Fed. Cir. 2004); *Invitrogen Corp. v. Biocrest Mfg. LP*, 327 F.3d 1364, 1368 (Fed. Cir. 2003); *AFG Indus. v. Cardinal IG Co.*, 239 F.3d 1239, 1244-45 (Fed. Cir. 2001); *PPG Indus. v. Guardian Indus. Corp.*, 156 F.3d 1351, 1354 (Fed. Cir. 1998); *Moleculon Research Corp. v. CBS, Inc.*, 793 F.2d 1261, 1271 (Fed. Cir. 1986); *AB Dick Co. v. Burroughs Corp.*, 713 F.2d 700, 703 (Fed. Cir. 1983).

> **Practice Note:** If the accused product or method includes all of the elements of the claim and also additional components or steps as well, the jury must find literal infringement as long as the additional elements do not negate any claim element.
> If the claim is literally infringed, there is no need to resort to the doctrine of equivalents. Similarly, the doctrine of equivalents is available only if one or more of the claim elements is not literally met. The patentee should be required to state their theory of infringement prior to trial and the jury should be charged on only the theory of infringement—literal and/or equivalents—that is adequately supported by the evidence.

3.6 Direct Infringement – Infringement Under the Doctrine of Equivalents[29]

If you decide that [the Defendant]'s [[product] [method]] does not literally infringe an asserted patent claim, you must then decide whether it is more probable than not that [[product] [method]] infringes the asserted claim under what is called the "doctrine of equivalents." Under the doctrine of equivalents, the [[product] [method]] can infringe an asserted patent claim if it includes [[parts] [steps]] that are equivalent to those elements of the claim that are not literally present in the [[product][method]]. If the [[product] [method]] is missing an equivalent [[part] [step]] to even one [[part] [step]] of the asserted patent claim, the [[product] [method]] cannot infringe the claim under the doctrine of equivalents. Thus, in making your decision under the doctrine of equivalents, you must look at each individual element of the asserted patent claim and decide whether the [[product] [method]] has an equivalent [[part] [step]] to the individual claim element(s) that are not literally present in the [[product][method]].

An equivalent of an element is a [[component]][[action]] that is insubstantially different from the claimed element. One way of showing that an element is insubstantially different is to show that it performs substantially the same function, in substantially the same way, to achieve substantially the same result as would be achieved by the element that is not literally present in the accused [[product]][[method]].

In deciding whether any difference between a claim requirement and the [[product] [method]] is not substantial, you may consider whether, at the time of the alleged infringement, persons of ordinary skill in the field would have known of the interchangeability of the [[part] [step]] with the claimed requirement. The known interchangeability between the claim requirement and the [[part] [step]] of the [[product] [method]] is not necessary to find infringement under the doctrine of equivalents.

---

29. This additional Instruction on equivalents should be given only if infringement under the doctrine of equivalents is properly before the court.

[Further, the same [[element] [method step]] of the accused [[product] [method]] may satisfy more than one element of a claim. If you find that all of the remaining elements of the claim are present in the accused [[product] [method]] and, further, that these differences are insubstantial, you may find infringement under the doctrine of equivalents.][30]

[Further, two [[elements] [methods]] of the accused [[product] [method] may satisfy a single claimed. If you find that all of the remaining elements of the claim are present in the accused [[product] [method]] and, further, that these differences are insubstantial, you may find infringement under the doctrine of equivalents.][31]

Warner-Jenkinson Co., Inc. v. Hilton Davis Chem. Co., 520 U.S. 17 (1997); *Graver Tank & Mfg. Co, v. Linde Air Prods. Co.*, 339 U.S. 605, 609 (1950); *Johnson & Johnston Assoc. v. R.E. Serv. Co.*, 285 F.3d 1046, 1053-54 (Fed. Cir. 2002) (*en banc*); *Multiform Desiccants, Inc. v. Medzam, Ltd.*, 133 F.3d 1473, 1480 (Fed. Cir. 1998); *Dolly, Inc. v. Spalding & Evenflo Cos.*, 16 F.3d 394, 397 (Fed. Cir. 1994); *Datascope Corp. v. SMEC, Inc.*, 776 F.2d 320, 325 (Fed. Cir. 1985); *Eagle Comtronics, Inc. v. Arrow Commc'n. Labs., Inc.*, 305 F.3d 1303, 1316-17 (Fed. Cir. 2002); *DeMarini Sports, Inc. v. Worth, Inc.*, 239 F.3d 1314, 1332, 57 USPQ2d 1889, 1900 (Fed. Cir. 2001) (citing *Dolly, Inc. v. Spalding & Evenflo Cos., Inc.*, 16 F.3d 394, 398, 29 USPQ2d 1767, 1769-70 (Fed. Cir. 1994)).

a. Limitations on the Doctrine of Equivalents – Prior Art[32]

The patentee is not entitled to a scope of equivalents under the "doctrine of equivalents" that is so broad that the claim would cover [[products] [methods]] that were already in the prior art. In this case, [the Defendant] alleges that the scope of the claim under the doctrine of equivalents asserted by [the Plaintiff] would cover the prior art, namely, ____.
In order to show that [the Plaintiff] is not entitled to this scope of equivalents, [the Defendant] must prove to you that ________________________________
was in the prior art.[33] [The Defendant] must show that it was in the prior art by a

---

30. *Eagle Comtronics, Inc. v. Arrow Commc'n. Labs., Inc.*, 305 F.3d 1303, 1316-17 (Fed. Cir. 2002); *DeMarini Sports, Inc. v. Worth, Inc.*, 239 F.3d 1314, 1332, 57 USPQ2d 1889, 1900 (Fed. Cir. 2001) (citing *Dolly, Inc. v. Spalding & Evenflo Cos., Inc.*, 16 F.3d 394, 398, 29 USPQ2d 1767, 1769-70 (Fed. Cir. 1994)).

31. *Id.*

32. This Instruction should be given only if the Defendant has identified sufficient evidence that this issue is genuinely disputed.

33. Although "ensnarement" is a question of law, a court may obtain an Advisory Verdict on this question necessitating inclusion of Instruction 3.7. In particular, the Federal Circuit has held that the question of whether the scope of a claim under the doctrine of equivalents ensnares the prior art is "ultimately . . . a question of law for the court, not the jury, to decide," but "[i]f a district court believes that an advisory verdict would be helpful, and that a 'hypothetical' claim construct would not unduly confuse the jury as to equivalence and va-

preponderance of the evidence. This is different, and lower, namely, more likely than not, than the burden Defendant has to prove invalidity by clear and convincing evidence.

If you find that the claim including the alleged equivalent, namely, _______ ________________________ was in the prior art, then you must find that [the Defendant] does not infringe the claim under the doctrine of equivalents. If you find that [the Defendant] has not proven to you that it is more likely than not that ____ is in the prior art, you may consider that [the Defendant] has not established this defense.

DePuy Spine, Inc. v. Medtronic Sofamor Danek, Inc., 567 F.3d 1314, 1322-24 (Fed. Cir. 2009); *Fiskars, Inc. v. Hunt Mfg. Co.*, 221 F.3d 1318, 1323 (Fed. Cir. 2000); *Conroy v. Reebok Int'l, Ltd.*, 14 F.3d 1570, 1576-77 (Fed. Cir. 1994); *Wilson Sporting Goods Co. v. David Geoffrey & Assocs.*, 904 F.2d 677, 683-85 (Fed. Cir. 1990).

> **Practice Note**: The doctrine of prosecution history estoppel is determined by the Court. The following Instruction should be given only if the Court has determined that the doctrine of prosecution history estoppel applies as a matter of law. Specifically, this requires that the patentee made a representation or argument, or that an amendment to the claim was made for reasons related to patentability, and the presumption that the equivalent subject matter has been surrendered by the patentee has not been rebutted.

3.8 Limitations on the Doctrine of Equivalents – Prosecution History Estoppel[34]

In this case, I have determined, as a matter of law, that the doctrine of equivalents cannot be applied to certain elements of the asserted claims. I am instructing you that the following elements cannot be considered equivalents to elements of the asserted claims:

[List Elements on a claim by claim basis]

Consequently, each of the elements above must be literally present within [the Defendant]'s [[product] [method]] for there to be infringement of the claim.

As for the remaining elements of the asserted claims not listed above, you are permitted to find these elements with the doctrine of equivalents analysis that I instructed you on earlier.

---

lidity, then one may be obtained under Federal Rule of Civil Procedure 39(c)." *DePuy Spine, Inc. v. Medtronic Sofamor Danek, Inc.*, 567 F.3d 1314, 1324 (Fed. Cir. 2009).

34. This Instruction should be given only if the Defendant has identified sufficient evidence that this issue is genuinely disputed.

Festo Corp. v. Shoketsu Kinzoku Kogyo Kabushiki Co., 535 U.S. 722 (2002); *Warner-Jenkinson Co. v. Hilton Davis Chem. Co.*, 520 U.S. 17, 30-34 (1997); *Festo Corp. v. Shoketsu Kinzoku Kogyo Kabushiki Co.*, 344 F.3d 1359, 1366-67 (Fed. Cir. 2003) (*en banc*).

3.9 Limitations on the Doctrine of Equivalents – Subject Matter Dedicated to the Public[35]

When a patent discloses subject matter but does not include it within its claims, the patentee has dedicated the unclaimed subject matter to the public. If [the Patentee] alleges that a [[component] [step]] of [the Defendant]'s [product] [method] that [the patent] discloses but does not claim is equivalent to a limitation of the claim that is missing from [the Defendant]'s [product] [method] the [component] [step] cannot be an equivalent. Instead, the subject matter that was disclosed but not claimed is dedicated to the public. This is true even if the failure to claim the subject matter was wholly unintentional.

In this case, I have determined as a matter of law, that certain subject matter from the patent has been dedicated to the public and the doctrine of equivalents analysis cannot be applied to the following elements of the asserted claims:

[LIST ELEMENTS ON A CLAIM-BY-CLAIM BASIS]

Unless you find that each of the elements of the claims is literally present in [the Defendant]'s [[product] [method]], you must find that there is no infringement. *Pfizer, Inc. v. Teva Pharms., USA, Inc.*, 429 F.3d 1364, 1378-79 (Fed. Cir. 2005); *Toro Co. v. White Consol. Indus., Inc.*, 383 F.3d 1326 (Fed. Cir. 2004); *Johnson & Johnston Assocs. Inc. v. R.E. Serv. Co.*, 285 F.3d 1046, 1054-55 (Fed. Cir. 2002) (*en banc*).

> **Practice Note:** The concepts of direct infringement based on joint infringement (Instruction 3.2) and indirect infringement based on inducement to infringe are closely-related and may be confusing to the jury. Care should be taken to be clear regarding the instructions on each issue and what findings the jury is being asked to make. Only if these theories of infringement are alleged and have been adequately supported by sufficient evidence should these instructions be given. If both instructions are being given, consideration should be given to instructing on joint infringement (Instruction 3.2) and inducement to infringe back-to-back and in a manner that readily allows the jury to appreciate the difference between the two theories, the evidence required to support each, and the specific findings they are being asked to make on each

---

35. This Instruction should be given only if the Defendant has identified sufficient evidence that this issue is genuinely disputed.

3.10 Actively Inducing Patent Infringement

In this case, [the Defendant] is accused of actively inducing [another entity] to directly infringe [the Plaintiff]'s patent, either literally or under the doctrine of equivalents. To find that [the Defendant] actively induced infringement, it is not necessary to show that [the Defendant] personally directly infringed, provided: (1) a single actor is responsible for direct infringement, namely, all of the [components] [steps] of the [product] [method] accused of infringing the patent; and (2) [the Defendant] actively induced these acts of infringement by [another entity]. If you do not find that there is direct infringement by a single actor, or if you do not find that [the Defendant] actively induced these acts, you must find that [the Defendant] did not induce infringement of the patent.[36]

To prove active inducement, [the Plaintiff] must establish that it is more likely than not that:

1. [the Defendant] aided, instructed, or otherwise acted with the intent to cause acts by [alleged direct infringer] that would constitute direct infringement of the patent;

2. [the Defendant] knew of the patent, or showed willful blindness to the existence of the patent, at that time;

3. [the Defendant] knew, or showed willful blindness that it consciously ignored the possibility that its actions would infringe at least one claim of the patent; and

4. [alleged direct infringer] infringed at least one patent claim.

To find willful blindness: (1) [the Defendant] must have subjectively believed that there was a high probability that a patent existed covering [the accused product/process]; and (2) [the Defendant] must have taken deliberate actions to avoid learning of the patent.

35 U.S.C. § 271(b); *Limelight Networks, Inc. v. Akamai Techs., Inc.*, 572 U.S. ___, 134 S. Ct. 2111, 189 L.Ed.2d 52 (2014); *Global-Tech Appliances, Inc., v. SEB, S.A.*, 563 U.S. ___, 131 S. Ct. 2060 (2011); *Commil USA, LLC v. Cisco Sys., Inc.*, 720 F.3d 1361, 1368 (Fed. Cir. 2013); *DSU Medical Corp. v. JMS Co.*, 471 F.3d 1293, 1304-05 (Fed. Cir. 2006) (en banc) (quoting *Metro-Goldwyn-Mayer Studios, Inc. v. Grokster, Ltd.*, 545 U.S. 913, 936 (2005)); *Metabolite Labs., Inc. v. Lab. Corp. of Am. Holdings*, 370 F.3d 1354, 1365 (Fed. Cir. 2004); *Ferguson Beauregard/Logic Controls, Div. of Dover Res., Inc. v. Mega Sys., LLC*, 350 F.3d 1327, 1342 (Fed. Cir. 2003); *Manville Sales Corp. v. Paramount Sys., Inc.*, 917 F.2d 544, 553 (Fed. Cir.

---

36. The issue of active inducement to infringe is currently the subject of a petition for a writ of certiorari to the Federal Circuit, in *Commil v. Costco,* Docket No. 13-896,

1990); *Hewlett-Packard Co. v. Bausch & Lomb, Inc.*, 909 F.2d 1464, 1468-69 (Fed. Cir. 1990).

Bard Peripheral Vascular, Inc. v. W.L. Gore & Assocs., Inc., 682 F.3d 1003, 1006-08 (Fed. Cir. 2012); *Powell v. Home Depot USA, Inc.*, 663 F.3d. 1221, 1236-37 (Fed. Cir. 2011); *i4i Ltd. P'Ship. v. Microsoft Corp.*, 598 F.3d 831, 859-60 (Fed. Cir. 2010); *Spine Solutions, Inc. v. Medtronic Sofamor Danek USA, Inc.*, 620 F.3d 1305, 1319 (Fed. Cir. 2010); *In re Seagate Tech., LLC*, 497 F.3d 1360 (Fed. Cir. 2007) (*en banc*); *Knorr-Bremse Systeme Fuer Nutzfahrzeuge GmbH v. Dana Corp.*, 383 F.3d 1337, 1347 (Fed. Cir. 2004) (*en banc*).

> **Practice Note:** Each of the theories of indirect infringement has a number of elements and the Instructions tend to be complex. In order to avoid the risk of jury confusion, it is important to instruct the jury on only those issues that are properly before the Court. Consideration should be given to using case management techniques, such as charging the jury and having the jury deliberate on specific issues separately, to reduce the risk of confusion

3.11 Infringement by Supply of all or a Substantial Portion of the Components of a Patented Invention to Another Country (§ 271(f)(1))

[Plaintiff] asserts that [Defendant] infringed the [abbreviated patent number] patent by supplying [or causing to be supplied] all or a substantial portion of the components of the patented product from the United States to another country and actively inducing the assembly of those components into a product that would infringe the [abbreviated patent number] patent if they had been assembled in the United States.

To show infringement under Section 271(f)(1), [the Plaintiff] must prove that each of the following is more likely than not:

1. the product, as it was intended to be assembled outside the United States, [included][would have included] all limitations of at least one of claims ____ of the [abbreviated patent number] patent;

2. [the Defendant] supplied [or caused to be supplied] components from the United States that made up all or a substantial portion of the invention of any one of claims _____ of the [abbreviated patent number] patent; and

3. [the Defendant] specifically intended to induce the combination of the components into a product that would infringe the [abbreviated patent number] patent if the components had been combined in the United States.

35 U.S.C. § 271(f)(1); *Cardiac Pacemakers, Inc. v. St. Jude Medical, Inc.* 576 F.3d 1348, 1359-67 (Fed. Cir. 2009); *Microsoft Corp. v. AT&T Corp.*, 550 U.S. 437, 453-56 (2007); *Minn. Mining & Mfg. Co. v. Chemque, Inc.*, 303 F.3d 1294, 1304-05 (Fed. Cir. 2002).

3.12 Contributory Infringement

[The Plaintiff] asserts that [the Defendant] has contributed to infringement by another person.

To establish contributory infringement, [the Plaintiff] must prove that it is more likely than not that [the Defendant] had knowledge of both the patent and direct infringement of that patent. Plaintiff must prove that each of the following is more likely than not:

1. someone other than [the Defendant] has directly infringed the [abbreviated patent number] patent;

2. [the Defendant] sold, offered for sale, or imported within the United States a component of the infringing product or an apparatus for use in the infringing process;

3. the component or apparatus is not a staple article or commodity of commerce capable of substantial non-infringing use;

4. the component or apparatus constitutes a material part of the patented invention; and

5. [the Defendant] knew that the component was especially made or adapted for use in an infringing [[product] [method]].

Proof of [the Defendant's] knowledge may be shown with evidence of willful blindness where [the Defendant] consciously ignored the existence of both the patent and direct infringement of that patent. To find willful blindness: (1) [the Defendant] must have subjectively believed that there was a high probability that a patent existed covering [the accused product/process] and (2) [the Defendant] must have taken deliberate actions to avoid learning of the patent.

A "staple article or commodity of commerce capable of substantial non-infringing use" is something that has uses [[other than as a part or component of the patented product] [other than in the patented method]], and those other uses are not occasional, farfetched, impractical, experimental, or hypothetical.

To find contributory infringement, it is not necessary to show that [the Defendant] has directly infringed as long as you find that someone has directly infringed. If you find that there is no direct infringement by any one single entity, you must find that [the Defendant] did not contribute to the infringement of the patent.

35 U.S.C. § 271(c); *Global-Tech Appliances, Inc., v. SEB, S.A.*, 563 U.S. ___, 131 S. Ct. 2060, 2068-70 (2011); *Aro Mfg. Co. v. Convertible Top Replacement Co.*, 377 U.S. 476, 488 (1964); *Commil USA, LLC v. Cisco Sys., Inc.*, 720 F.3d 1361, 1368 (Fed. Cir. 2013); *Toshiba Corp. v. Imation Corp.*, 681 F.3d 1358, 1362 (Fed. Cir. 2012); *R+L Carriers, Inc. v. DriverTech LLC*, 681 F.3d 1323, 1337 (Fed. Cir. 2012); *Spansion, Inc. v. Int'l Trade Comm'n*, 629 F.3d 1331, 1353 (Fed. Cir. 2010); *Fujitsu Ltd. v. Netgear Inc.*, 620 F.3d 1321, 1326 (Fed. Cir. 2010).

3.13 Infringement by Supply of Components Especially Made or Adapted for Use in the Patented Invention into Another Country (§ 271(f)(2))

[The Plaintiff] asserts that [the Defendant] infringed the [abbreviated patent number] patent by supplying [or causing to be supplied] [a component][components] of an invention covered by at least one claim of the [abbreviated patent number] patent from the United States into a foreign country, where the exported component[s] [was][were] especially made or especially adapted for use in an invention covered by the [abbreviated patent number] patent and [has][have] no substantial non-infringing use[s], and where [the Defendant] knew the component[s] [was][were] especially made or adapted for use in the patented invention and intended for the component[s] to be combined in a way that would have infringed the [abbreviated patent number] patent if the combination had occurred in the United States.

To show infringement under Section 271(f)(2), [the Plaintiff] must prove that each of the following is more likely than not:

1. [the Defendant] actually supplied the components from the United States into a foreign country or caused them to be supplied from the United States to a foreign country;

2. [the Defendant] knew or should have known that the components were especially made or adapted for use in a product that infringes the [abbreviated patent number] patent;

3. those components have no substantial non-infringing use; and

4. [the Defendant] intended for the components to be combined into that product . It is not necessary for you to find that the components actually were combined into an infringing product, as long as you find that [Defendant] intended the components to be combined into a product that would have infringed the [abbreviated patent number] patent if they had been combined in the United States.

35 U.S.C. § 271(f)(2); *Cardiac Pacemakers, Inc. v. St. Jude Medical, Inc.* 576 F.3d 1348, 1359-67 (Fed. Cir. 2009); *Microsoft Corp. v. AT&T Corp.*, 550 U.S. 437, 453-56 (2007); *Waymark Corp. v. Porta Sys. Corp.*, 245 F.3d 1364, 1367-69 (Fed. Cir.

2001); *Rotec Indus., Inc. v. Mitsubishi Corp.*, 215 F.3d 1246, 1257-58 (Fed. Cir. 2000)

3.14 Infringement by Import, Sale, Offer for Sale or Use of Product Made by Patented Process (§ 271(g))

[Plaintiff] asserts that [Defendant] infringed the [abbreviated patent number] patent by [importing][selling][offering for sale][using] a product that was made by a process covered by one or more claims of the [abbreviated patent number] patent.

To show infringement under Section 271(g), [the Plaintiff] must prove that each of the following is more likely than not:

1. [the Defendant] [imported][sold][offered for sale][used] a product that was made by a process that includes all steps of at least one claim of the [abbreviated patent number] patent;

2. the product was made between [issue date of patent] and [expiration date of patent][date of trial];

3. [the Defendant] [imported][sold][offered for sale][used] the product between [issue date of patent] and [expiration date of patent][date of trial].

You must decide whether the evidence presented at trial establishes that the product [imported][sold][offered for sale][used] by the Defendant was "made by" the patented process. However, if you find that either: (a) the product [imported][sold][offered for sale][used] was materially changed by later processes, or (b) the product is only a trivial or non-essential part of another product, you must find that the product [imported][sold][offered for sale][used] by the Defendant was not "made by" by the patented process.[37]

35 U.S.C. § 271(g); *Amgen Inc., v. F. Hoffman-La Roche Ltd.*, 580 F.3d 1340 (Fed. Cir. 2009); *Mycogen Plant Sci., Inc. v. Monsanto Co.*, 252 F.3d 1306 (Fed. Cir. 2001); *Biotec Biologische Naturvenpackungen GmbH v. BioCorp., Inc.*, 249 F.3d 1341 (Fed. Cir. 2001); *Eli Lilly & Co. v. American Cyanamid Co.*, 82 F.3d 1568 (Fed. Cir. 1996); *Bio-Technology Gen. Corp. v. Genentech, Inc.*, 80 F.3d 1553 (Fed. Cir. 1996).

4. Summary of Invalidity Defense

[The Defendant] contends that the asserted claim[s] of the patent[s]-in-suit are invalid. [The Defendant] must prove that it is highly probable that each asserted claim is invalid.

---

37. In cases where the patentee is unable to determine the process by which the product at issue is made, and the prerequisites of 35 U.S.C. § 295 are satisfied, the presumption of Section 295 may also need to be included in this instruction, requiring the accused infringer to rebut a presumption that the product was made by the patented process.

Claims of an issued patent may be found to be invalid. Thus, you must determine whether each of [the Plaintiff]'s claims is invalid.

[The Defendant] contends that patent claims [insert claim numbers] are invalid for the following reasons:

[Insert invalidity contentions]

I will now instruct you in more detail why [the Defendant] alleges that the asserted claim[s] of the [abbreviated patent numbers] is/are invalid.

> **Practice Note:** Jury Instructions on prior art are always complex and potentially confusing. Following implementation of the AIA, different legal principles are applicable to pre-AIA and post-AIA claims, requiring multiple instructions on similar issues, under different controlling legal principles. Consideration should be given by the Court whether to bifurcate the issues of validity of pre-AIA claims from post-AIA claims, or to separately instruct and have the jury deliberate to a verdict on these issues, in order to avoid undue burden and jury confusion. At a minimum, the issues that the jury needs to decide must be clearly identified and the instructions limited to these issues.

5. Prior Art

5.0 Prior Art Defined (For patent claims having a priority date before March 16, 2013)

Prior art includes any of the following items received into evidence during trial:

1. any [product] [method] that was publicly known or used by others in the United States before the patented invention was made;
2. patents that issued more than one year before the filing date of the patent, or before the invention was made;
3. publications having a date more than one year before the filing date of the patent, or before the invention was made;
4. any [product] [method] that was in public use or on sale in the United States more than one year before the patent was filed;
5. any [product] [method] that was made by anyone before the named inventors created the patented [product] [method] where the [product] [method] was not abandoned, suppressed, or concealed.

In this case, [the Defendant] contends that the following items are prior art:

[Identify the prior art admitted into evidence by name]

35 U.S.C. § 102 (pre-AIA).

5.0 Prior Art Defined (For patent claims having a priority date after March 16, 2013)

1. any claimed invention that was patented, described in a printed publication, or in public use, on sale, or otherwise available to the public anywhere in the world before the effective filing date of the current patent; or

2. any claimed invention that was described in a patent, or in an application for patent published or deemed published, in which the patent or application names another inventor and was filed before the effective filing date of the current patent;

Exceptions to Prior Art:

1. A disclosure made 1 year or less before the effective filing date of the current claim[s] shall not be prior art to claim[s] ___________ of the [abbreviated patent number] patent if:

   A. the disclosure was made by the inventor or joint inventor named in the current patent or by another person who obtained the subject matter disclosed directly or indirectly from such inventor; or

   B. the subject matter disclosed had, before such disclosure, been publicly disclosed by the inventor or another person who obtained the subject matter disclosed directly or indirectly from such inventor.

2. A disclosure shall not be prior art to claim[s] _________ of the [abbreviated patent number] if:

   A. the subject matter disclosed was obtained directly or indirectly from the inventor or joint inventor named in the [abbreviated patent number] patent;

   B. the subject matter disclosed had, before the effective filing date of the current patent, been publicly disclosed by the inventor or joint inventor named in the [abbreviated patent number] patent or another person who obtained the subject matter disclosed directly or indirectly from such inventor; or

   C. the subject matter disclosed and the claimed invention, not later than the effective filing date of the [abbreviated patent number] patent, were owned by the same person or subject to an obligation of assignment to the same person.

> **Practice Note:** While AIA § 102(a) does not use the term "disclosure," that section expressly identifies as "prior art" things existing before the effective filing date of the application claiming the invention that have been: (i) patented, (ii) described in a printed publication, (iii) in public use, (iv) on sale, or (v) otherwise available to the public. The term "disclosure" is used in AIA § 102(b) to describe "exceptions" to one of the disclosure means identified in AIA § 102(a) which made the claimed invention (or elements thereof) publicly accessible. This is consistent with the USPTO's AIA Examination Guidelines, 78 Fed. Reg. 11059, Feb. 14, 2013. Some commentators still question whether the AIA repudiated the doctrine of *Metallizing Engineering Co. v. Kenyon Bearing & Auto Parts*, 153 F.2d 516 (2d Cir. 1945), which barred patentability where an inventor/patentee (but not third parties) secretly, but commercially, practiced a claimed invention more than one year before its filing date

In this case, [the Defendant] contends that the following items are prior art: [identify prior art by name]

35 U.S.C. § 102 as amended by the Leahy-Smith America Invents Act of 2011.

COMMENTS:

"Effective filing date" is defined under 35 U.S.C. § 100(i).

> **Practice Note:** The issues on which the jury is being asked to make factual findings should be identified clearly and concisely. For example, if the parties dispute the status of a reference as prior art due to its date, public availability, or other factors, these issues should be identified clearly to the jury in the instructions in order to avoid jury confusion.

5.1 Prior Art Considered or Not Considered by the USPTO

Regardless whether particular prior art reference[s] was/were considered by the USPTO Examiner during the prosecution of the application which matured into the [the abbreviated number] patent, [the Defendant] must prove that the challenged claim[s] is/are invalid. [The Defendant] must do so by clear and convincing evidence. This burden of proof on [the Defendant] never changes regardless whether or not the Examiner considered the reference.

Microsoft Corp. v. i4i Ltd. P'ship., 564 U.S. __, 131 S. Ct. 2238, 2251 (2011); *Sciele Pharma Inc. v. Lupin LTD*, 684 F.3d 1253, 1260 (Fed. Cir. 2012; *SIBIA Neurosciences, Inc. v. Cadus Pharm. Corp.*, 225 F.3d 1349, 1355-56 (Fed. Cir. 2000); *Grp. One, Ltd. v. Hallmark Cards, Inc.*, 407 F.3d 1297, 1306 (Fed. Cir. 2005).

5.2 Invalidity of Independent and Dependent Claims

There are two different types of claims in the patent. One type is called an independent claim. The other is called a dependent claim.

An independent claim does not refer to any other claim of the patent. For example, [Independent Claim] is an independent claim. An independent claim must be read separately from the other claims to determine the scope of the claim.

A dependent claim refers to at least one other claim in the patent. For example, [Dependent Claim] is a dependent claim that refers to claim [Independent Claim]. A dependent claim includes all of the elements recited in the dependent claim, as well as all of the elements of [Independent Claim] the claim to which it refers.

[IDENTIFY THE DIFFERENCES BETWEEN [Independent Claim] AND [Dependent Claim]]. [Dependent Claim] requires each of the elements of [Dependent Claim], as well as all of the additional elements of [Independent Claim].

You must evaluate the invalidity of each asserted claim separately. Even if an independent claim is invalid, this does not mean that the dependent claims that depend from it are automatically invalid. Rather, you must consider the validity of each claim, separately. You must decide this issue of validity on a claim-by-claim basis. However, if you find that a dependent claim is invalid, then you must find that the independent claim from which it depends is also invalid. The dependent claim includes all of the elements of the independent claim from which it depends.

Comaper Corp. v. Antec. Inc., 596 F.3d 1343, 1350 (Fed. Cir. 2010); *Callaway Golf Co. v. Acushnet Co.*, 576 F.3d 1331, 1344 (Fed. Cir. 2009); *Ormco Corp. v. Align Tech., Inc.*, 498 F.3d 1307, 1319 (Fed. Cir. 2007).

5.3 Person of Ordinary Skill in the Art (For patent claims having a priority date before March 16, 2013)

The question of invalidity of a patent claim is determined from the perspective of a person of ordinary skill in the art in the field of the asserted invention as of [date].

You must determine the level of ordinary skill in the field of the invention. The higher the level of ordinary skill, the easier it may be to establish that an invention would have been obvious. Persons having a greater level of education, training, or experience in the field will more readily appreciate technical details that may be more challenging for persons having a lower level of skill. On the other hand, persons having a lower level of skill may not perceive as obvious technical details that would be apparent to persons having greater skill. In order to determine the obviousness of the invention you will be asked to determine what the ordinary level of skill was in the field of the invention. Regardless whether you decide to articulate in your verdict what you believe was the level of ordinary skill in the field of the invention, you must consider and assess this factor before reaching your conclusion in this case.

35 U.S.C. § 103 (pre-AIA).

5.3 Person of Ordinary Skill in the Art (For patent claims having a priority date on or after March 16, 2013)

The question of invalidity of a patent claim is determined from the perspective of a person of ordinary skill in the art in the field of the asserted invention as of [the effective filing date of the patent(s)].

You must determine the level of ordinary skill in the field of the invention. In order to determine the obviousness of the invention you will be asked to determine what the ordinary level of skill was in the field of the invention. Regardless whether you decide to articulate in your verdict what you believe was the level of ordinary skill in the field of the invention, you must consider and assess this factor before reaching your conclusion in this case.

35 U.S.C. § 103 as amended by the Leahy-Smith America Invents Act of 2011.

6. Anticipation

6.0 Anticipation

If a device or process has been previously invented and disclosed to the public, then it is not new, and therefore the claimed invention is "anticipated" by the prior invention. Simply put, the invention must be new to be entitled to patent protection under the U.S. patent laws. To prove anticipation, [the Defendant] must prove by clear and convincing evidence, namely, evidence that leaves you with a clear conviction, that the claimed invention is not new.

In this case, [the Defendant] contends that [some/all of] the claims of the [abbreviated patent number] patent are anticipated. [DESCRIBE BRIEFLY EACH BASIS FOR THE DEFENDANT'S INVALIDITY DEFENSE, FOR EXAMPLE: "First, [the Defendant] contends that the invention of claims 1, 2, and 3 of the ____ patent was described in the July, 1983 article published by Jones in THE JOURNAL OF ENDOCRINOLOGY."]

To anticipate a claim, each and every element in the claim must be present in a single item of prior art, and arranged or combined in the same way as recited in the claim. You may not combine two or more items of prior art to find anticipation. In determining whether every one of the elements of the claimed invention is found in the prior [[publication] [patent] [etc.]], you should take into account what a person of ordinary skill in the art would have understood from his or her review of the particular [[publication] [patent] [etc.]].

> **Practice Note:** If one or more elements of the claim are alleged by the Defendant to be inherent in a single prior art reference, the jury will

need to be instructed on inherency. Care should be taken to limit this instruction as appropriate to the evidence admitted in the case and to make this instruction as clear as possible. This Instruction should be given only if the issue is properly before the Court.

Inherency: In determining whether the single item of prior art anticipates a patent claim, you should take into consideration not only what is expressly disclosed in the particular prior art reference [[publication] [invention] [etc.]] but also what is inherently present or disclosed in that prior art or inherently results from its practice. Prior art inherently anticipates a patent claim if the missing element or feature would necessarily result from what the prior art teaches to persons of ordinary skill in the art. A party claiming inherent anticipation must prove by clear and convincing evidence that the allegedly inherent element necessarily is present. Evidence outside of the prior art reference itself [including experimental testing] may be used to show that elements that are not expressly disclosed in the reference are inherent in it. In order to be inherent, the feature that is alleged to have been inherent must necessarily have existed in the prior art reference. The fact that it was likely is not sufficient. It is not required, however, that persons of ordinary skill actually recognized or appreciated the inherent disclosure at the time the prior art was first known or used. Thus, the prior use of the patented invention that was unrecognized and unappreciated can still be an invalidating anticipation, provided the allegedly inherent feature was necessarily present in the reference.

You must keep these requirements in mind and apply them to each kind of anticipation you consider in this case. There are additional requirements that apply to the particular categories of anticipation that [the Defendant] contends apply in this case. I will now instruct you about these.

Net MoneyIN, Inc. v. Verisign, Inc., 545 F.3d 1359, 1369-70 (Fed. Cir. 2008); *Toro Co. v. Deere & Co.*, 355 F.3d 1313, 1320-21 (Fed. Cir. 2004); *Schering Corp. v. Geneva Pharms., Inc.*, 339 F.3d 1373, 1377-78 (Fed. Cir. 2003); *In re Robertson*, 169 F.3d 743, 745 (Fed. Cir. 1999); *Atlas Powder Co. v. IRECO Inc.*, 190 F.3d 1342, 1347-48 (Fed. Cir. 1999); *Glaverbel Societe Anonyme v. Northlake Mktg. & Supply, Inc.*, 45 F.3d 1550, 1554 (Fed. Cir. 1995); *Minn. Mining & Mfg. Co. v. Johnson & Johnson Orthopaedics, Inc.*, 976 F.2d 1559, 1565 (Fed. Cir. 1992); *Cont'l Can Co. USA v. Monsanto Co.*, 948 F.2d 1264, 1267-69 (Fed. Cir. 1991); *Buildex, Inc. v. Kason Indus., Inc.*, 849 F.2d 1461, 1463 (Fed. Cir. 1988).

6.1 Prior Public Knowledge (Pre-AIA)

[The Defendant] contends that claim __________ of the [abbreviated patent number] patent was anticipated because the invention defined in that claim was publicly known by others in the United States before it was invented by the inventor(s).

> **Practice Note:** If there is a factual issue to be resolved by the jury as to the date of invention, the jury should be instructed here as to how they should determine the date of invention. Otherwise, the Court should instruct the jury as follows: "The invention defined by claim _____ of the [abbreviated patent number] patent was invented on [invention date]."

A patent claim is invalid if the invention defined in that claim was publicly known by others in the United States before it was invented by [the patentee].

35 U.S.C. § 102(a) (pre-AIA); *Minnesota Mining and Manuf. Co. v. Chemque, Inc.*, 303 F.3d 1294, 1301, 1306 (Fed. Cir. 2002); *Ecolochem, Inc. v. Southern Cal. Edison Co.*, 227 F.3d 1361, 1369 (Fed. Cir. 2000); *Woodland Trust v. Flowertree Nursery*, 148 F.3d 1368, 1370 (Fed. Cir. 1998).

6.1 Prior Public Knowledge (Post-AIA):

[The Defendant] contends that claim ____ of the [abbreviated patent number] patent was anticipated because the invention defined in that claim was available to the public before the effective filing date of the claimed invention.

> **Practice Note:** If there is a factual issue to be resolved by the jury as to whether the prior public knowledge is the result of a disclosure made within one (1) year or less of the effective filing date by the inventor, or by another who obtained the subject matter disclosed directly from the inventor, or is subject matter which had previously been disclosed by the inventor, the jury should be instructed here as to exceptions under § 102(b).

You are instructed that the [abbreviated patent number] patent has an effective filing date of [effective filing date].

A patent claim is invalid if the invention defined in that claim was available to the public before the effective filing date of the claimed invention.

35 U.S.C. § 102(a)(1) (post-AIA); *Minnesota Mining and Manuf. Co. v. Chemque, Inc.*, 303 F.3d 1294, 1301, 1306 (Fed. Cir. 2002); *Ecolochem, Inc. v. Southern Cal. Edison Co.*, 227 F.3d 1361, 1369 (Fed. Cir. 2000); *Woodland Trust v. Flowertree Nursery*, 148 F.3d 1368, 1370 (Fed. Cir. 1998).

6.2 Prior Public Use (Pre-AIA):

[The Defendant] contends that claim _____ of the [abbreviated patent number] patent was anticipated because the invention defined in that claim [was publicly used by others in the United States before it was invented by [the patentee]] [was publicly used in the United States more than one year before [the patentee] filed his patent application on [effective filing date]].

> **Practice Note:** If there is a factual issue to be resolved by the jury as to the date of invention of the patent claims in suit, the jury should be instructed here as to how they should determine that date of invention. Otherwise, the Court should instruct the jury as follows: "The invention defined by claim _____ of the [abbreviated patent number] patent was invented on [invention date]."

A patent claim is invalid if more than one year before the filing date of the patent an embodiment of the claimed invention was both:

1. accessible to the public or commercially exploited in the United States; and
2. ready for patenting.

An invention was in public use if the claimed invention was accessible to the public or commercially exploited. Factors relevant to determining whether a use was public include: the nature of the activity that occurred in public; public access to the use; confidentiality obligations imposed upon observers; commercial exploitation; and the circumstances surrounding testing and experimentation.

An invention is publicly used if it is used by the inventor or by a person who is not under any limitation, restriction, or obligation of secrecy to the inventor. The absence of affirmative steps to conceal the use of the invention is evidence of a public use. However, secret use by a third party is not public, unless members of the public or employees of the third party have access to the invention.

In order to be a public use, the invention also must have been ready for patenting at the time of the alleged public use. An invention is ready for patenting either when it is reduced to practice or when the inventor has prepared drawings or other descriptions of the invention sufficient to allow a person of ordinary skill in the art to make or use the invention. An invention is reduced to practice when it has been: (1) constructed or performed within the scope of the patent claims; and (2) determined that it works for its intended purpose. The claimed invention is ready for patenting when there is reason to believe it would work for its intended purpose.

35 U.S.C. § 102(a), (b) (pre-AIA); *Clock Spring, L.P. v. Wrapmaster, Inc.*, 560 F.3d 1317, 1325-27 (Fed. Cir. 2009); *American Seating Co. v. USSC Grp., Inc.*, 514 F.3d 1262, 1267 (Fed. Cir. 2008); *Invitrogen Corp. v. Biocrest Manuf., L.P.*, 424 F.3d 1374, 1379-82 (Fed. Cir. 2005); *SmithKline Beecham Corp. v. Apotex Corp.*, 365 F.3d 1306, 1316-20 (Fed. Cir. 2004); *Netscape Commc'ns Corp. v. Konrad*, 295 F.3d 1315, 1320-23 (Fed. Cir. 2002); *Cooper v. Goldfarb*, 154 F.3d 1321, 1327 (Fed. Cir. 1998) (as to reduction to practice); *Grain Processing Corp. v. Am. Maize-Prods. Co.*, 840 F.2d 902, 906 (Fed. Cir. 1988); *Moleculon Research Corp. v. CBS, Inc.*, 793 F.2d 1261, 1265-67 (Fed. Cir. 1986); *Kinzenbaw v. Deere & Co.*, 741 F.2d 383, 390-91 (Fed. Cir. 1984); *TP Lab., Inc. v. Prof'l Positioners, Inc.*, 724 F.2d 965,

970-72 (Fed. Cir. 1984); *WL Gore & Assocs., Inc. v. Garlock, Inc.*, 721 F.2d 1540, 1549-50 (Fed. Cir. 1983); *In re Smith*, 714 F.2d 1127, 1134-37 (Fed. Cir. 1983).

6.2 Prior Public Use (Post-AIA):

[The Defendant] contends that claim ____ of the [abbreviated patent number] patent was anticipated because the invention defined in that claim was in public use anywhere in the world before the effective filing date of the claimed invention.

> **Practice Note:** If there is a factual issue to be resolved by the jury as to whether the prior public use is the result of a disclosure made within one (1) year or less of the effective filing date by the inventor, or by another who obtained the subject matter disclosed directly from the inventor, or subject matter which had previously been disclosed by the inventor, the jury should be instructed here as to exceptions under § 102(b).

You are instructed that the [abbreviated patent number] patent has an effective filing date of [effective filing date].

A patent claim is invalid if the claimed invention was in public use before the effective filing date of the claimed invention.

An invention was in public use if the claimed invention was accessible to the public or commercially exploited anywhere in the world. Factors relevant to determining whether a use was public include the nature of the activity that occurred in public; public access to the use; confidentiality obligations imposed upon observers; commercial exploitation; and the circumstances surrounding testing and experimentation. An invention is publicly used if it is used by the inventor or by a person who is not under any limitation, restriction, or obligation of secrecy to the inventor. The absence of affirmative steps to conceal the use of the invention is evidence of a public use. However, secret use by a third party is not public, unless members of the public or employees of the third party have access to the invention.

In order to be a public use, the invention also must have been ready for patenting at the time of the alleged public use. An invention is ready for patenting either when it is reduced to practice or when the inventor has prepared drawings or other descriptions of the invention sufficient to allow a person of ordinary skill in the art to make or use the invention. An invention is reduced to practice when it has been: (1) constructed or performed within the scope of the patent claims; and (2) determined that it works for its intended purpose. The claimed invention is ready for patenting when there is reason to believe it would work for its intended purpose.

35 U.S.C. § 102(a)(2) (post-AIA); *Clock Spring, L.P. v. Wrapmaster, Inc.*, 560 F.3d 1317, 1325-27 (Fed. Cir. 2009); *American Seating Co. v. USSC Grp., Inc.*, 514 F.3d 1262, 1267 (Fed. Cir. 2008); *Invitrogen Corp. v. Biocrest Manuf., L.P.*, 424 F.3d 1374, 1379-82 (Fed. Cir. 2005); *SmithKline Beecham Corp. v. Apotex Corp.*, 365

F.3d 1306, 1316-20 (Fed. Cir. 2004); *Netscape Commc'ns Corp. v. Konrad*, 295 F.3d 1315, 1320-23 (Fed. Cir. 2002); *Grain Processing Corp. v. Am. Maize-Prods. Co.*, 840 F.2d 902, 906 (Fed. Cir. 1988); *Moleculon Research Corp. v. CBS, Inc.*, 793 F.2d 1261, 1265-67 (Fed. Cir. 1986); *Kinzenbaw v. Deere & Co.*, 741 F.2d 383, 390-91 (Fed. Cir. 1984); *TP Lab., Inc. v. Prof'l Positioners, Inc.*, 724 F.2d 965, 970-72 (Fed. Cir. 1984); *WL Gore & Assocs., Inc. v. Garlock, Inc.*, 721 F.2d 1540, 1549-50 (Fed. Cir. 1983); *In re Smith*, 714 F.2d 1127, 1134-37 (Fed. Cir. 1983).

6.3 On Sale Bar (Pre-AIA):

[The Defendant] contends that claim __________ of the [abbreviated patent number] patent was anticipated because the invention defined in that claim was on sale in the United States more than one year before [the patentee] filed his U.S. patent application on [U.S. filing date].

A patent claim is invalid if more than one year before the filing date of the patent an embodiment of the claimed invention was both: (1) subject to commercial offer for sale in the United States; and (2) ready for patenting.

A commercial "offer for sale" was made if another party could make a binding contract by simply accepting the offer. An invention was subject to an "offer for sale" if the claimed invention was embodied in an item that was actually sold or offered for sale. It is not required that a sale was actually made. The essential question is whether there was an attempt to obtain a commercial benefit from the invention.

The invention also must have been "ready for patenting" more than one year before the filing date of the patent. An invention is ready for patenting either when it is reduced to practice or when the inventor has prepared drawings or other descriptions of the invention that were sufficiently specific to enable a person of ordinary skill in the art to practice the invention. An invention is reduced to practice when it has been (1) constructed or performed within the scope of the patent claims; and (2) determined that it works for its intended purpose. The claimed invention is ready for patenting when there is reason to believe it would work for its intended purpose.

35 U.S.C. § 102(b) (pre-AIA); *Pfaff v. Wells Elecs.*, 525 U.S. 55, 67-68 (1998); *August Tech v. Camtek*, 655 F.3d 1278, 1288-89 (Fed. Cir. 2011); *Atlanta Attachment Co., v. Leggett & Platt, Inc.*, 516 F.3d 1361, 1365 (Fed. Cir. 2008); *Board of Educ. ex rel Bd. Of Trustees of Florida State University v. American Bioscience, Inc.*, 333 F.3d 1330, 1338 (Fed. Cir. 2003) (as to conception); *Allen Eng'g Corp. v. Bartell Indus., Inc.*, 299 F.3d 1336, 1352-55 (Fed. Cir. 2002); *Linear Tech. Corp. v. Micrel, Inc.*, 275 F.3d 1040, 1047-54 (Fed. Cir. 2001); *Robotic Vision Sys., Inc., v. View Eng'g, Inc.*, 249 F.3d 1307, 1312 (Fed. Cir. 2001); *Grp. One, Ltd. v. Hallmark Cards, Inc.*, 254 F.3d 1041, 1045-49 (Fed. Cir. 2001; *Cooper v. Goldfarb*, 154 F.3d 1321, 1327 (Fed. Cir. 1998) (as to reduction to practice).

6.3 On Sale Bar (Post-AIA):

[The Defendant] contends that claim __________ of the [abbreviated patent number] patent was anticipated because the invention defined in that claim was on sale before the effective filing date of the claimed invention.

You are instructed that the [abbreviated patent number] patent has an effective filing date of [effective filing date].

A patent claim is invalid if it was on sale before the effective filing date of the claimed invention.

A commercial "offer for sale" was made if another party could make a binding contract by simply accepting the offer. An invention was subject to an "offer for sale" if the claimed invention was embodied in an item that was actually sold or offered for sale. It is not required that a sale was actually made. The essential question is whether there was an attempt to obtain a commercial benefit from the invention.

A commercial "offer for sale" was made by the inventor both:

1. if the claimed invention was embodied in an item that was actually sold or offered for sale; and
2. the invention was "ready for patenting"

more than one year before the effective filing date of the claimed invention. An invention is ready for patenting either when it is reduced to practice or when the inventor has prepared drawings or other descriptions of the invention that was sufficiently specific to enable a person of ordinary skill in the art to practice the invention. An invention is reduced to practice when it has been: (1) constructed or performed within the scope of the patent claims; and (2) determined that it works for its intended purpose. The claimed invention is ready for patenting when there is reason to believe it would work for its intended purpose.

35 U.S.C. § 102(a)(1) (post-AIA); *Pfaff v. Wells Elecs.*, 525 U.S. 55, 67-68 (1998); *August Tech v. Camtek*, 655 F.3d 1278, 1288-89 (Fed. Cir. 2011); *Atlanta Attachment Co., v. Leggett & Platt, Inc.*, 516 F.3d 1361, 1365 (Fed. Cir. 2008); *Board of Educ. ex rel Bd. Of Trustees of Florida State University v. American Bioscience, Inc.*, 333 F.3d 1330, 1338 (Fed. Cir. 2003) (as to conception); *Allen Eng'g Corp. v. Bartell Indus., Inc.*, 299 F.3d 1336, 1352-55 (Fed. Cir. 2002); *Linear Tech. Corp. v. Micrel, Inc.*, 275 F.3d 1040, 1047-54 (Fed. Cir. 2001); *Robotic Vision Sys., Inc., v. View Eng'g, Inc.*, 249 F.3d 1307, 1312 (Fed. Cir. 2001); *Grp. One, Ltd. v. Hallmark Cards, Inc.*, 254 F.3d 1041, 1045-49 (Fed. Cir. 2001; *Cooper v. Goldfarb,* 154 F.3d 1321, 1327 (Fed. Cir. 1998) (as to reduction to practice).

6.4 Experimental Use

[The Plaintiff] contends that ________________ should not be considered [[a prior public use of the invention] [placing the invention on sale]] because that [[use] [sale]] was experimental. The law recognizes that the inventor must be given the opportunity to develop the invention through experimentation. Certain activities are experimental if they are a legitimate effort to test claimed features of the invention or to determine if the invention will work for its intended purpose. So long as the primary purpose is experimentation, it does not matter that the public used the invention or that the inventor incidentally derived profit from it.

Only experimentation by or under the control of the inventor of the patent [or his assignee] qualifies for this exception. Experimentation by [third party], for its own purposes, does not. The experimentation must relate to the features of the claimed invention, and it must be for the purpose of technological improvement, not commercial exploitation. If any commercial exploitation does occur, it must be merely incidental to the primary purpose of experimentation. A test done primarily for marketing, and only incidentally for technological improvement, is not an experimental use.

If you find that [the Defendant] has shown by clear and convincing evidence that there was a [[prior public use] [prior sale]], then the burden is on [the Plaintiff] to come forward with evidence showing that the purpose of [the prior public use] [prior sale]] was experimental. If the evidence of the experimental use produced by [the Plaintiff] is strong enough that you find that [the Defendant] has not met its burden of establishing a [[prior public use][prior sale]] by clear and convincing evidence, you may find that______________ does not constitute [[a prior public use of the invention][placing the invention on sale]].

City of Elizabeth v. Am. Nicholson Pavement Co., 97 U.S. 126, 134-35 (1877); *Clock Spring, L.P. v. Wrapmaster, Inc.*, 560 F.3d 1317, 1327 (Fed. Cir. 2009); *Lisle Corp. v. A.J. Mfg. Co.*, 398 F.3d 1306, 1316 (Fed. Cir. 2005); *Allen Eng'g Corp. v. Bartell Indus., Inc.*, 299 F.3d 1336, 1353-55 (Fed. Cir. 2002); *LaBounty Mfg., Inc. v. U.S. Int'l Trade Comm'n*, 958 F.2d 1066, 1071-72 (Fed. Cir. 1992); *Manville Sales Corp. v. Paramount Sys., Inc.*, 917 F.2d 544, 549-51 (Fed. Cir. 1990); *U.S. Envtl. Prods. Inc. v. Westall*, 911 F.2d 713, 716 (Fed. Cir. 1990); *In re Hamilton*, 882 F.2d 1576, 1580-83 (Fed. Cir. 1989); *Grain Processing Corp. v. Am. Maize-Prods. Co.*, 840 F.2d 902, 906 (Fed. Cir. 1988); *Hycor Corp. v. Schlueter Co.*, 740 F.2d 1529, 1535-37 (Fed. Cir. 1984); *Pennwalt Corp. v. Akzona Inc.*, 740 F.2d 1573, 1580-81 (Fed. Cir. 1984); *In re Smith*, 714 F.2d 1127, 1134-37 (Fed. Cir. 1983).

6.5 Printed Publication (Pre-AIA):

[The Defendant] contends that claim __________ of the [abbreviated patent number] patent was anticipated because the invention defined in that claim was described in a printed publication [[more than one year before [the patentee] filed the U.S. patent application on [U.S. filing date]] [before [the patentee] invented the invention]].

A patent claim is invalid if the invention defined by that claim was described in a printed publication [[before it was invented by [the patentee]] [more than one year prior to the filing date of the U.S. application]].

Practice Note: If there is a factual issue to be resolved by the jury as to the date of invention of the patent claims in suit, the jury should be instructed here as to how they should determine that date of invention. Otherwise, the Court should instruct the jury as follows: "The invention defined by claim _____ of the [abbreviated patent number] patent was invented on [invention date]."

A printed publication must have been maintained in some tangible form, such as [[printed pages] [typewritten pages] [magnetic tape] [microfilm] [photographs] [internet publication] [photocopies]], and must have been sufficiently accessible to persons interested in the subject matter of its contents.

Practice Note: In the event accessibility is disputed, it is appropriate to give the following additional Instruction.

Information is publicly accessible if it was distributed or otherwise made available to the extent that persons interested and ordinarily skilled in the subject matter exercising reasonable diligence can locate it. It is not necessary for the printed publication to have been available to every member of the public. An issued patent is a printed publication. A published patent application is a printed publication as of its publication date.

The disclosure of the claimed invention in the printed publication must be complete enough to enable one of ordinary skill in the art to use the invention without undue experimentation. In determining whether the disclosure is enabling, you should take into account what would have been within the knowledge of a person of ordinary skill in the art [[one year before the application for the [abbreviated patent number] patent was filed] [at the time the invention of the [abbreviated patent number] patent was made]], and you may consider evidence that sheds light on the knowledge such a person would have had.

35 U.S.C. § 102(a), (b) (pre-AIA); *In re NTP, Inc.*, 654 F.3d 1279, 1296-97 (Fed. Cir. 2011); *Orion IP v. Hyundai Motor America*, 605 F.3d 967 (Fed. Cir. 2010); *In re Lister*, 583 F.3d 1307, 1311-12 (Fed. Cir. 2009); *Kyocera Wireless Corp. v. Int'l Trade Comm.*, 545 F.3d 1340, 1350 (Fed. Cir. 2008); *Finisar Corp. v. DirectTV Grp., Inc.*, 523 F.3d 1323, 1334 (Fed. Cir. 2008); *SRI Int'l, Inc. v. Internet Sec. Sys., Inc.*, 511 F.3d 1186 (Fed. Cir. 2008); *In re Klopfenstein*, 380 F.3d 1345, 1352 (Fed. Cir. 2004); *Glaverbel Societe Anonyme v. Northlake Mktg. & Supply, Inc.*, 45 F.3d 1550, 1554-55 (Fed. Cir. 1995); *Scripps Clinic & Research Found. v. Genentech, Inc.*, 927 F.2d 1565, 1576 (Fed. Cir. 1991); *Constant v. Advanced Micro-Devices, Inc.*, 848 F.2d 1560, 1568-69 (Fed. Cir. 1988); *Akzo N.V. v. U.S. Int'l Trade Comm'n*, 808 F.2d 1471, 1479 (Fed. Cir. 1986); *In re Hall*, 781 F.2d 897, 898-899 (Fed. Cir. 1986); *In re Donohue*, 766 F.2d 531, 533-34 (Fed. Cir. 1985); *Studiengesellschaft Kohle mbH v. Dart Indus., Inc.*, 726 F.2d 724, 727 (Fed. Cir. 1984).

6.5 Printed Publication (Post-AIA):

[The Defendant] contends that claim __________ of the [abbreviated patent number] patent was anticipated because the invention defined in that claim was described in a printed publication before the effective filing date of the claimed invention.

You are instructed that the [abbreviated patent number] patent has an effective filing date of [effective filing date].

> **Practice Note:** If there is a factual issue to be resolved by the jury as to whether the printed publication is the result of a disclosure made within one (1) year or less of the effective filing date by the inventor, or by another who obtained the subject matter disclosed directly from the inventor, or subject matter which had previously been disclosed by the inventor, the jury should be instructed here as to exceptions under § 102(b)(1).

A patent claim is invalid if the invention defined by that claim was described in a printed publication before the effective filing date of the claimed invention.

A printed publication must have been maintained in some tangible form, such as [[printed pages] [typewritten pages] [magnetic tape] [microfilm] [photographs] [internet publication] [photocopies]], and must have been sufficiently accessible to persons interested in the subject matter of its contents .

> **Practice Note:** In the event accessibility is disputed, it is appropriate to give the following additional instruction on this issue.

Information is publicly accessible if it was distributed or otherwise made available to the extent that persons interested and ordinarily skilled in the subject matter exercising reasonable diligence can locate it. It is not necessary for the printed publication to have been available to every member of the public. An issued patent is a printed publication. A published patent application is a printed publication as of its publication date.

The disclosure of the claimed invention in the printed publication must be complete enough to enable one of ordinary skill in the art to use the invention without undue experimentation. In determining whether the disclosure is enabling, you should take into account what would have been within the knowledge of a person of ordinary skill in the art [[one year before the application for the [abbreviated patent number] patent was filed] [at the time the invention of the [abbreviated patent number] patent was made]], and you may consider evidence that sheds light on the knowledge such a person would have had.

35 U.S.C. § 102(a)(1) & (b)(1) (post-AIA); *In re NTP, Inc.*, 654 F.3d 1279, 1296-97 (Fed. Cir. 2011); *Orion IP v. Hyundai Motor America*, 605 F.3d 967 (Fed. Cir.

2010); *In re Lister*, 583 F.3d 1307, 1311-12 (Fed. Cir. 2009); *Kyocera Wireless Corp. v. Int'l Trade Comm.*, 545 F.3d 1340, 1350 (Fed. Cir. 2008); *Finisar Corp. v. DirectTV Grp., Inc.*, 523 F.3d 1323, 1334 (Fed. Cir. 2008); *SRI Int'l, Inc. v. Internet Sec. Sys., Inc.*, 511 F.3d 1186 (Fed. Cir. 2008); *In re Klopfenstein*, 380 F.3d 1345, 1352 (Fed. Cir. 2004); *Glaverbel Societe Anonyme v. Northlake Mktg. & Supply, Inc.*, 45 F.3d 1550, 1554-55 (Fed. Cir. 1995); *Scripps Clinic & Research Found. v. Genentech, Inc.*, 927 F.2d 1565, 1576 (Fed. Cir. 1991); *Constant v. Advanced Micro-Devices, Inc.*, 848 F.2d 1560, 1568-69 (Fed. Cir. 1988); *Akzo N.V. v. U.S. Int'l Trade Comm'n*, 808 F.2d 1471, 1479 (Fed. Cir. 1986); *In re Hall*, 781 F.2d 897, 898-899 (Fed. Cir. 1986); *In re Donohue*, 766 F.2d 531, 533-34 (Fed. Cir. 1985); *Studiengesellschaft Kohle mbH v. Dart Indus., Inc.*, 726 F.2d 724, 727 (Fed. Cir. 1984).

6.6 Prior Invention (pre-AIA Only)[38]

[The Defendant] contends that claim __________ of the [abbreviated patent number] patent was anticipated because the invention defined in that claim was invented by another person, [third party], before [the patentee] invented his invention.

A patent claim is invalid if the invention defined by that claim was invented by another person in the United States before it was invented by the patentee, [and that other person did not abandon, suppress, or conceal the invention].

[The Defendant] must show clear and convincing evidence *either* that before [the patentee] invented his invention, [third party] reduced to practice a [[product] [method]] that included all of the elements of claim ___ of the [abbreviated patent number] patent or that [third party] was first to conceive the invention and that he exercised reasonable diligence in later reducing the invention to practice. In addition, [the Defendant] must show that [third party]'s device was sufficiently developed that one skilled in the art would have recognized that it would work for its intended purpose.

> **Practice Note:** This defense may be negated if the invention was abandoned, suppressed, or concealed. In the event this issue is properly asserted and there is sufficient evidentiary support to submit this issue to the jury the following additional Instructions should be given.

38. In cases where priority of invention is an issue to be submitted to the jury, further instructions will be required. For example, the jury will need to consider not only the dates when the respective inventions were conceived, but also when the inventions were reduced to practice. An inventor who claims to be the first to conceive of a prior invention but was the last to reduce to practice must also show reasonable diligence from a time just before the other party entered the field until his own reduction to practice in order for the "prior invention" to anticipate the claimed invention in suit.

If the prior invention was abandoned, suppressed, or concealed, it does not anticipate the [abbreviated patent number] patent. It is not necessary that [the patentee] had knowledge of that prior invention.[39]

You may find that an invention was abandoned, suppressed, or concealed if you find that: (1) the prior inventor actively concealed the invention from the public; or (2) the prior inventor unreasonably delayed in making the invention publicly known. These facts must be proven by clear and convincing evidence. Generally, an invention was not abandoned, suppressed, or concealed if the invention was made public, sold, or offered for sale, or otherwise used for a commercial purpose. A period of delay does not constitute abandonment, suppression, or concealment, provided the prior inventor was engaged in reasonable efforts to bring the invention to market during this period.

35 U.S.C. § 102(a), (g) (pre-AIA); *Teva Pharm. v. Astrazeneca Pharms.*, 661 F.3d 1378 (Fed. Cir. 2011); *Solvay S.A. v. Honeywell Int'l. Inc.*, 622 F.3d 1367, 1376 (Fed. Cir. 2010); *Rosco, Inc. v. Mirror Lite Co.*, 304 F.3d 1373, 1381 (Fed. Cir. 2002); *Dow Chemical Co. v. Astro-Valcour, Inc.*, 267 F.3d 1334, 1343 (Fed. Cir. 2001); *Monsanto Co. v. Mycogen Plant Sci., Inc.*, 261 F.3d 1356, 1361-63 (Fed. Cir. 2001); *Apotex USA, Inc. v. Merck & Co.*, 254 F.3d 1031, 1035-40 (Fed. Cir. 2001); *E.I. du Pont de Nemours & Co. v. Phillips Petroleum Co.,* 849 F.2d 1430, 1436-37 (Fed. Cir.1988); *Kimberly-Clark Corp. v. Johnson & Johnson,* 745 F.2d 1437, 1444-46 (Fed. Cir. 1984).

6.6 Prior Invention (post-AIA Only)

Practice Note: The prior invention defense was eliminated by the AIA. The prior invention defense is no longer a basis for invalidity and no instruction should be given on this issue for Post-AIA claims.

6.7 Prior Patent (Pre-AIA):

[The Defendant] contends that claim __________ of the [abbreviated patent number] patent was anticipated because the invention defined in that claim was patented by [third party] [[before it was invented by [the patentee]] [more than one year before [the patentee] filed his United States patent application on [U.S. filing date]].

39. If abandonment, suppression or concealment are at issue in the case, these terms should be defined for the jury. *See Dow Chem. Co. v. Astro-Valcour Inc.*, 267 F.3d 1334, 1342 (Fed. Cir. 2001); *Checkpoint Sys., Inc. v. United States Int'l Trade Comm'n*, 54 F.3d 756, 761-62 (Fed. Cir. 1995).

A patent claim is invalid if the invention defined by that claim was patented in the United States or a foreign country [[before it was invented by [the patentee]] [more than one year before [the patentee] filed his United States patent application]].

> **Practice Note:** If there is a factual issue to be resolved by the jury as to the date of invention of the patent claims in suit, the jury should be instructed here as to how they should determine that date of invention. Otherwise, the court should instruct the jury as follows: "The invention defined by claim _____ of the [abbreviated patent number] patent was invented on [invention date]."

35 U.S.C. § 102(a)-(b) (pre-AIA); *Adv. Display Sys., Inc. v. Kent State Univ.*, 212 F.3d 1272, 1287-83 (Fed. Cir. 2000); *In re Carlson*, 983 F.2d 1032, 1035-36 (Fed. Cir. 1992).

6.7 Prior Patent (Post-AIA):

[The Defendant] contends that claim __________ of the [abbreviated patent number] patent was anticipated because the invention defined in that claim was patented by [third party] before the effective filing date of the claimed invention.

> **Practice Note:** If there is a factual issue to be resolved by the jury as to whether the disclosure appearing in a patent is the result of a disclosure made within one (1) year or less of the effective filing date by the inventor, by another who obtained the subject matter disclosed directly from the inventor, or if the subject matter disclosed and the claimed invention were owned by the same person or subject to an obligation of assignment to the same person, the jury should be instructed here as to exceptions under § 102(b)(2).

A patent claim is invalid if the invention defined by that claim was patented in the United States or a foreign country before the effective filing date of the claimed invention.

You are instructed that the [abbreviated patent number] patent has an effective filing date of [effective filing date].

You are further instructed that patent [patent number] issued to [third party] has an effective filing date of [effective filing date].

35 U.S.C. § 102(a)(1), (a)(2) & (d) (post-AIA).

6.8 Prior U.S. Application (Pre-AIA)

[The Defendant] contends that claim __________ of the [abbreviated patent number] patent was anticipated because the invention defined in that claim was described in United States [[published patent application] [patent]] [[published application number] [anticipating patent number]], and because [[the published patent application [published application number]] [application for the [anticipating patent number] patent] was filed before [the patentee] made his invention.

A claim of the [abbreviated patent number] patent would be invalid if the invention defined by that claim was described in a [[published United States patent application] [United States patent]] filed by another person before the invention was made by [the patentee].

> **Practice Note:** if there is a factual issue to be resolved by the jury as to the date of invention of the patent claims in suit, the jury should be instructed here as to how they should determine that date of invention. Otherwise, the court should instruct the jury as follows: "The invention defined by claim [____] of the [abbreviated patent number] patent was invented on [invention date]"

35 U.S.C. §§ 102(e)(1) and (2) (pre-AIA); *In re Giacomini*, 612 F.3d 1380, 1383-84 (Fed. Cir. 2010); *Sun Studs, Inc. v. ATA Equip. Leasing, Inc.*, 872 F.2d 978, 983-84 (Fed. Cir. 1989) (*overruled on other grounds*); *In re Wertheim*, 646 F.2d 527, 536-37 (C.C.P.A. 1981).

6.8 Prior U.S. Application (Post-AIA):

[The Defendant] contends that claim __________ of the [abbreviated patent number] patent was anticipated because the invention defined in that claim was described in a patent application [published application number] published in the United States, and because the published patent application [published application number] was filed before the effective filing date of the claimed invention.

A claim of the [abbreviated patent number] patent would be invalid if the invention defined by that claim was described in a published patent application filed by another person before the effective filing date of the claimed invention.

> **Practice Note:** If there is a factual issue to be resolved by the jury as to whether the disclosure appearing in a patent application is the result of a disclosure made within one (1) year or less of the effective filing date by the inventor, by another who obtained the subject matter disclosed directly from the inventor, or if the subject matter disclosed and the claimed invention were owned by the same person or subject to an obligation of assignment to the same person, the jury should be instructed here as to exceptions under § 102(b)(2).

You are instructed that the [abbreviated patent number] patent has an effective filing date of [effective filing date].

You are further instructed that the published patent application [published application number] has an effective filing date of [effective filing date].

35 U.S.C. § 102(a)(2), (b)(2) & (d) (post-AIA).

7. Obviousness

> **Practice Note:** Obviousness is a mixed question of fact and law. Failing to move for judgment as a matter of law may waive the issue of obviousness on an appeal. Careful consideration should be given to the Court's and the Jury's respective roles in determining this issue and the jury should be instructed accordingly.

7.0 Obviousness

[The Defendant] contends that claim(s) [numbers] of the [abbreviated patent number] patent are invalid because the claimed invention(s) is "obvious."

A claimed invention is invalid as "obvious" if it would have been obvious to a person of ordinary skill in the art of the claimed invention at the time the invention was made. Unlike anticipation, which allows consideration of only one item of prior art, obviousness may be shown by considering more than one item of prior art.

In deciding obviousness, you must avoid using hindsight; that is, you should not consider what is known today or what was learned from the teachings of the patent. You should not use the patent as a road map for selecting and combining items of prior art. You must put yourself in the place of a person of ordinary skill in the art at the time the invention was made.

The following factors must be evaluated to determine whether [the Defendant] has established that the claimed invention(s) is obvious:

1. the scope and content of the prior art relied upon by [the Defendant];
2. the difference or differences, if any, between each claim of the [abbreviated patent number] patent that [the Defendant] contends is obvious and the prior art;
3. the level of ordinary skill in the art at the time the invention of the [abbreviated patent number] patent was made; and
4. additional considerations, if any, that indicate that the invention was obvious or not obvious.

Each of these factors must be evaluated, although they may be analyzed in any order, and you must perform a separate analysis for each of the claims.

[The Defendant] must prove by clear and convincing evidence that the invention would have been obviousness.

I will now explain each of the four factors in more detail.

KSR Int'l Co. v. Teleflex Inc., 550 U.S. 398, 405 and 421 (2007); *Graham v. John Deere Co.*, 383 U.S. 1, 17-18 (1966); *Otsuka Pharm. Co., Ltd. v. Sandoz, Inc.*, 678 F.3d 1280, 1296 (Fed. Cir. 2012); *Leapfrog Enters., Inc. v. Fisher-Price, Inc.*, 485

F.3d 1157, 1161-62 (Fed. Cir. 2007); *Ruiz v. A.B. Chance Co.*, 234 F.3d 654, 662-63 (Fed. Cir. 2000); *Arkies Lures, Inc. v. Gene Larew Tackle, Inc.*, 119 F.3d 953, 955 (Fed. Cir. 1997); *Ryko Mfg. Co. v. Nu-Star, Inc.*, 950 F.2d 714, 716 (Fed. Cir. 1991); *Nutrition 21 v. U.S.*, 930 F.2d 867, 871 n.2 (Fed. Cir. 1991); *Newell Cos. v. Kenney Mfg. Co.*, 864 F.2d 757, 764 (Fed. Cir. 1988); *Structural Rubber Prods. Co. v. Park Rubber Co.*, 749 F.2d 707, 718-19 (Fed. Cir. 1984); *Orthopedic Equip. Co. v. All Orthopedic Appliances, Inc.*, 707 F.2d 1376, 1382-83 (Fed. Cir. 1983); *Stratoflex, Inc. v. Aeroquip Corp.*, 713 F.2d 1530, 1538-40 (Fed. Cir. 1983).

7.1 The First Factor: Scope and Content of the Prior Art

The prior art that you considered previously for anticipation purposes is also prior art for obviousness purposes. The prior art includes the following items received into evidence during the trial:

[LIST PRIOR ART STIPULATED TO BY THE PARTIES].

[IF PARTIES DISPUTE THE PRIOR ART, USE THE FOLLOWING]. You must determine what is the prior art that may be considered in determining whether the [abbreviated patent number] patent is obvious. A prior art reference may be considered if it discloses information designed to solve any problem or need addressed by the patent or if the reference discloses information that has obvious uses beyond its main purpose that a person of ordinary skill in the art would reasonably examine to solve any problem or need addressed by the patent.

[ADD INSTRUCTIONS ON PRIOR ART CONTENTIONS, E.G., PUBLICATION AND ON-SALE BAR, AND INHERENCY, IF ASSERTED]

KSR Int'l Co. v. Teleflex Inc., 127 S. Ct. 1727, 1742 (2007); *Ruiz v. A.B. Chance Co.*, 234 F.3d 654, 664-65 (Fed. Cir. 2000); *Wang Labs., Inc. v. Toshiba Corp.*, 993 F.2d 858, 864 (Fed. Cir. 1993); *In re Clay,* 966 F.2d 656, 658-59 (Fed. Cir. 1992); *In re Wood,* 599 F.2d 1032, 1036-37 (C.C.P.A. 1979).

7.2 The Second Factor: Differences Between the Claimed Invention and the Prior Art

You should analyze whether there are any relevant differences between the prior art and the claimed invention from the view of a person of ordinary skill in the art at the time of the invention. Your analysis must determine the impact, if any, of such differences on the obviousness or nonobviousness of the invention as a whole, and not merely some portion of it.

> **Practice Note:** In the event inherency if properly asserted and adequately supported by the evidence, the following instruction should be given:
>
> "In comparing the scope and content of each prior art reference to a patent claim, you may find that inherency may supply a claim element that is otherwise missing from the explicit disclosure of a prior art reference. The

inherent presence of an element so found by you may be used in your evaluation of whether the claimed invention would have been obvious in view of the prior art. But, to rely on inherency to establish the existence of a claim limitation in the prior art in an obviousness analysis, that limitation necessarily must be present in, or the natural result of, the combination of elements explicitly disclosed by the prior art. Inherency may not be established by probabilities or possibilities. The mere fact that a certain thing *may* result from an explicit disclosure is not sufficient to find inherency. However, if the disclosure is sufficient to show that the natural result flowing from the explicit disclosure *would* result in the claim limitation in question, inherency may be found. Something inherent from the explicit disclosure of the prior art must be limited when applied in an obviousness analysis and used only when the inherent limitation is the natural result of the combination of prior art elements explicitly disclosed."

Par Pharm., Inc. v. TWI Pharms., Inc., 773 F.3d 1186, 1194-1196 (Fed. Cir. 2014); *Alcon Research, Ltd. v. Apotex Inc.*, 687 F.3d, 1362 (Fed. Cir. 2012); *In re Kubin,* 561 F.3d 1351, 1357 (Fed. Cir. 2009); and cases cited therein.

In analyzing the relevance of the differences between the claimed invention and the prior art, you do not need to look for precise teaching in the prior art directed to the subject matter of the claimed invention. You may take into account the inferences and creative steps that a person of ordinary skill in the art would have employed in reviewing the prior art at the time of the invention. For example, if the claimed invention combined elements known in the prior art and the combination yielded results that were predictable to a person of ordinary skill in the art at the time of the invention, then this evidence would make it more likely that the claim was obvious. On the other hand, if the combination of known elements yielded unexpected or unpredictable results, or if the prior art teaches away from combining the known elements, then this evidence would make it more likely that the claim that successfully combined those elements was not obvious.

Importantly, a claim is not proved obvious merely by demonstrating that each of the elements was independently known in the prior art. Most, if not all, inventions rely on building blocks long-known, and claimed discoveries almost of necessity will likely be combinations of what is already known. Therefore, you should consider whether a reason existed at the time of the invention that would have prompted a person of ordinary skill in the art in the relevant field to combine the known elements in the way the claimed invention does. The reason could come from the prior art, the background knowledge of one of ordinary skill in the art, the nature of any problem or need to be addressed, market demand, or common sense. You may also consider whether the problem or need was known, the possible approaches to solving the problem or addressing the need were known and finite, and the solution was predictable through use of a known option.

If you find that a reason existed at the time of the invention to combine the elements of the prior art to arrive at the claimed invention, this evidence would make it more likely that the claimed invention was obvious. Again, you must undertake this analysis separately for each claim that [the Defendant] contends is obvious.

KSR Int'l Co. v. Teleflex Inc., 127 S. Ct. 1727, 1742-43 (2007); *Abbott Labs. v. Sandoz, Inc.*, 544 F.3d 1341, 1351 (Fed. Cir. 2008); *Graham v. John Deere Co.*, 383 U.S. 1, 17-18 (1966); *Stratoflex, Inc. v. Aeroquip Corp.*, 713 F.2d 1530, 1536-37 (Fed. Cir. 1983); *Medtronic, Inc., v. Cardiac Pacemakers, Inc.*, 721 F.2d 1563, 1567-68 (Fed. Cir. 1983).

7.3 The Third Factor: Level of Ordinary Skill

The determination of whether a claimed invention is obvious is based on the perspective of a person of ordinary skill in the [pertinent art field]. The person of ordinary skill is presumed to know all prior art that you have determined to be reasonably relevant. The person of ordinary skill is also a person of ordinary creativity that can use common sense to solve problems.

[If the parties have agreed to the level of ordinary skill in the art, then the instruction should include: "[The Plaintiff] and [the Defendant] contend that the level of ordinary skill in the art is [insert proposal]]."

[If the parties have not agreed to the level of ordinary skill in the art, then the instruction should continue as follows].

When determining the level of ordinary skill in the art, you should consider all the evidence submitted by the parties, including evidence of:

1. the level of education and experience of persons actively working in the field at the time of the invention, including the inventor;
2. the types of problems encountered in the art at the time of the invention; and
3. the sophistication of the technology in the art at the time of the invention, including the rapidity with which innovations were made in the art at the time of the invention.

KSR Int'l Co. v. Teleflex Inc., 127 S. Ct. 1727, 1742-43 (2007); *Graham v. John Deere Co.*, 383 U.S. 1, 17-18 (1966); *Ruiz v. A.B. Chance Co.*, 234 F.3d 654, 666-67 (Fed. Cir. 2000); *Envtl Designs, Ltd. v. Union Oil Co.*, 713 F.2d 693, 696-97 (Fed. Cir. 1983).

7.4 The Fourth Factor: Other Considerations

Before deciding the issue of obviousness, you must also consider certain factors, which may help to determine whether or not the invention would have been obvious. No factor alone is dispositive, and you must consider the obviousness or nonobviousness of the invention as a whole.

> **Practice Note:** Careful consideration should be given to the Court's role in determining the admissibility of evidence of secondary considerations. In addition, the materiality of the evidence depends on the existence of a nexus between the consideration and the invention as opposed to other factors. Only if the Court determines that there is a sufficient nexus that a consideration is admissible should the jury be instructed on it.

[PROVIDE ONLY THOSE INSTRUCTIONS THAT ARE APPROPRIATE.]

1. Were products covered by the claim commercially successful due to the merits of the claimed invention rather than due to advertising, promotion, salesmanship, or features of the product other than those found in the claim?
2. Was there long felt need for a solution to the problem facing the inventors, which was satisfied by the claimed invention?
3. Did others try, but fail, to solve the problem solved by the claimed invention?
4. Did others copy the claimed invention?
5. Did the claimed invention achieve unexpectedly superior results over the closest prior art?
6. Did others in the field, or [the Defendant] praise the claimed invention or express surprise at the making of the claimed invention?
7. Did others accept licenses under [abbreviated patent number] patent because of the merits of the claimed invention?

Answering all, or some, of these questions "yes" may suggest that the claim was not obvious. Answering all, or some, of these questions "no" may suggest that the claims would have been obvious. These factors are relevant only if there is a connection, or nexus, between the factor and the invention covered by the patent claims. Even if you conclude that some of the above indicators have been established, those factors should be considered along with all the other evidence in the case in determining whether [the defendant] has proven that the claimed invention would have been obvious.

Graham v. John Deere Co., 383 U.S. 1, 17-18 (1966); *United States v. Adams*, 383 U.S. 39, 52 (1966); *Perkin-Elmer Corp. v. Computervision Corp.*, 732 F.2d 888, 894-95 (Fed. Cir. 1984); *Envtl. Designs, Ltd. v. Union Oil Co.*, 713 F.2d 693, 697 (Fed. Cir. 1983); *WL Gore & Assocs., Inc. v. Garlock, Inc.*, 721 F.2d 1540, 1555-56 (Fed. Cir. 1983); *Stratoflex, Inc., v. Aeroquip Corp.*, 713 F.2d 1530, 1538-39 (Fed. Cir. 1983).

8. Enablement

> **Practice Note:** Enablement is a question of law for the Court. The jury should be instructed on subsidiary fact issues only if, and only to the extent, that there is a specific issue of fact that the jury must decide that bears on the issue of enablement. If not, this instruction should not be given.

[The defendant] contends that claim[s] ____ of the [abbreviated patent number] patent [is] [are] invalid for lack of enablement. [The defendant] bears the burden of establishing lack of enablement by the highly probable standard.

A patent must disclose sufficient information to enable or teach persons of ordinary skill in the field of the invention, at the time the [priority] patent application was filed, to make and use the full scope of the claimed invention without undue experimentation. This requirement is known as the enablement requirement. If a patent claim is not enabled, it is invalid.

In considering whether a patent complies with the enablement requirement, you must keep in mind that patents are written for persons of ordinary skill in the field of the invention. Thus, a patent need not expressly state information that persons of ordinary skill would be likely to know or could obtain.

The fact that some experimentation may be required for a person of ordinary skill to practice the claimed invention does not mean that a patent does not meet the enablement requirement. Factors that you may consider in determining whether persons of ordinary skill in the field of the invention would require undue experimentation to make and use the full scope of the claimed invention include:

1. the quantity of experimentation necessary and whether that experimentation involves only known or commonly used techniques. [The question of undue experimentation is a matter of degree. Even extensive experimentation does not necessarily make the experiments unduly extensive where the experiments are routine, such as repetition of known or commonly used techniques. But permissible experimentation is not without bounds.[40]
2. the amount of direction or guidance disclosed in the patent;
3. the presence or absence of working examples in the patent;
4. the nature of the invention;
5. the state of the prior art;
6. the relative skill of those in the art;

---

40. *Cephalon, Inc. v. Watson Pharm., Inc.*, 707 F.3d 1330, 1338 (Fed. Cir. 2013); *see also Johns Hopkins Univ. v. CellPro, Inc.*, 152 F.3d 1342, 1360-61 (Fed. Cir. 1998).]].

7. the predictability of the art; and
8. the breadth of the claims.

Practice Note: This Instruction should be modified to identify the fact issues the jury is being asked to determine. The ultimate issue of enablement is a question of law to be decided by the Court.

35 U.S.C. § 112; *Streck, Inc. v. Research & Diagnostic Sys.*, 665 F.3d 1269, 1288-89 (Fed. Cir. 2012); *Transocean Offshore Deepwater Drilling, Inc. v. Maersk Contractors USA, Inc.*, 617 F.3d 1296, 1305-07 (Fed. Cir. 2010); *ALZA Corp. v. Andrx Pharms., LLC*, 603 F.3d 935, 939-43 (Fed. Cir. 2010); *Martek Biosciences Corp. v. Nutrinova, Inc.*, 579 F.3d 1363, 1377-79 (Fed. Cir. 2009); *Sitrick v. Dreamworks, LLC*, 516 F.3d 993, 999-1002 (Fed. Cir. 2008); *Liebel-Flarsheim Co. v. Medrad, Inc.*, 481 F.3d 1371, 1380 (Fed. Cir. 2007); *AK Steel Corp. v. Sollac & Ugine*, 344 F.3d 1234, 1244 (Fed. Cir. 2003); *Durel Corp. v. Osram Sylvania Inc.*, 256 F.3d 1298, 1306 (Fed. Cir. 2001); *Union Pac. Resources Co. v. Chesapeake Energy Corp.*, 236 F.3d 684, 690-92 (Fed. Cir. 2001); *Ajinomoto Co. v. Archer- Daniels-Midland Co.*, 228 F.3d 1338, 1345-46 (Fed. Cir. 2000); *Nat'l Recovery Techs., Inc. v. Magnetic Separation Sys., Inc.*, 166 F.3d 1190, 1195-98 (Fed. Cir. 1999); *Enzo Biochem, Inc. v. Calgene, Inc.*, 188 F.3d 1362, 1371 (Fed. Cir. 1999); *In re Wands*, 858 F.2d 731, 737 (Fed. Cir. 1988); *Amgen, Inc. v. Chugai Pharm.* Co., 927 F.2d 1200, 1213 (Fed. Cir. 1991).

9. Written Description Requirement

Practice Note: Written description is a question of fact for the finder of fact. The jury should be instructed on these issues only if, and only to the extent, that specific claims are challenged for lack of written description support and there is sufficient evidentiary support for these arguments.

The [Defendant] contends that claim[s] ____ of the [abbreviated patent number] patent [is] [are] invalid for failure to satisfy the written description requirement. [The defendant] bears the burden of establishing lack of written description by clear and convincing evidence.

A patent must contain a written description of the [product or process] claimed in the patent. The written description requirement helps to ensure that the patent applicant actually invented the claimed subject matter. To satisfy the written description requirement, the patent specification must describe each and every limitation of a patent claim, in sufficient detail, although the exact words found in the claim need not be used. When determining whether the specification discloses the invention, the claim must be viewed as a whole,.

The written description requirement is satisfied if persons of ordinary skill in the field of the invention would recognize, from reading the patent specification, that the inventor possessed the subject matter finally claimed in the patent. The written description requirement is satisfied if the specification shows that the inventor possessed his or her invention as of the date the [priority] patent application was filed, even though the claims themselves may have been changed or new claims added since that time.

It is unnecessary to spell out every detail of the invention in the specification, and specific examples are not required; only enough must be included in the specification to convince persons of ordinary skill in the art that the inventor possessed the full scope of the invention. In evaluating whether the specification has provided an adequate written description, you may take into account such factors as:

1. the nature and scope of the patent claims;
2. the complexity, predictability, and maturity of the technology at issue;
3. the existing knowledge in the relevant field; and
4. the scope and content of the prior art.

The issue of written description is decided on a claim-by-claim basis, not as to the entire patent or groups of claims.

If you find that [the defendant] has proven by clear and convincing evidence that the [abbreviated patent number] patent does not contain a written description for the invention[s] of claims _____, then you must find that the claim[s] [is] [are] invalid.

35 U.S.C. § 112; *Bard Peripheral Vascular, Inc. v. W.L. Gore & Assocs.*, 670 F.3d 1171, 1188-89 (Fed. Cir. 2012), aff'd on reh'g, 682 F.3d 1003, 1005 (Fed. Cir. 2012); *Streck, Inc. v. Research & Diagnostic Sys.*, 665 F.3d 1269, 1284-87 (Fed. Cir. 2012); *Atl. Research Mktg. Sys. v. Troy*, 659 F.3d 1345, 1353-55 (Fed. Cir. 2011); *Boston Sci. Corp. v. Johnson & Johnson*, 647 F.3d 1353, 1361-63 (Fed. Cir. 2011); *Crown Packaging Tech. v. Ball Metal Bev. Container Corp.*, 635 F.3d 1373, 1379-80 (Fed. Cir. 2011); *Centocor Ortho Biotech, Inc. v. Abbott Labs.*, 636 F.3d 1341, 1347-48 (Fed. Cir. 2011); *Ariad Pharms., Inc. v. Mass. Instit. of Tech.*, 598 F.3d 1336, 1351-52 (Fed. Cir. 2010) (en banc); *Research Corp. Techs., Inc. v. Microsoft Corp.*, 627 F.3d 859, 870 (Fed. Cir. 2010); *Laryngeal Mask Co. v. Ambu A/S*, 618 F.3d 1367, 1373-74 (Fed. Cir. 2010); *Revolution Eyewear, Inc. v. Aspex Eyewear, Inc.*, 563 F.3d 1358, 1366 (Fed. Cir. 2009); *PowerOasis, Inc. v. T-Mobile USA, Inc.*, 522 F.3d 1299, 1306 (Fed. Cir. 2008); *Falko-Gunter Faulkner v. Inglis*, 448 F.3d 1357, 1366 (Fed. Cir. 2006); *Kao Corp. v. Unilever U.S., Inc.*, 441 F.3d 963, 968 (Fed. Cir. 2006); *Monsanto Co. v. Scruggs*, 459 F.3d 1328, 1336 (Fed. Cir. 2006); *Univ. of Rochester v. G.D. Searle & Co.*, Inc., 358 F.3d 916, 922-28 (Fed. Cir. 2004); *Enzo Biochem, Inc. v. Gen-Probe Inc.*, 323 F.3d 956, 964 (Fed. Cir. 2002).

10. Unenforceability (Inequitable Conduct)

Practice Note: Inequitable conduct is an equitable issue that is decided by the Court, in its discretion.[41] There is no right to a jury trial on inequitable conduct. Although the issue is sometimes submitted to the finder of fact for an Advisory Verdict, the issue must be decided by the Court, either with or without and Advisory Verdict. If the court elects to request and Advisory Verdict, the Court should consider whether to charge the jury on the entire issue, or solely on the materiality and/or intent to deceive issues. The verdict form should include separate questions on each of the issues on which the jury is charged, *i.e.*, materiality, intent, and/or balancing the equities.

The Court should consider carefully whether to request an Advisory Verdict. The issues are complex and potentially confusing. A clear-and-convincing-evidence standard applies to the inequitable conduct defense while the preponderance-of-the-evidence standard applies to the issue of whether the Patent and Trademark Office would have issued the patent "but for" the failure to disclose.[42] In addition, the USPTO employs a "broadest reasonable interpretation" standard for claim construction, which may conflict with the Court's construction of the claims. Submitting the issue for an Advisory Verdict increases the complexity of the Instructions, has the potential to confuse the jury, and may bias the jury's consideration of other issues that it is required to decide. Federal Circuit authority establishes an objective threshold issue of whether the reference or conduct would have been a basis to deny patentability.[43] If this threshold issue is not satisfied, submitting the issue for an Advisory Verdict is not appropriate.

If an Advisory Verdict is requested, care must be taken to ensure that the issue(s) is properly raised and that there is sufficient evidence to support the defense.

---

41. *Flex-Rest, LLC v. Steelcase, Inc.*, 455 F.3d 1351, 1357 (Fed. Cir. 2006).
42. *Therasense, Inc. v. Becton Dickinson & Co.*, 649 F.3d 1276 (Fed. Cir. 2011) (*en banc*).
43. *Id.*

10.0 Inequitable Conduct – Generally

[The Defendant] contends that [the Plaintiff] may not enforce the [abbreviated patent number] patent against [the Defendant] because individuals substantively involved in the prosecution of the [abbreviated patent number] patent engaged in inequitable conduct before the Patent and Trademark Office during prosecution of that patent.

Applicants for a patent have a duty to prosecute patent applications in the Patent and Trademark Office with candor and good faith. This duty of candor and good faith extends to all inventors named on a patent application, all patent attorneys and patent agents involved in preparing and prosecuting the application, and every other individual involved in a substantial way with the prosecution of the patent application. An intentional failure to meet this duty of candor and good faith is referred to as "inequitable conduct."

[In this case, [the Defendant] asserts that [DESCRIBE BRIEFLY EACH BASIS FOR [THE DEFENDANT]'S UNENFORCEABILITY DEFENSE].]

[The Defendant] must prove inequitable conduct by clear and convincing evidence. To determine whether the [abbreviated patent number] patent was obtained through inequitable conduct, you must determine:

1. whether an individual or individuals having this duty of candor and good faith [engaged in affirmative acts of egregious misconduct or] withheld or misrepresented information, or submitted false information, that was material to the examination of the patent application; and
2. that this individual or individuals acted with the specific intent to deceive or mislead the Patent and Trademark Office.

Therasense, Inc. v. Becton Dickinson & Co., 649 F.3d 1276 (Fed. Cir. 2011) (*en banc*); *Avid Identification Sys., Inc. v. Crystal Import Corp.*, 603 F.3d 967, 973-74 (Fed. Cir. 2010); *eSpeed, Inc. v. BrokerTec USA, L.L.C.*, 480 F.3d 1129, 1135 (Fed. Cir. 2007); *Digital Control, Inc. v. Charles Mach. Works*, 437 F.3d 1309, 1313 (Fed. Cir. 2006); *Purdue Pharma L.P. v. Endo Pharm., Inc.*, 438 F.3d 1123, 1128 (Fed. Cir. 2006); *Bristol-Myers Squibb Co. v. Rhone-Poulenc Rorer, Inc.*, 326 F.3d 1226, 1233 (Fed. Cir. 2003).

10.1 Materiality (Non-disclosure cases only)

[Defendant] contends that ______________________ was information [known to] [misrepresented by] an individual having the duty of good faith and candor to the Patent and Trademark Office, and that such information was [withheld from] [misrepresented to] the Patent and Trademark Office during the prosecution of the [abbreviated patent number] patent. If you find that an individual having this duty of good faith and candor [withheld] [misrepresented] information when applying for the [abbreviated patent number] patent, you must also determine whether that information was material information.

Information is material if "but for" the individual's [failure to disclose] [misrepresentation of] the information during the prosecution, the Patent and Trademark Office would not have allowed one or more claims of the [abbreviated patent number] patent. In other words, information is material if it is more likely than not that the Patent and Trademark Office would not have allowed one or more claims of the [abbreviated patent number] patent if it had been aware of the [withheld] [true] information. To decide whether the Patent and Trademark Office would not have allowed one or more claims if it had been aware of the [withheld] [true] information, you should use the broadest reasonable interpretation of the claim or claims under consideration and apply the "more likely than not" standard, as the Patent and Trademark Office would have done.

If you decide that the Patent and Trademark Office would not have allowed one or more claims applying this standard, then the individual's [failure to disclose] [misrepresentation of] the information during the prosecution is material, whether or not you also find the claims invalid under the standards for finding claims invalid in this lawsuit. This does not change the [Defendant]'s overall burden, however, to prove its inequitable conduct defense by the highly probable standard of proof.

Therasense, Inc. v. Becton Dickinson & Co., 649 F.3d 1276 (Fed. Cir. 2011) (*en banc*).

10.2 Materiality (Affirmative Egregious Misconduct cases only)

In this case, [the Defendant] alleges that [individual(s) accused of inequitable conduct] engaged in affirmative acts of egregious misconduct during the prosecution of the [abbreviated patent number] patent. Specifically, [the Defendant] alleges [summarize alleged affirmative acts of egregious misconduct]. If you are left with a clear conviction that [accused individual(s)] engaged in the conduct as alleged by [the Defendant], and that the conduct rises to the level of affirmative egregious misconduct, then you must find that the misconduct was material.

To assist you in your deliberation, examples of affirmative acts of egregious conduct would be perjury, including filing an unmistakably false affidavit in the Patent and Trademark Office during prosecution of the [abbreviated patent number], or fabricating evidence presented to the Patent and Trademark Office during prosecution of the [abbreviated patent number]. Affirmative acts of egregious conduct may also include deliberately planned and executed schemes to defraud the Patent and Trademark Office.

On the other hand, examples of things that do not rise to the level of affirmative acts of egregious conduct would be mere nondisclosure of prior art references to the Patent and Trademark Office, failure to submit references that are duplicative or cumulative of references of which the Patent and Trademark Offfice was already aware, or failure to mention prior art references in an affidavit during prosecution of the [abbreviated patent number].

Therasense, Inc. v. Becton Dickinson & Co., 649 F.3d 1276 (Fed. Cir. 2011) (*en banc*).

10.3 Intent to Deceive or Mislead

If you find by clear and convincing evidence that material information was withheld from or misrepresented to the Patent and Trademark Office, or that [accused individual(s)] engaged in affirmative egregious misconduct, you must next determine whether this was done with a specific intent to deceive or mislead the Patent and Trademark Office. You may find intent to deceive or mislead the Patent and Trademark Office from direct evidence. You may also infer intent to deceive or mislead the Patent and Trademark Office from the facts and surrounding circumstances. Whether based on direct or circumstantial evidence, the evidence must leave you with a clear conviction that material information was withheld from or misrepresented to the Patent and Trademark Office in order for you to find an intent to deceive or mislead.

For example, when a patentee has knowingly misrepresented a material fact or submitted false material information, and when the natural consequence of those intentional acts would be to deceive or mislead the Patent and Trademark Office, an inference that [the accused individual(s)] intended to deceive the Patent and Trademark Office may be appropriate.

When the individual having a duty of good faith and candor has deliberately withheld or misrepresented known material information from the Patent and Trademark Office, you may find that he or she acted with intent to deceive or mislead the Patent and Trademark Office if and only if that is the single most reasonable inference to be drawn from the evidence. If there are multiple reasonable inferences that may be drawn, you cannot find an intent to deceive or mislead. You may not infer that the individual acted with intent to deceive or mislead based solely on the fact or facts that the information withheld was material, or even highly material, or that the individual has not provided a good faith explanation for the withholding. Nor may you infer intent solely on the basis of gross negligence or negligence in withholding material information.

For example, it is not enough that the individual knew of a reference, should have known of its materiality, and did not submit it to the Patent and Trademark Office. Instead, you need to determine whether or not the individual knew of the withheld or misrepresented information, knew the information was material, and made a deliberate and conscious decision to withhold or misrepresent the information. In determining whether there was an intent to deceive or mislead the Patent and Trademark Office, you should consider the totality of the circumstances, including the nature of the conduct and whether that conduct occurred in good faith.

Therasense, Inc. v. Becton Dickinson & Co., 649 F.3d 1276 (Fed. Cir. 2011)(*en banc*); *Intellect Wireless, Inc. v. HTC Corp.*, 732 F.3d 1339, 1345 (Fed. Cir. 2013); *Larson Mfg. Co. of S.D. v. Aluminart Prods. Ltd.*, 559 F.3d 1317, 1340-41 (Fed. Cir. 2009); *Star Scientific, Inc. v. R.J. Reynolds Tobacco Co.*, 537 F.3d 1357, 1366, 1368

(Fed. Cir. 2008); *eSpeed, Inc. v. BrokerTec USA, L.L.C.*, 480 F.3d 1129, 1137-38 (Fed. Cir. 2007); *Purdue Pharma L.P. v. Endo Pharm. Inc.*, 438 F.3d 1123, 1133-34 (Fed. Cir. 2006); *PerSeptive Biosystems, Inc. v. Pharmacia Biotech, Inc.*, 225 F.3d 1315, 1319-20 (Fed. Cir. 2000); *Molins PLC v. Textron, Inc.*, 48 F.3d 1172, 1180-82 (Fed. Cir. 1995).

11. Damages

11.0 Damages – Generally

If you find that the accused [[device] [method]] infringes any of the claims of the [abbreviated patent number] patent, and that those claims are not invalid, you must determine the amount of damages to be awarded [the Plaintiff] for the infringement. On the other hand, if you find that each of the asserted patent claims is either invalid or is not infringed, then you need not consider damages in your deliberations.

[The Plaintiff] must prove each element of its damages—including the amount of the damages—by a preponderance of the evidence, which means more likely true than not.

If proven by the Plaintiff, damages must be in an amount adequate to compensate [the Plaintiff] for the infringement. The purpose of a damage award is to put [the Plaintiff] in about the same financial position it would have been in if the infringement had not happened. But, the damage award cannot be less than a reasonable royalty. You may not add anything to the amount of damages to punish an accused infringer or to set an example. You also may not add anything to the amount of damages for interest.

The fact that I am instructing you on damages does not mean that the Court believes that one party or the other should win in this case. My instructions about damages are for your guidance only in the event you find in favor of [the Plaintiff]. You will need to decide the issue of damages only if you find that one or more of the asserted claims are both not invalid and infringed.

Powell v. Home Depot U.S.A., Inc., 663 F.3d 1221, 1238 (Fed. Cir. 2011); *ResQNet.com, Inc. v. Lansa, Inc.*, 594 F.3d 860, 868 (Fed. Cir. 2010); *Lucent Techs., Inc. v. Gateway, Inc.*, 580 F.3d 1301, 1325 (Fed. Cir. 2009); 35 U.S.C. § 284 (2004); *Aro Mfg. Co. v. Convertible Top Replacement Co.*, 377 U.S. 476, 507 (1964); *Dow Chem. Co. v. Mee Indus., Inc.*, 341 F.3d 1370, 1381-82 (Fed. Cir. 2003); *Vulcan Eng'g Co. v. FATA Aluminum, Inc.*, 278 F.3d 1366, 1376 (Fed. Cir. 2002); *Grain Processing Corp. v. Am. Maize-Prods. Co.*, 185 F.3d 1341, 1349 (Fed. Cir. 1999); *Maxwell v. J. Baker, Inc.*, 86 F.3d 1098, 1108-09 (Fed. Cir. 1996); *Hebert v. Lisle Corp.*, 99 F.3d 1109, 1119 (Fed. Cir. 1996); *Rite-Hite Corp. v. Kelley Co.*, 56 F.3d 1538, 1544-45 (Fed. Cir. 1995); *Wang Labs., Inc. v. Toshiba Corp.*, 993 F.2d 858, 870 (Fed. Cir. 1993); *Fromson v. W. Litho Plate & Supply Co.*, 853 F.2d 1568, 1574 (Fed. Cir. 1988), *overruled on other grounds by Knorr-Bremse Systeme Fuer Nutzfahrzeuge v. Dana Corp.*, 383 F.3d 1337, 1342 (Fed. Cir 2004); *Del Mar Avionics, Inc. v. Quinton Instrument Co.*, 836 F.2d 1320, 1326 (Fed. Cir. 1987).

11.1 Date Damages Begin

11.1.1 Alternate A – When the Date of the Notice of Infringement is Stipulated

The date that [the Plaintiff] first notified [the Defendant] of its claim of patent infringement is the date for the start of damages calculations. The parties agree that date is [infringement notice date].

11.1.2 Alternate B – When the Date of the Notice of Infringement is Disputed – Product Claims

The date that [the Plaintiff] first notified [the Defendant] of its claim for patent infringement is the date for the start of damages. The parties do not agree on that date, and it is up to you to determine what that date is. [The Plaintiff] must prove that it is more likely than not that the [Defendant] actually was notified of the claim for patent infringement as of the date alleged by [the Plaintiff].

[The Plaintiff] can give notice in two ways. The first way is to give notice to the public in general. [The Plaintiff] can do this by marking substantially all of the products that it sold which included the patented invention, or including on the labeling of substantially all of the products, the word "patent" or the abbreviation "PAT" with the number of the patent. [The Plaintiff] also may give notice by marking substantially all of the products with "Patent" or "Pat" and a free internet address where there is a posting that connects the product with the patent number. [Licensees of the [abbreviated patent number] patent who use the patented invention must also mark substantially all of their products that include the patented invention with the patent number.] This type of notice starts from the date [the Plaintiff] [and its licensees] began to mark substantially all of its products that use the patented invention with the patent number. If [the Plaintiff] [and its licensees] did not mark substantially all of those products with the patent number, then [the Plaintiff] did not provide notice in this way.[44]

A second way [the Plaintiff] can give notice of its patent[s] is to notify [the Defendant] directly with a specific claim that the [allegedly infringing product] infringed the [abbreviated patent number] patent. This type of notice starts from the date [Defendant] received the notice. If you find that [the Plaintiff], before filing this lawsuit, did not properly mark its products and did not notify [the Defendant] with a specific charge that the [allegedly infringing product] infringed, then [the Plaintiff] can only recover damages for infringement that occurred after it sued [the Defendant] on [lawsuit filing date].

---

44. If there is an issue of fact regarding the adequacy of [the Patentee's marking], additional instructions will be required.

11.1.3 Alternate C – When the Date Damages Begin is the Date the Lawsuit was Filed

The date that damages begin to be calculated in this case is the date this lawsuit was filed, which is [the lawsuit filing date].

35 U.S.C. § 287(a); *Funai Elec. Co., Ltd. v. Daewoo Electronics Corp.*, 616 F.3d 1357, 1373-74 (Fed. Cir. 2010); *Gart v. Logitech, Inc.*, 254 F.3d 1334, 1345 (Fed. Cir. 2001); *Lans v. Digital Equip. Corp.*, 252 F.3d 1320, 1327-28 (Fed. Cir. 2001); *Crystal Semiconductor Corp. v. TriTech Microelecs. Int'l, Inc.*, 246 F.3d 1336, 1353 (Fed. Cir. 2001); *Amsted Indus., Inc. v. Buckeye Steel Castings Co.*, 24 F.3d 178, 184-87 (Fed. Cir. 1994); *Devices for Med., Inc. v. Boehl,* 822 F.2d 1062, 1066 (Fed. Cir. 1987).

11.2 Damages – Types of Damages That May be Recovered

> **Practice Note:** The issue of damages is rapidly evolving at both the Federal Circuit and Supreme Court. The courts have recently supported vigorous examination of the plaintiff's damages theory before submitting this issue to the jury. Only if the plaintiff's damages theory is admissible and supported by sufficient evidence should it be submitted to the jury. In addition, in order to avoid undue burden and jury confusion, the jury should be instructed on only those theories of recovery that the Court has determined are admissible.

There are several types of damages that are available for patent infringement.

One type of patent damages is lost profits. Lost profits are the additional profits that the patent owner would have made if the defendant had not infringed. In this connection, you may hear references to the "but for" test—which means, "what profits would the patent owner have made 'but for' the alleged infringement?"

A second type of patent damages is price suppression. The patentee may have been forced to reduce its price for the patented product or other related products in order to compete with the infringer. Again, the patentee must prove to you by a preponderance of the evidence what price concessions it was forced to give that are due to the infringement as opposed to other factors.

A third measure of damages is convoyed sales. A patentee may have lost sales of other related products other than the patented product, if these products are typically sold together.

Finally, another measure of damages is a reasonable royalty. A reasonable royalty is the reasonable amount that someone wanting to use the patented invention would have agreed to pay to the patent owner and the patent owner would have accepted. A reasonable royalty is the minimum amount of damages that a patent owner can receive for an infringement.

11.3 Lost Profits – "But-For" Test

[The Plaintiff] is seeking lost profits damages in this case. To prove lost profits, [the Plaintiff] must show that, but for [the Defendant]'s infringement, [the Plaintiff] would have made additional profits through the sale of all or a portion of the sales of [the allegedly infringing products] made by [the Defendant]. Plaintiff must prove this by a preponderance of the evidence, more likely than not. Part of your job is to determine what the customers who purchased the [allegedly infringing product] [from the Defendant] would have done if the alleged infringement had not occurred. It is important to remember that the profits I have been referring to are the profits allegedly lost by [the Plaintiff], not the profits, if any, made by [the Defendant] on the allegedly infringing sales.

Siemens Med. Solutions USA, Inc. v. Saint-Gobain Ceramics & Plastics, Inc., 637 F.3d 1269, 1289 (Fed. Cir. 2011); *American Seating Co. v. USSC Grp., Inc.*, 514 F.3d 1262 (Fed. Cir. 2008); *Aro Mfg. Co. v. Convertible Top Replacement Co.*, 377 U.S. 476, 507 (1964); *Micro Chem. v. Lextron, Inc.*, 318 F.3d 1119, 1122-25 (Fed. Cir. 2003); *Ferguson Beauregard/Logic Controls v. Mega Sys., L.L.C.*, 350 F.3d 1327, 1345-46 (Fed. Cir. 2003); *Ericsson, Inc. v. Harris Corp.*, 352 F.3d 1369, 1377 (Fed. Cir. 2003); *Tate Access Floors, Inc. v. Maxcess Techs., Inc.*, 222 F.3d 958, 971 (Fed. Cir. 2000); *Grain Processing Corp. v. Am. Maize-Prods. Co.*, 185 F.3d 1341, 1349 (Fed. Cir. 1999); *King Instruments Corp. v. Perego*, 65 F.3d 941, 952 (Fed. Cir. 1995); *State Indus., Inc. v. Mor-Flo Indus., Inc.*, 883 F.2d 1573, 1577 (Fed. Cir. 1989); *Ryco, Inc. v. Ag-Bag Corp.*, 857 F.2d 1418, 1428 (Fed. Cir. 1988); *King Instrument Corp. v. Otari Corp.*, 767 F.2d 853, 863-64 (Fed. Cir. 1985); *Paper Converting Mach. Co. v. Magna-Graphics Corp.*, 745 F.2d 11, 21 (Fed. Cir. 1984); *Am. Hoist & Derrick Co. v. Sowa & Sons, Inc.*, 725 F.2d 1350, 1365 (Fed. Cir. 1984); *Central Soya Co. v. Geo A Hormel & Co.*, 723 F.2d 1573, 1578-79 (Fed. Cir. 1983).

11.4 Lost Profits – Panduit Factors

[The Plaintiff] has proven its lost profits if you find that [the Plaintiff] has proven each of the following factors by the more likely than not standard:

1. the demand for the patented [[product] [method]],
2. absence of acceptable non-infringing substitutes,
3. that [the Plaintiff] had the manufacturing and marketing ability to make all or a part of the infringing sales actually made by [the Defendant], and
4. the amount of profit that [the Plaintiff] would have made if it were not for [the Defendant]'s infringement.

I will now explain each of these factors.

Siemens Med. Solutions USA, Inc. v. Saint-Gobain Ceramics & Plastics, Inc., 637 F.3d 1269, 1287 (Fed. Cir. 2011); *DePuy Spine, Inc. v. Medtronic Sofamor Danek, Inc.*, 567 F.3d 1314, 1329 (Fed. Cir. 2009); *Tate Access Floors, Inc. v. Maxcess Techs., Inc.*, 222 F.3d 958, 971 (Fed. Cir. 2000); *Gargoyles, Inc. v. United States*, 113 F.3d 1572, 1577-79 (Fed. Cir. 1997); *Stryker Corp. v. Intermedics Orthopedics, Inc.*, 96 F.3d 1409, 1417-18 (Fed. Cir. 1996); *Rite-Hite Corp. v. Kelley Co.*, 56 F.3d 1538, 1545 (Fed. Cir. 1995); *State Indus., Inc. v. Mor-Flo Indus., Inc.*, 883 F.2d 1573, 1577 (Fed. Cir. 1989); *Yarway Corp. v. Eur-Control USA, Inc.*, 775 F.2d 268, 275 (Fed. Cir. 1985); *Panduit Corp. v. Stahlin Bros. Fibre Works, Inc.*, 575 F.2d 1152, 1156 (6th Cir. 1978).

11.5 Lost Profits – Panduit Factors – Demand

The first factor asks whether there was demand for the patented product in the relevant market. [The Plaintiff] can prove demand for the patented product by showing significant sales of [the Plaintiff]'s own patented product. [The Plaintiff] also can prove demand for the patented product by showing significant sales of [the Defendant]'s products that are covered by the patent in suit. To use sales of [the Defendant]'s products as proof of this demand, however, [the Plaintiff]'s and [the Defendant]'s product must be sufficiently similar to compete against each other in the same market or market segment. You also should not consider sales of products mainly due to advertising and marketing, and unpatented features of the products as evidence of demand for the patented product.

DePuy Spine, Inc. v. Medtronic Sofamor Danek, Inc., 567 F.3d 1314, 1330 (Fed. Cir. 2009); *Rite-Hite Corp. v. Kelley Co.*, 56 F.3d 1538, 1548-49 (Fed. Cir. 1995); *BIC Leisure Prods., Inc. v. Windsurfing Int'l, Inc.*, 1 F.3d 1214, 1218-19 (Fed. Cir. 1993); *SmithKline Diagnostics, Inc. v. Helena Labs. Corp.*, 926 F.2d 1161, 1165 n.3 (Fed. Cir. 1991); *Gyromat Corp. v. Champion Spark Plug Co.*, 735 F.2d 549, 552 (Fed. Cir. 1984).

11.6 Lost Profits – Panduit Factors – Acceptable Non-Infringing Substitutes

The second factor asks whether there were non-infringing, acceptable substitutes for the patented products in the market place and the impact of such substitute products on the marketplace absent the sale of [Defendant]'s products. If the realities of the marketplace are that competitors other than [the Plaintiff] would likely have captured some or all of the sales made by the [Defendant], even despite a difference in the products, then [the Plaintiff] is not entitled to lost profits on those sales.

To be an acceptable substitute, the products must have had one or more of the advantages of the patented invention that were important to the actual buyers of the infringing products, not the public in general. The acceptable substitutes also must not infringe the patent because they were licensed under the patent or they did not include all the features required by the patent. The acceptable substitutes, in addition, must have been available during the damages period. An acceptable non-infringing substitute is available if, during the damages period, a competitor or [the Defendant] had all the necessary equipment, materials, know-how, and experience to design and manufacture the substitute and sell such substitute instead of its infringing sales at the time those infringing sales were made. If you determine that some of [the Defendant]'s customers would just as likely have purchased a non-infringing acceptable product, then [the Plaintiff] has not shown it lost those sales but for [the Defendant]'s sales.

Even if you find that [the Plaintiff]'s and [the Defendant]'s products were the only ones with the advantages of the patented invention, [the Plaintiff] is nonetheless required to prove to you that it in fact would have made the [the Defendant]'s infringing sales.

SynQor, Inc. v. Aresyn Techs., Inc., 709 F.3d 1365, 1383 (Fed. Cir. 2013); *DePuy Spine, Inc. v. Medtronic Sofamor Danek, Inc.*, 567 F.3d 1314, 1331-32 (Fed. Cir. 2009); *American Seating Co. v. USSC Grp., Inc.*, 514 F.3d 1262, (Fed. Cir. 2008); *Mars, Inc. v. Coin Acceptors, Inc.*, 527 F.3d 1359, 1372-73 (Fed. Cir. 2008); *Grain Processing Corp. v. Am. Maize-Prods. Co.*, 185 F.3d 1341, 1349 (Fed. Cir. 1999); *Gargoyles, Inc. v. United States*, 113 F.3d 1572, 1577-78 (Fed. Cir. 1997); *Uniroyal, Inc. v. Rudkin-Wiley Corp.*, 939 F.2d 1540, 1545-46 (Fed. Cir. 1991); *Standard Havens Prods., Inc. v. Gencor Indus.*, 953 F.2d 1360, 1373 (Fed. Cir. 1991); *Kaufman Co. v. Lantech, Inc.*, 926 F.2d 1136, 1142-43, 1143 n.17 (Fed. Cir. 1991); *SmithKline Diagnostics, Inc. v. Helena Lab. Corp.*, 926 F.2d 1161, 1166 (Fed. Cir. 1991); *TWM Mfg. Co. v. Dura Corp.*, 789 F.2d 895, 901-02 (Fed. Cir. 1986).

11.7 Lost Profits – Market Share

If you find that there were other acceptable non-infringing substitute products in the market, then [the Plaintiff] may be entitled to lost profits on a portion of [the Defendant]'s infringing sales. The burden is on [the Plaintiff] to prove that it is more likely than not that the patented product competed in the same market as [the Defendant]'s infringing product, and that [the Plaintiff] would have made a portion of the infringing sales equal to at least [the Plaintiff]'s share of that market but for [the Defendant]'s infringement. It is not necessary for [the Plaintiff] to prove that [the Plaintiff] and [the Defendant] were the only two suppliers in the market for [the Plaintiff] to demonstrate entitlement to lost profits. The burden is on [the Plaintiff], however, to show that it is more likely than not that it would have sold that portion had [the Defendant]'s product never existed. In a two-supplier marker, the burden is on [the Plaintiff] to show that its product competed in the same market with the [the Defendant]'s product and that it would have made those sales if the infringement had not occurred.

DePuy Spine, Inc. v. Medtronic Sofamor Danek, Inc., 567 F.3d 1314, 1330 (Fed. Cir. 2009); *Ericsson, Inc. v. Harris Corp.*, 352 F.3d 1369, 1377-78 (Fed. Cir. 2003); *Crystal Semiconductor Corp. v. Tritech Microelecs. Int'l, Inc.*, 246 F.3d 1336, 1353-57 (Fed. Cir. 2001); *BIC Leisure Prods., Inc. v. Windsurfing Int'l, Inc.*, 1 F.3d 1214

(Fed. Cir. 1993); *State Indus., Inc. v. Mor-Flo Indus., Inc.*, 883 F.2d 1573, 1577-78 (Fed. Cir. 1989).

11.8 Lost Profits – Panduit Factors – Capacity

The third factor asks whether [the Plaintiff] had the manufacturing and marketing ability to actually make the sales it allegedly lost due to [the Defendant]'s infringement. [The Plaintiff] must prove that it could have supplied the additional patented products needed to make the sales [the Plaintiff] said it lost, or that someone working with [the Plaintiff] could have supplied the additional patented products. [The Plaintiff] also must prove that it more likely than not had the ability to market and sell these additional patented products.

Wechsler v. Macke Int'l Trade, Inc., 486 F.3d 1286, 1293 (Fed. Cir. 2007); *Gargoyles, Inc. v. United States*, 113 F.3d 1572, 1577-78 (Fed. Cir. 1997); *Fonar Corp. v. Gen. Elec. Co*, 107 F.3d 1543, 1553 (Fed. Cir. 1997); *Kearns v. Chrysler Corp.*, 32 F.3d 1541, 1551 (Fed. Cir. 1994); *Datascope Corp. v. SMEC, Inc.*, 879 F.2d 820, 825 (Fed. Cir. 1989); *Gyromat Corp. v. Champion Spark Plug Co.*, 735 F.2d 549, 554 (Fed. Cir. 1984).

11.9 Lost Profits – Panduit Factors – Amount of Profit Incremental Income Approach

[The Plaintiff] may calculate the amount of its lost profits by calculating its lost sales for the patented product and subtracting from that amount any additional costs or expenses that [the Plaintiff] would have had to pay to make the lost sales. This might include additional costs for making the products, and additional sales costs, additional packaging costs, additional shipping costs, etc. Any costs that do not change when more products are made, such as taxes, insurance, rent and administrative overhead, should not be subtracted from the lost sales amount. The amount of lost profits cannot be speculative but it need not be proved with unerring certainty.

Sensonics, Inc. v. Aerosonic Corp., 81 F.3d 1566, 1572 (Fed. Cir. 1996); *Oiness v. Walgreen Co.*, 88 F.3d 1025, 1030 (Fed. Cir. 1996); *Beatrice Foods Co. v. New England Printing & Lithographing Co.*, 923 F.2d 1576, 1579 (Fed. Cir. 1991); *Kalman v. Berlyn Corp.*, 914 F.2d 1473, 1482-83 (Fed. Cir. 1990); *State Indus., Inc. v. Mor-Flo Indus., Inc.*, 883 F.2d 1573, 1579-80 (Fed. Cir. 1989); *Ryco, Inc. v. Ag-Bag Corp.*, 857 F.2d 1418, 1428 (Fed. Cir. 1988); *Del Mar Avionics, Inc. v. Quinton Instrument Co.*, 836 F.2d 1320, 1327 (Fed. Cir. 1987); *King Instrument Corp. v. Otari*, 767 F.2d 853, 863-64 (Fed. Cir. 1985); *Gyromat Corp. v. Champion Spark Plug Co.*, 735 F.2d 549, 554-55 (Fed. Cir. 1984); *Paper Converting Mach. Co. v. Magna-Graphics Corp.*, 745 F.2d 11, 22 (Fed. Cir. 1984); *Bio-Rad Labs., Inc. v. Nicolet Inst. Corp.*, 739 F.2d 604 (Fed. Cir. 1984); *Lam, Inc. v. Johns-Manville Corp.*, 718 F.2d 1056, 1065 (Fed. Cir. 1983).

11.10 Price Erosion

[The Plaintiff] is entitled to recover additional damages if it can show that it is more likely than not that, but for [the Defendant]'s infringement, [the Plaintiff] [[would have been able to charge higher prices] [would not have had to lower its prices]] for its patented products. If you find that [the Plaintiff] has met its burden of proof, then you may award as additional damages an amount equal to the difference between the profits that [the Plaintiff] would have made at the higher price and the profits [the Plaintiff] actually made selling its patented products at the lower price that [the Plaintiff] charged for its patented product. This type of damage is referred to as price erosion damages.

If you find that [the Plaintiff] suffered price erosion damages, then you also may use the higher price that [the Plaintiff] would have charged in determining [the Plaintiff]'s lost sales and lost profits due to [the Defendant]'s infringement. However, if you calculate price erosion or lost profits damages using the higher price for the patented product, then you also must take into account any decrease in [the Plaintiff]'s sales that might have occurred due to the higher price for the patent products. In order to award lost profits based on price erosion, it is not required that [the Plaintiff] knew that [the Defendant]'s competing product infringed the patent, if [the Plaintiff] reduced its price to meet [the Defendant]'s prices.

Power Integrations, Inc. v. Fairchild Semiconductor Int'l, Inc., 711 F.3d 1348, 1377-80 (Fed. Cir. 2013); *Siemens Med. Solutions USA, Inc. v. Saint-Gobain Ceramics & Plastics, Inc.*, 637 F.3d 1269, 1287 (Fed. Cir. 2011); *Ericsson, Inc. v. Harris Corp.*, 352 F.3d 1369, 1378-79 (Fed. Cir. 2003); *Vulcan Eng'g Co. v. FATA Aluminum, Inc.*, 278 F.3d 1366, 1377 (Fed. Cir. 2002); *Rite-Hite Corp. v. Kelley Co.*, 56 F.3d 1538, 1544 (Fed. Cir. 1995) (*en banc*) (applying test articulated in *Panduit Corp. v. Stahlin Bros. Fibre Works, Inc.*, 575 F.2d 1152 (6th Cir. 1978)); *BIC Leisure, Inc. v. Windsurfing Int'l, Inc.*, 1 F.3d 1214, 1218 (Fed. Cir. 1993); *Minn. Mining & Mfg. Co. v. Johnson & Johnson Orthopaedics, Inc.*, 976 F.2d 1559, 1578-79 (Fed. Cir. 1992); *Amstar Corp. v. Envirotech Corp.*, 823 F.2d 1538, 1543 (Fed. Cir. 1987); *Lam, Inc. v. Johns-Manville Corp.*, 718 F.2d 1056, 1065 (Fed. Cir. 1983).

11.11 Cost Escalation

[The Plaintiff] can recover additional damages if it can show that it also lost profits because its costs—such as additional marketing costs—went up as a result of [the Defendant]'s infringement of [the Plaintiff]'s patent. [The Plaintiff] must prove that it was more likely than not that its costs went up because of [the Defendant]'s actions, and not for some other reason.

Amstar Corp. v. Envirotech Corp., 823 F.2d 1538, 1543 (Fed. Cir. 1987); *Lam, Inc. v. Johns-Manville Corp.*, 718 F.2d 1056, 1064-65 (Fed. Cir. 1983).

11.12 Convoyed Sales

In this case, [the Plaintiff] contends that the patented product is ordinarily sold along with other products, namely [collateral products]. These other products are called "collateral products." It is part of your job to determine whether [the Plaintiff] has proved that it is entitled to damages for the lost sales of any collateral products.

To recover lost profits for lost sales of any collateral products, [the Plaintiff] must prove two things. First, [the Plaintiff] must prove that it is more likely than not that it would have sold the collateral products but for the infringement. Second, the collateral products and the patented product must be so closely related that they effectively act or are used together for a common purpose. Damages for lost collateral sales, if any, are calculated in the same way as for calculating lost profits on the patented product.

Aro Mfg. Co. v. Convertible Top Replacement Co., 377 U.S. 476, 507 (1964); *DePuy Spine, Inc. v. Medtronic Sofamor Danek, Inc.*, 567 F.3d 1314, 1333 (Fed. Cir. 2009); *Rite-Hite Corp. v. Kelley Co.*, 56 F.3d 1538, 1549-51 (Fed. Cir. 1995); *State Indus., Inc. v. Mor-Flo Indus., Inc.*, 883 F.2d 1573, 1580 (Fed. Cir. 1989); *Kori Corp. v. Wilco Marsh Buggies & Draglines, Inc.*, 761 F.2d 649, 656 (Fed. Cir. 1985); *Paper Converting Mach. Co. v. Magna-Graphics Corp.*, 745 F.2d 11, 22-23 (Fed. Cir. 1984).

11.13 Reasonable Royalty – Generally

If you find that [the Plaintiff] has not proven its claim for lost profits, or if you find that [the Plaintiff] has proven its claim for lost profits for only a portion of the infringing sales, then you must consider the issue of a reasonable royalty.

The patent law provides that the amount of damages that [the Defendant] should pay [the Plaintiff] for infringing [the Plaintiff]'s patent must be enough to compensate for the infringement, but may not be less than a reasonable royalty for the use of [the Plaintiff]'s invention.

You must award the [the Plaintiff] a reasonable royalty in the amount that the [the Plaintiff] has proved it could have earned on any infringing sales for which you have not already awarded lost profit damages. A royalty is a payment made to a patent owner by someone else in exchange for the rights to [make, use, sell, or import] a patented product.

The reasonable royalty award must be based on the incremental value that the patented invention adds to the end product. When the infringing products have both patented and unpatented features, measuring this value requires a determination of the value added by the patented features. The ultimate combination of royalty base and royalty rate must reflect the value attributable to the infringing features of the product, and no more.

35 U.S.C. § 284; *Ericsson, Inc. v. D-Link Syss., Inc.*, No. 10-CV-0473, 2014 U.S. App. LEXIS 22778 *at *53, 54* (Fed. Cir. 2014); *VirnetX, Inc. v. Cisco Sys., Inc.*, 767 F.3d 1308, 1326 (Fed. Cir. 2014); *Apple Inc. et al v. Motorola Inc., et al.*, ___ F.3d ____ (Fed. Cir. Apr. 25, 2014); *Uniloc USA, Inc. v. Microsoft Corp.*, 632 F.3d 1292, 1312 (Fed. Cir. 2011); *Lucent Techs., Inc. v. Gateway, Inc.*, 580 F.3d 1301, 1324-25 (Fed. Cir. 2009); *Fromson v. W. Litho Plate & Supply Co.*, 853 F.2d 1568, 1574 (Fed. Cir. 1998) overruled on other grounds by Knorr-Bremse Systeme Fuer Nutzfahrzeuge v. Dana Corp., 383 F.3d 1337, 1342 (Fed. Cir 2004); *Minco, Inc. v. Combustion Eng'g, Inc.*, 95 F.3d 1109, 1119 (Fed. Cir. 1996); *Mahurkar v. C.R. Bard, Inc.*, 79 F.3d 1572, 1579 (Fed. Cir. 1996); *Rite-Hite Corp. v. Kelley Co.*, 56 F.3d 1538, 1554 (Fed. Cir. 1995) (*en banc*).

11.14 Reasonable Royalty Definition – Using the "Hypothetical Negotiation" Method

A reasonable royalty is the royalty that would have resulted from a hypothetical license negotiation between [the Plaintiff] and [the Defendant]. Of course, we know that they did not agree to a license and royalty payment. But, in order to decide on the amount of reasonable royalty damages, you should assume that that the parties did negotiate a license just before the infringement began. This is why it is called a "hypothetical" license negotiation. You should assume that both parties to the hypothetical negotiation understood that the patent was valid and infringed and both were willing to enter into a license. You should also presume that the parties had full knowledge of the facts and circumstances surrounding the infringement at the time of the hypothetical negotiation.

Apple Inc. et al v. Motorola Inc., et al., ___ F.3d ____ (Fed. Cir. Apr. 25, 2014); *LaserDynamics, Inc. v. Quanta Computer, Inc. et al*, 694 F.3d 51, 75 (Fed. Cir. 2012); *Uniloc USA, Inc. v. Microsoft Corp.*, 632 F.3d 1292, 1311 (Fed. Cir. 2011); *Fujifilm Corp. v. Benun*, 605 F.3d 1366, 1372 (Fed. Cir. 2010); *Lucent Techs., Inc. v. Gateway, Inc.*, 580 F.3d 1301, 1324-25 (Fed. Cir. 2009); *Mahurkar v. C.R. Bard, Inc.*, 79 F.3d 1572, 1579 (Fed. Cir. 1996); *Maxwell v. J. Baker, Inc.*, 86 F.3d 1098, 1109-10 (Fed. Cir. 1996); *Rite-Hite Corp. v. Kelley Co.*, 56 F.3d 1538, 1554 (Fed. Cir. 1995) (*en banc*); *Wang Labs., Inc. v. Toshiba Corp.*, 993 F.2d 858, 870 (Fed. Cir. 1993).

11.15 Relevant Factors if Using the Hypothetical Negotiation Method

In determining the amount of a reasonable royalty, you may consider evidence on any of the following factors, in addition to any other evidence presented by the parties on the economic value of the patent:

1. Any royalties received by the licensor for the licensing of the patent-in-suit, proving or tending to prove an established royalty.
2. The rates paid by [the Defendant] to license other patents comparable to the [abbreviated patent number] patent.

3. The nature and scope of the license, as exclusive or non-exclusive, or as restricted or non-restricted in terms of its territory or with respect to whom the manufactured product may be sold.
4. The licensor's established policy and marketing program to maintain its right to exclude others from using the patented invention by not licensing others to use the invention, or by granting licenses under special conditions designed to preserve that exclusivity.
5. The commercial relationship between the licensor and the licensee, such as whether or not they are competitors in the same territory in the same line of business.
6. The effect of selling the patented product in promoting sales of other products of the licensee; the existing value of the invention to the licensor as a generator of sales of its non-patented items; and the extent of such collateral sales.
7. The duration of the [abbreviated patent number] patent and the term of the license.
8. The established profitability of the product made under the [abbreviated patent number] patent; its commercial success; and its current popularity.
9. The utility and advantages of the patented invention over the old modes or devices, if any that had been used for achieving similar results.
10. The nature of the patented invention; the character of the commercial embodiment of it as owned and produced by the licensor; and the benefits to those who have used the invention.
11. The extent to which [the Defendant] has made use of the invention; and any evidence that shows the value of that use.
12. The portion of the profit or of the selling price that may be customary in the particular business or in comparable businesses to allow for the use of the invention or analogous inventions.
13. The portion of the profit that arises from the patented invention itself as opposed to profit arising from unpatented features, such as the manufacturing process, business risks, or significant features or improvements added by the accused infringer.
14. The opinion testimony of qualified experts.
15. The amount that a licensor and a licensee (such as [the Defendant]) would have agreed upon (at the time the infringement began) if both sides had been reasonably and voluntarily trying to reach an agreement; that is, the amount which a prudent licensee—who desired, as a business proposition, to obtain a license to manufacture and sell a

particular article embodying the patented invention—would have been willing to pay as a royalty and yet be able to make a reasonable profit and which amount would have been acceptable by a patentee who was willing to grant a license.

16. Any other economic factor that a normally prudent business person would, under similar circumstances, take into consideration in negotiating the hypothetical license.

Ericsson, Inc. v. D-Link Sys., Inc., No. 10-CV-0473, 2014 U.S. App. LEXIS 22778 at *65-69 (Fed. Cir. 2014); *Apple Inc. et al v. Motorola Inc., et al.*, ___ F.3d ____ (Fed. Cir. Apr. 25, 2014); *LaserDynamics, Inc. v. Quanta Computer, Inc. et al*, 694 F.3d 51, 60 (Fed. Cir. 2012); *Wordtech Sys., Inc. v. Integrated Networks Solutions, Inc.*, 609 F.3d 1308, 1319 (Fed. Cir. 2010); *ResQNet.com, Inc. v. Lansa, Inc.*, 594 F.3d 860, 869-73 (Fed. Cir. 2010); *Monsanto Co. v. McFarling*, 488 F.3d 973 (Fed. Cir. 2007); *Maxwell v. J. Baker, Inc.*, 86 F.3d 1098, 1108-10 (Fed. Cir. 1996); *TWM Mfg. Co. v. Dura Corp.*, 789 F.2d 895, 898-900 (Fed. Cir. 1986); *Georgia-Pacific Corp. v. United States Plywood Corp.*, 318 F. Supp. 1116 (S.D.N.Y. 1970), *modified and aff'd sub nom., Georgia Pacific Corp. v. United States Plywood Champion Papers, Inc.*, 446 F.2d 295 (2d Cir. 1971).

11.16 Reasonable Royalty – Attribution

The amount you find as damages must be the value attributable to the patented technology, as distinct from other unpatented features of the accused product, or other factors such as marketing or advertising, or [the Patentee]'s size or market position. In determining the appropriate royalty base and the appropriate royalty rate, the ultimate combination of both the royalty rate and the royalty based must reflect the value attributable to the patented technology. It is not sufficient to use a royalty base that is too high and adjust the damages downward by applying a lower royalty rate. Similarly, it is not appropriate to select a royalty base that is too low and adjust it upward by applying a higher royalty rate. Rather, you must determine an appropriate royalty rate and an appropriate royalty base that reflect the value attributable to the patented technology.

VirnetX, Inc. v. Cisco Sys., Inc., 767 F.3d 1308 (Fed. Cir. 2014); *LaserDynamics, Inc. v. Quanta Computer, Inc. et al*, 694 F.3d 51, 60 (Fed. Cir. 2012).

11.17 Reasonable Royalty – Entire Market Value Rule

A product may have both infringing and non-infringing components. In such products, royalties should be based not on the entire product, but instead on the "smallest salable unit" that practices the patent and has close relation to the claimed invention. Where the smallest salable unit is, in fact, a multi-component product containing several non-infringing features with no relation to the patented feature, damages must only be based on portion of the value of that product is attributable to the patented technology. This may involve estimating the value of a feature that may not have ever been individually sold.

The entire market value rule is a narrow exception to this general rule. In order to recover damages as a percentage of revenues or profits attributable to the entire product, [the Patentee] must establish that it is more likely than not that the patented feature drives the demand for an entire multi-component product.

VirnetX, Inc. v. Cisco Sys., Inc., 767 F.3d 1308, 1326-29 (Fed. Cir. 2014); *LaserDynamics, Inc. v. Quanta Computer, Inc. et al*, 694 F.3d 51, 67 (Fed. Cir. 2012); *Uniloc USA, Inc. v. Microsoft Corp.*, 632 F.3d 1292, 1318 (Fed. Cir. 2011); *Lucent Techs., Inc. v. Gateway, Inc.*, 580 F.3d 1301, 1336-37 (Fed. Cir. 2009); *Rite-Hite Corp. v. Kelley Co.*, 56 F.3d 1538, 1549-51 (Fed. Cir. 1995) (*en banc*).

11.18 Reasonable Royalty – *Multiple Patents*

If you find that [the Defendant] infringed multiple patents, even by a single infringing act and if you award a reasonable royalty for the infringement, then you may award separate royalties to [the Plaintiff] for each patent that was infringed. You also may consider the number of patent licenses that are needed for the allegedly infringing product and the effect on the hypothetical negotiation of having to pay a royalty for each of those licenses.

Stickle v. Heublein, Inc., 716 F.2d 1550, 1561 n.8 (Fed. Cir. 1983); *Integra Lifesciences I, Ltd. v. Merck KGaA*, 331 F.3d 860, 871 (Fed. Cir. 2003), *reversed on other ground, Merck KGaA v. Integra Lifesciences I., Ltd.*, 545 U.S. 193 (2005); *Verizon Servs. Corp. v. Vonage Holdings Corp.*, 503 F.3d 1295, 1310 (Fed. Cir. 2007).

11.19 Reasonable Royalty – Timing

Although the relevant date for the hypothetical license negotiation is just before the infringement began, you may consider evidence relating to events after the infringement began, any actual profits made by [the Defendant] due to its infringement and any commercial success of the patented invention or the infringing products after that date

Lucent Techs., Inc. v. Gateway, Inc., 580 F.3d 1301, 1324-25 (Fed. Cir. 2009); *TWM Mfg. Co. v. Dura Corp.*, 789 F.2d 895, 898-900 (Fed. Cir. 1986); Studiengesellschaft Kohle, mbH v. Dart Indus., Inc., 862 F.2d 1564, 1570-72 (Fed. Cir. 1988*); Fromson v. W. Litho Plate & Supply Co.*, 853 F.2d 1568, 1575-76 (Fed. Cir. 1988), overruled on other grounds by Knorr-Bremse Systeme Fuer Nutzfahrzeuge v. Dana Corp., 383 F.3d 1337, 1342 (Fed. Cir 2004).

11.20 Reasonable Royalty – Availability of Non-Infringing Substitutes

In determining a reasonable royalty, you may also consider evidence concerning the availability and cost of non-infringing alternatives to the patented invention. A non-infringing alternative must be an acceptable product that is licensed under the patent or that does not infringe the patent.

Uniloc USA, Inc. v. Microsoft Corp., 632 F.3d 1292, 1313 (Fed. Cir. 2011); *Mars, Inc. v. Coin Acceptors, Inc.*, 527 F.3d 1359, 1372-73 (Fed. Cir. 2008); *Zygo v. Wyko*, 79 F.3d 1563, 1571-72 (Fed. Cir. 1996).

11.21 Reasonable Royalty – Use of Comparable License Agreements

When determining a reasonable royalty, you may consider evidence concerning the amounts that other parties have paid for rights to the patent[s] in question, or for rights to similar technologies. A license agreement must not be perfectly comparable to a hypothetical license that would be negotiated between [the Plaintiff] and [the Defendant] in order for you to consider it. However, if you choose to rely upon evidence from any other license agreements, you must account for any differences between those licenses and the hypothetically negotiated license between [the Plaintiff] and [the Defendant], in terms of the technologies and economic circumstances of the contracting parties, when you make your reasonable royalty determination.

Ericsson, Inc. v. D-Link Sys., Inc., No. 10-CV-0473, 2014 U.S. App. LEXIS 22778 at *57-59 (Fed. Cir. 2014); *VirnetX, Inc. v. Cisco Sys., Inc.*, 767 F.3d 1308, 1330-31 (Fed. Cir. 2014); *Apple Inc. et al v. Motorola Inc., et al.*, 757 F.3d 1286, 1325-26 (Fed. Cir. Apr. 25, 2014); *LaserDynamics, Inc. v. Quanta Computer, Inc. et al*, 694 F.3d 51, 77-81 (Fed. Cir. 2012); *ResQNet.com, Inc. v. Lansa, Inc.*, 594 F.3d 860, 869-70 (Fed. Cir. 2010); *Lucent Techs., Inc. v. Gateway, Inc.*, 580 F.3d 1301, 129, 1336 (Fed. Cir. 2009).

11.22 Doubts Resolved Against Infringer

Any doubts that you may have on the issue of damages due to [the Defendant]'s failure to keep proper records should be decided in favor of [the Plaintiff]. Any confusion or difficulties caused by [the Defendant]'s records also should be held against [the Defendant], not [the Plaintiff].

Sensonics, Inc. v. Aerosonic Corp., 81 F.3d 1566, 1572-73 (Fed. Cir. 1996); *Lam, Inc. v. Johns-Manville Corp.*, 718 F.2d 1056, 1065 (Fed. Cir. 1983).

11.23 Standards Essential Patents

Practice Note: Substantial recent attention has been given to the appropriate royalty rate for Standards-Essential Patents (SEPs). Although several district courts have applied the *Georgia-Pacific* factors in assessing a Fair Reasonable and Non-Discriminatory (FRAND or RAND) royalty rate, the Federal Circuit has held some *Georgia-Pacific* factors may not be relevant. Rather, the jury must be instructed on the particulars of the FRAND commitment

> made by the patentee, on established principles of patent law, and on those *Georgia-Pacific* factors that may be relevant. The jury must not be instructed on any factors that are not relevant to the determination of the royalty. The jury must be instructed on apportionment of the value of the portion of the standard as a whole to which the patented technology relates. Finally, the jury must be instructed on apportionment of the value of the patented technology and not the value added by standardization. These will typically be fact-specific issues that will depend on the facts of the individual case. *Ericsson, Inc. v. D-Link Systems, Inc.*, 773 F.3d 1201 (Fed. Cir 2014).

12. Willful Infringement

12.0 Willful Infringement – Generally

> **Practice Note:** The following instruction should be given only if the patent owner contends willful infringement and has introduced sufficient evidence to support this contention.

If you find that it is more likely than not that [the Defendant] infringed [the Plaintiff]'s patent, either literally or under the doctrine of equivalents, then you must also determine whether or not [the Defendant]'s infringement was willful. In contrast to proving that infringement is more likely than not, [the Patentee] must prove willfulness by clear and convincing evidence. Willfulness requires clear and convincing evidence that:

1. [The Defendant] acted despite an objectively high likelihood that its actions infringed a valid patent; and

2. This objectively high likelihood of infringement was either known or so obvious that it should have been known to [the Defendant].

In making the determination of whether [the Defendant] acted despite an objectively high likelihood that its actions infringed a valid patent, you are to consider what a reasonable person would have believed and are not to consider [the Defendant]'s actual state of mind.

> **Practice Note:** In *Bard,* the Federal Circuit stated "the objective determination of recklessness, ... is best decided by the judge....,"682 F.3d at 1007, and that "the judge may when the defense is a question of fact or a mixed question of law and fact allow the jury to determine the underlying facts relevant to the defense in the first instance.... But, ... the ultimate legal question of whether a reasonable person would have considered there to be a high likeli-

hood of infringement of a valid patent should always be decided as a matter of law by the judge." *Id.* at 1008. "The judge remains the final arbiter of whether the defense was reasonable, even when the underlying fact question is sent to a jury." *Id.* at 1007. *But cf. Powell v. Home Depot USA, Inc.*, 663 F.3d. 1221, 1236-37 (Fed. Cir. 2011) ("Under the objective prong, the answer to whether an accused infringer's reliance on a particular issue or defense is reasonable is a question for the court when the resolution of that particular issue or defense is a matter of law.

Should the court determine that the infringer's reliance on a defense was not objectively reckless, the question of willfulness should not be sent to the jury because the objective prong is a predicate to the subjective prong. When the resolution of a particular issue or defense is a factual matter, however, such as whether or not reliance on that issue or defense was reasonable under the objective prong, the issue is properly considered by the jury.

In circumstances, then, where separate issues of fact and law are presented by an alleged infringer as defenses to willful infringement, the objective recklessness inquiry may require analysis by both the court and the jury. For instance, in this case, certain components of the case were before the jury, while others were not. The court decided issues of claim construction and inequitable conduct, neither of which was before the jury. Thus, while the jury was in a position to consider how the infringement case weighed in the objective prong analysis, on other components—such as claim construction—the objective prong question was properly considered by the court.") (citations omitted).[45]

In determining whether [the Defendant] knew of the objectively high likelihood of infringement or whether the likelihood was so obvious that [the Defendant] should have known of that likelihood, you must consider the totality of the circumstances. The totality of the circumstances comprises a number of factors, which include, but are not limited to, whether [the Defendant] intentionally copied the claimed invention or a product covered by patent, whether [the Defendant] relied on competent legal advice, and whether [the Defendant] presented a substantial defense to infringement, including the defense that the patent is invalid [or unenforceable].

---

45. As the earlier case, *Powell* is controlling precedent. *See Deckers Corp. v. U.S.*, No. 2013-1356, Slip. Op. at *27 (Fed. Cir. May 13, 2014) ("We have also adopted the rule that a panel of this court—which normally sits in panels of three, and not en banc—is bound by the precedential decisions of prior panels unless and until overruled by an intervening Supreme Court or en banc decision."). *Compare Scripps Clinic & Res. Found v. Genentech*, Inc., 927 F.2d 1565 (Fed. Cir. 1991) *with Atlantic Thermoplastics Co. v. Faytex Corp.*, 970 F.2d 834 (Fed. Cir. 1992).

Bard Peripheral Vascular, Inc. v. W.L. Gore & Assocs., Inc., 682 F.3d 1003, 1006-08 (Fed. Cir. 2012); *Powell v. Home Depot USA, Inc.*, 663 F.3d. 1221, 1236-37 (Fed. Cir. 2011); *i4i Ltd. P'Ship. v. Microsoft Corp.*, 598 F.3d 831, 859-60 (Fed. Cir. 2010); *Spine Solutions, Inc. v. Medtronic Sofamor Danek USA, Inc.*, 620 F.3d 1305, 1319 (Fed. Cir. 2010); *In re Seagate Tech., LLC*, 497 F.3d 1360 (Fed. Cir. 2007) (*en banc*); *Knorr-Bremse Systeme Fuer Nutzfahrzeuge GmbH v. Dana Corp.*, 383 F.3d 1337, 1347 (Fed. Cir. 2004) (*en banc*).

12.1 Willful Infringement – Absence of Legal Opinion

> **Practice Note:** The following instruction should be given only if the Defendant does not claim reliance on a legal opinion to rebut willfulness.

In considering the totality of the circumstances whether [the Defendant] acted willfully, you may consider as one factor whether [the Defendant] obtained a competent legal opinion. The absence of a legal opinion is one factor that may be considered.

You may not assume that merely because [the Defendant] did not obtain a legal opinion, that the opinion would have been unfavorable. The absence of a lawyer's opinion is not sufficient for you to find that [the Defendant] acted willfully. Rather, the issue is whether the Defendant had a good faith belief that they were not infringing or that the asserted patent was invalid. An opinion of counsel is not necessary for [the Defendant] to establish this defense.

Spectralytics, Inc. v. Cordis Corp., 649 F.3d 1336, 1347-48 (Fed. Cir. 2011); *Aspex Eyewear, Inc. v. Clariti Eyewear, Inc.*, 605 F.3d 1305, 1313 (Fed. Cir. 2010); *In re Seagate Tech., LLC*, 497 F.3d 1360 (Fed. Cir. 2007) (*en banc*).

* * *

VI. Acknowledgments

The contributions of the following attorneys to the drafting and commenting on of these model jury instructions are gratefully acknowledged.

The 1997 Version

Mark Abate
Ken R. Adamo
Joseph Z. Allen
Robert L. Baechtold
Russell J. Barron
Christopher R. Benson
David J. Brezner
Henry L. Brinks
Jeffrey N. Costakos
John F. Delaney
Bradford J. Duft
Donald R. Dunner
Richard D. Fladung
Floyd A. Gibson
Eileen M. Herlihy
Roy E. Hofer
Michael K. Kirschner
Steven S. Korniczky
William E. Lahey
Bradley G. Lane
Robert C. Laurenson
Gary H. Levin
Jeffrey I.D. Lewis
Brent P. Lorimer
Don W. Martens
Alice O. Martin
Clifton E. McCann
Gaynell C. Methvin
Frederick G. Michaud, Jr.
Jeffrey D. Mills
John B. Pegram
Michael F. Petock
Peter H. Priest
Jerrold B. Reilly
Daniel M. Riess
William C. Rooklidge
Alan J. Ross
John M. Skenyon
Allan Sternstein
Lawrence M. Sung
Jennifer A. Tegfeldt
David C. Wright

The 2005 version

Kley Achterhof
Stephanie Barbosa
Kelli Deasy
Denise DeFranco
Barbara Fiacco
Katherine Fick
Mareesa Frederick
Stephanie Harris
Wendell Harris
Andrew Lagatta
Christy Lea
Kalun Lee
Rashida MacMurray
Steven Maslowski
William McGeveran
George Medlock
Mary Beth Noonan
Matthew Pearson
Mark Schuman
Steve Sheldon
Sean Seymour
John Skenyon
Stephen Timmins
Hema Viswanathan
Aaron Weiss
Elizabeth Wright
Jeremy Younkin

The 2007 version

Aaron Barlow
Dave Bennett
Elaine Hermann Blais
Walter Bookhardt
Scott Breedlove
Patrick Coyne
John Crossan
Elizabeth Day
Conor Farley
John Hintz
Scott Howard
Kirby Lee
Gregory Lyons
Joshua Masur
Clifton McCann
Tim Meece
Heather Mewes
Joe Miller
Kenneth Mitchell
John Moran
Jeff Nichols
Scott Pivnick
Mirriam Quinn
Amber Rovner
Michael Sacksteder
John Scheibeler
John Schneider
Mark Schuman
Jeff Sheldon
John Skenyon
Steve Swinton
Tim Teter
Kurt Van Thomme
David Todd
Michael Valek
Alastair Warr
Adam Wichman
Daniel Winston
Steven Zeller

The 2012 version

Matthew Blackburn
Elaine Blais
Carrie Beyer
Gary Buccigross
Brian Butler
Justin Cohen
Danielle Coleman
Craig Countryman
Tom Davison
David DeBruin
Evan Finkel
Glenn Forbis
Nicolas Gikkas
Aleksander Goranin
Angie Hankins
Ben Hanrahan
Ben Hodges
Lisa Kattan
William Lenz
Greg Lewis
Robert Matthews
John Moy
Paul Overhauser
Ajeet Pai
John Pinkerton
Scott J. Pivnick
William Poynter
Woody Pollack
Joe Richetti
Spencer Ririe
John Skenyon
Laura Smalley
Andrew Stein
Steve Swinton
Lynn Tyler
Jennifer Vein, Smr. Assoc.
Jose Villareal
Steven Zeller

The 2015 version

Ken Adamo
Aden Allen
Alan Anderson
Matt Bernstein
Felicia Boyd
Joshua Brady
Cheryl Burgess
Kristin Cleveland
Patrick J. Coyne
David De Bruin
Denise DeFranco
Larry DeMeo
Alper Ertas
Peter Forrest
Aaron Frankel
Gary Frischling
Mel Garner
Derek Gilliland
James Goggin
David Harth
Anthony Hartmann
Rudy Hofmann
Daniel Holmander
Travis Jensen
Neil Jones
James Kamp
Karen Keller
Nicholas Kim
Suzanne Konrad
Samuel Lewis
David Moore
Jeffrey Mote
Don Niles
Eric Osterberg
Paul Overhauser
Ajeet Pai
Henrik Parker
Ken Parker
Roger Parkhurst
John Pegram
Rafael A. Perez-Pineiro
Scott J. Pivnick
Connie Ramos
Russell Rigby
Spencer Ririe
Victor Rodriguez Reyes
David Ruschke
Jeffrey Sadowski
Javier Sobrado
Kim Schenk
Michael Strapp
Mark Supko
Stephen Swinton
Jamaica Szeliga
Peter Toren
Christopher Tokarczyk
Steven Trybus
Colette Verkuil
Mark Whitaker
A. Robert Weaver
Steven McMahon Zeller
RJ Zayed

Table of Cases

Hayes Microcomputer Products, *In re*, 982 F.2d 1527 (Fed. Cir. 1992), 6-5

Haynes v. Dart, No. 08 C 4834, 2010 WL 140387 (N.D. Ill. Jan. 11, 2010), 4-41

Hazel-Atlas Glass Co. v. Hartford-Empire Co., 322 U.S. 238 (1944), 1-8

Hazelquist v. Guchi Moochie Tackle Co., 437 F.3d 1178 (Fed. Cir. 2006), 2-47

Hearing Components, Inc. v. Shure Inc., 600 F.3d 1357 (Fed. Cir. 2010), 14-75

Hearing Components, Inc. v. Shure, Inc., 2008 U.S. Dist. LEXIS 109230, 2008 WL 2485426 (E.D. Tex. June 13, 2008), 2-11

Heart Seed Co. v. Seeds, Inc., No. C-84-336-SPM, 1987 WL 41982, 1987 U.S. Dist. LEXIS 13969 (E.D. Wash. Jan. 29, 1987), 12-10

Hechinger Investment Co. of Delaware, Inc., *In re*, 489 F.3d 568 (3d Cir. 2007), 4-37

Helman v. Murry's Steaks, Inc., 728 F. Supp. 1099 (D. Del. 1990), 4-11

Helmsderfer v. Bobrick Washroom Equip., Inc., 527 F.3d 1379 (Fed. Cir. 2008), 5-60

Henry Hanger & Display Fixture Corp. of Am. v. Sel–O–Rak Corp., 270 F.2d 635 (5th Cir. 1959), 11-14

Henry v. Gill Indus., 983 F.2d 943 (9th Cir. 1993), 4-43

Hess v. Adv. Cardiovascular Systems, Inc., 106 F.3d 976 (Fed. Cir. 1997), 6-8

Hewlett-Packard Co. v. Acceleron LLC, 587 F.3d 1358 (Fed. Cir. 2009), 2-33

Hewlett-Packard Co. v. Bausch & Lomb, Inc., 882 F.2d 1556 (Fed. Cir. 1989), 14-20

Hewlett-Packard Co. v. Bausch & Lomb, Inc., 909 F.2d 1464 (Fed. Cir. 1990), 5-52

Hewlett-Packard Co. v. Repeat-O-Type Stencil Mfg. Co., 123 F.3d 1445 (Fed. Cir. 1997), 14-90

Hickman v. Taylor, 329 U.S. 495 (1947), 2-43

High Point Design LLC v. Buyers Direct, Inc., 730 F.3d 1301 (Fed. Cir. 2013), 11-12

High Tech Medical Instrumentation, Inc. v. New Image Indus., Inc., 49 F.3d 1551 (Fed. Cir. 1995), 3-12, 3-13

Highmark Inc. v. Allcare Health Management System, Inc., 134 S. Ct. 1744 (2014), 1-2, 9-12, 14-112

Hilgraeve, Inc. v. Symantec Corp., 272 F. Supp. 2d 613 (E.D. Mich. 2003), 8-40

Hilleby v. FMC Corp., No. C-91-0568 FMS (CW), 1992 U.S. Dist. LEXIS 20835, 1992 WL 455436 (N.D. Cal. May 13, 1992), 8-8

Hill-Rom Services, Inc. v. Stryker Corp., 755 F.3d 1367 (Fed. Cir. 2014), 5-38, 5-42, 5-64

Hilton v. Braunskill, 481 U.S. 770 (1987), 3-30

Hirst v. Gertzen, 676 F.2d 1252 (9th Cir. 1982), 8-4

Hoechst Celanese Corp. v. BP Chems. Ltd., 78 F.3d 1575 (Fed. Cir. 1996), 3-17

Hoffer v. Microsoft Corp., 405 F.3d 1326 (Fed. Cir. 2005), 5-76, 5-84

Hoffman v. Blaski, 363 U.S. 335 (1960), 2-61

Hoffmann–La Roche Inc., *In re*, 587 F.3d 1333 (Fed. Cir. 2009), 2-64

Holmes Group, Inc. v. Vornado Air Circulation Systems, Inc., 535 U.S. 826 (2002), 2-60, 14-116

Hologic, Inc. v. SenoRx, 639 F.3d 1329 (Fed. Cir. 2011), 5-67

Home Diagnostics Inc. v. Lifescan, Inc., 120 F. Supp. 2d 864 (N.D. Cal. 2000), 5-93

Home Gambling Network Inc. v. Piche, No. 05-cv-610, 2014 U.S. Dist. LEXIS 71071, 2014 WL 2170600 (D. Nev. May 21, 2014), 9-13

Homeland Housewares, LLC v. Sorensen Research & Dev. Tr., 581 F. App'x 877 (Fed. Cir. 2014), 9-12, 9-16

Honeywell Int'l Inc. v. Hamilton Sundstrand Corp., 370 F.3d 1131 (Fed. Cir. 2004), 8-40, 9-17

Honeywell Int'l, Inc. v. ITC, 341 F.3d 1332 (Fed. Cir. 2003), 5-86

Author Biographies

Peter S. Menell is the Koret Professor of Law at the University of California, Berkeley School of Law, where he specializes in intellectual property law. In 1995, he co-founded the Berkeley Center for Law & Technology, which has been instrumental in Berkeley Law being named the top intellectual property program in the nation for nearly two decades. Professor Menell earned his B.S. from M.I.T., M.A. and Ph.D. in Economics from Stanford University, and J.D. from Harvard Law School, where he served as an editor of the *Harvard Law Review*. After graduating from law school, he clerked for Judge Jon O. Newman of the Court of Appeals for the Second Circuit. Professor Menell has written more than 70 articles and 10 books, including *Intellectual Property in the New Technological Age* (with R. Merges and M. Lemley, now in its eighth edition, 2016) and *Software and Internet Law* (with M. Lemley, R. Merges, P. Samuelson, and B. Carver, 4th ed. 2011). Professor Menell has organized more than 50 intellectual property education programs for the Federal Judicial Center since 1998. Professor Menell founded and supervises the *Annual Review of Law and Technology* (now in its nineteenth year, published by the *Berkeley Technology Law Journal*). He has advised the U.S. Congress, federal agencies, state attorneys general, and technology and entertainment companies on a wide range of intellectual property and antitrust matters. He is a member of the District of New Jersey Local Patent Rules Advisory Committee and the Court of Federal Claims Advisory Council. He served from 2012–2013 as one of the inaugural scholars in the USPTO's Thomas Alva Edison Visiting Professionals Program.

Lynn H. Pasahow is a partner in the Litigation Group at Fenwick & West, where he specializes in patent litigation. He has represented cutting-edge technology companies and universities and their Nobel laureate and other inventors in patent and other intellectual property litigation in the software, Internet, and biotech industries. Mr. Pasahow is a coauthor, with Judge William W Schwarzer, of *Civil Discovery: A Guide to Efficient Practice*. He co-teaches an intellectual property course at the University of California, San Francisco, and regularly lectures about intellectual property law subjects to groups that have included the Federal Judicial Center, the American Association for the Advancement of Science, the American Law Institute, the Practising Law Institute, and the University of California, Berkeley School of Law. Mr. Pasahow earned his B.A. from Stanford University and his J.D. from the University of California, Berkeley School of Law.

James Pooley advises clients on patent and trade secret matters in Silicon Valley. He served from 2009 through 2014 as deputy director general, Innovation and Technology Section, at the World Intellectual Property Organization (WIPO). Prior to that appointment, Mr. Pooley was a partner at Morrison and Foerster, where he specialized in intellectual property and technology-related commercial litigation. Mr. Pooley is the author of the treatise *Trade Secrets* (Law Journal Press), *Secrets: Managing Information Assets in the Age of Cyberespionage* (Verus Press 2015), and numerous other professional publications in the field of intellectual property. He is a former president of the American Intellectual Property Law Association and the National Inventors Hall of Fame. Mr. Pooley has taught as an adjunct professor of law at the University of California, Berkeley School of Law. He is a fellow of the California Council on Science and Technology and a member of the National Academy of Sciences Committee on Intellectual Property Rights. Mr. Pooley conceived and scripted an instructional video for jurors in patent cases that was produced by the Federal Judicial Center. Mr. Pooley earned his B.A. from Lafayette College and his J.D. from Columbia University School of Law.

Matthew D. Powers is the lead partner at Tensegrity Law Group, LLP. He is one of the nation's most experienced patent trial lawyers. He has litigated and tried cases in jurisdictions nationwide involving a wide range of technologies, including semiconductor, biomedical, computer, computer peripherals, cellular, holographic, digital media and specialty chemical products. He has published articles on various aspects of intellectual property law and litigation. Mr. Powers has taught as an adjunct professor of law at the University of California, Berkeley School of Law. Mr. Powers earned his B.S. from Northwestern University and his J.D. from Harvard Law School.

Steven C. Carlson is managing partner in the Silicon Valley office of Kasowitz, Benson, Torres & Friedman LLP, where he specializes in patent litigation. He served as a judicial law clerk to Judge Roderick R. McKelvie of the U.S. District Court for the District of Delaware and to Judge Paul R. Michel of the U.S. Court of Appeals for the Federal Circuit. He earned his B.A. from Reed College and his J.D. from Yale Law School, where he served as an editor of the *Yale Law Journal.*

Jeffrey G. Homrig is a partner in the Silicon Valley office of Latham & Watkins LLP. He has extensive experience as a litigator and trial lawyer in complex and high-stakes patent cases for leading technology companies. He graduated from University of California, Berkeley School of Law, and holds a B.A. from the University of California, Berkeley.

George F. Pappas is a partner at Covington & Burling LLP, where he specializes in patent litigation. He is a fellow of the American College of Trial Lawyers and the chair of its Complex Litigation Committee. He also chairs the Editorial Committee and is one of the coauthors of *Anatomy of a Patent Case* (2d ed. 2012), published in conjunction with the Federal Judicial Center. He received his undergraduate and law degrees from the University of Maryland.

Carolyn Chang is a partner at Fenwick & West's Silicon Valley office, where she specializes in patent litigation. She received her B.A. from the University of California, Berkeley, and her J.D. from the University of California, Hastings College of the Law.

Colette Reiner Mayer is a partner at Morrison & Foerster's Silicon Valley office, where she specializes in patent litigation. She earned her B.S. from M.I.T. and her J.D. from Cardozo School of Law.

Marc David Peters is a partner at Morrison & Foerster's Silicon Valley office, where he specializes in patent and trade secret litigation. He earned his B.A. from Harvard University, his M.A. and Ph.D. in Physics from the University of California, Berkeley, and his J.D. from Stanford Law School.

Collaborator Profiles

Anita Choi is an associate at Morrison & Foerster's Silicon Valley office, where she focuses on clean technology, biofuels, agricultural biotechnology, life sciences, biotechnology, pharmaceuticals, molecular diagnostics, and material sciences. She earned her B.S. from the California Institute of Technology, her M.B.A. from the Wharton School of Business, and her J.D. from the University of Pennsylvania Law School.

John Fargo serves as the director of the Intellectual Property Staff within the Commercial Litigation Branch of the Civil Division at the U.S. Department of Justice. He specializes in intellectual property litigation at the Federal Court of Claims. He earned his B.S. in Industrial Engineering and his J.D. at the State University of New York at Buffalo.

Michael Sawyer is an associate in the Washington, D.C., office of Covington & Burling where he specializes in patent litigation. He served as a judicial law clerk to Judge William C. Bryson of the U.S. Court of Appeals for the Federal Circuit. He earned his B.S. in Computer Science and Mathematics at the University of Scranton and his J.D. from the University of California, Berkeley School of Law.

Allison A. Schmitt currently serves as a law clerk to the Honorable Stanley R. Chesler at the U.S. District Court for the District of New Jersey, after which she will be clerking for Judge Kathleen M. O'Malley of the U.S. Court of Appeals for the Federal Circuit. She earned her B.S. in Chemistry and Biochemistry from the University of Washington, her Ph.D. in Chemistry from Duke University, and her J.D. from the University of California, Berkeley School of Law.

Michael R. Ward is a partner at Morrison & Foerster's San Francisco office, where he specializes in intellectual property relating to plants and biotechnology. He earned his B.S. from the University of California, Berkeley, his M.S. in Agronomy and Ph.D. in Plant Physiology/Biochemistry from the University of California, Davis, and his J.D. from Golden Gate University School of Law.

Patricia Young is an associate at Latham & Watkins LLP, where she specializes in patent litigation. She received her S.B. from M.I.T. and her J.D. from Harvard Law School.

Made in the USA
Monee, IL
05 November 2026

67811027R10208